YELLOW FEVER AND THE SOUTH

HEALTH AND MEDICINE
IN AMERICAN SOCIETY SERIES

EDITORS
Judith Walzer Leavitt
Morris Vogel

MARGARET HUMPHREYS

YELLOW FEVER and the SOUTH

RUTGERS UNIVERSITY PRESS

NEW BRUNSWICK, NEW JERSEY

Library of Congress Cataloging-in-Publication Data

Humphreys, Margaret, 1955–
    Yellow fever and the South / Margaret Humphreys.
      p.   cm.—(Health and medicine in American society)
    Based on author's thesis (Ph.D.)—Harvard, 1983, presented under
title: Public health in the New South.
    Includes bibliographical references and index.
    ISBN 0-8135-1820-2
    1. Yellow fever—Southern States—History. I. Humphreys,
Margaret, 1955– Public health in the New South. II. Title.
III. Series.
    [DNLM: 1. Disease Outbreaks—prevention & control—Southeastern
United States. 2. History of Medicine, 19th Cent.—Southeastern
United States. 3. Public Health—history—Southeastern United
States. 4. Yellow Fever—history—Southeastern United States. WC
532 H927y]
    RA644.Y4H86 1992
    614.5'41'097509034—dc20
    DNLM/DLC
    for Library of Congress   91-41138
                                               CIP

British Cataloging-in-Publication information available

For my family:

K.B., MARY, BROOKS, CINDY, CONNOR, and KATE

CONTENTS

······························

ACKNOWLEDGMENTS

This study originated as a doctoral dissertation in the History of Science Department at Harvard University. My greatest debts are to Barbara Gutmann Rosenkrantz, John Harley Warner, and Judith Walzer Leavitt, who read multiple drafts of the manuscript and contributed immeasurably to its improvement. Allan Brandt, Charles Rosenberg, David Rosner, Morris Vogel, Everett Mendelsohn, and the anonymous reader for the press, who all read the text in its entirety, offered valuable comments and encouragement.

I am grateful to Drew Gilpin Faust and Ronald L. Numbers for reading and criticizing an earlier version of chapter two, which was presented in an abbreviated form at the biennial convention of the American Studies Association, Memphis, Tennessee, 1 November 1981. Parts of chapter one and chapter two were combined into a paper on public health in the old South and presented at the Second Barnard-Millington Symposium on Southern Science and Medicine, Jackson, Mississippi, 17–19 March 1983. At the latter meeting a number of scholars, including Dana Ketchum, Kenneth Kiple, and K. David Patterson, expressed welcome interest in my work, reassuring me that someone besides myself cared about yellow fever and southern public health. In early stages of my exploration of this topic, William Coleman fostered my enthusiasm for yellow fever; during the same period David Donald and Joel Williamson provided valuable guidance into the vast field of nineteenth century southern history.

The Educational Foundation of the American Association of University Women awarded me a predoctoral fellowship, which freed me from the burdens of teaching for the 1982–83 academic year. The Department of Health Policy and Social Medicine at Harvard Medical School supported the revision of the thesis during the summer of 1984.

Versions of some sections of this work have been previously published. Material from "Public Health in the Old South," now divided between the first two chapters is found in Ronald L. Numbers and Todd L. Savitt, eds., *Science and Medicine in the Old South* (Baton Rouge: Louisiana State University Press, 1989), 226–255. Chapter two contains extensive material from my "Local Control versus National Interest: The Debate over Southern Public Health, 1878–1884," *The Journal of Southern History* 50 (1984): 407–428. A few paragraphs in chapters one and two are found in similar form in "Hunting the Yellow Fever Germ: The Principle and Practice of Etiological Proof in Late Nineteenth-Century America," *Bulletin of the History of Medicine* 59 (1985): 361–382. All previously published material was under my former married name of Warner and is used with permission.

Medical school and residency training were largely remarkable for denying me the time to work on this project. I would like to thank Cynthia Whitman, Phyllis Jen, Shahram Khoshbin, and Thomas O'Brien for their friendship during this trying period and their encouragement of all my endeavors.

YELLOW FEVER AND THE SOUTH

INTRODUCTION

The imperative to control yellow fever fundamentally directed the development of southern and federal public health institutions in nineteenth-century America. The death and disorder yellow fever brought to the South made it the preeminent concern of southern boards of health from the 1840s through the first decade of the twentieth century, when the last yellow fever epidemic in the United States occurred in 1905. As a result, the objectives, attitudes, and achievements of southern public health officials were strikingly different from those of their northern counterparts. The studies upon which historians have based their assessment of American public health in the nineteenth century have focused heavily on the northeastern and midwestern states; an explication of the distinctive character of the southern public health endeavor is needed to redress this imbalance and facilitate a more complete understanding of the history of public health in America. In addition, the yellow fever story illuminates the origin of the United States Public Health Service by demonstrating that the Service's acquisition of funding, staffing, and authority during a period of impressive growth, 1878–1910, was strongly dependent upon its role in defending the nation against yellow fever.

The government involvement yellow fever commanded arose not so much out of the large numbers of deaths that occurred during epidemics—tuberculosis, smallpox, or typhoid might well kill as many or more every year yet fail to stir the public from apathy—but from the total disruption of the fabric of life that epidemics occasioned. Yellow fever was a disease whose presence often created mass panic, a response that brought commercial interactions to a standstill as many communities blockaded themselves against the world to keep out pestilence. This interference with the transportation of goods and passengers, and the cessation of ordinary local business during the three or four month duration of the typical epidemic, made yellow fever above all a commercial problem, the control of which was essential to the development and prosperity of the South. Accordingly, to control yellow fever legislators charged southern public health officials with two related duties: (1) to prevent the importation of the disease from the foreign cities where it was endemic, and (2) to limit an epidemic once it had begun by actions that would both protect the locality and the region from the spread of the disease as well as preserve to the maximum extent possible the flow of commerce. Every major epidemic was followed by exclamations that some solution had to be found to the yellow fever problem, for such destruction of life and trade could not be allowed to recur. This energy might be variously channeled toward calls for public health measures of either local, state, or national provenance, but inevitably each visitation generated an outcry for the elimination of yellow fever from the South.

The years encompassed by this narrative were ones of enormous change throughout the South. The region fought and lost a devastating war that was largely waged within its boundaries, destroying not only lives but infrastructure. A largely agricultural society moved slowly in the post-war years not only to reconstruct what was lost, but to venture into new realms of commerce and manufacturing. The assessment of the region's wealth in the antebellum period has been much discussed, complicated as it is by how to count the value of slaves as property,

varying estimates of the fertility of southern soil, and the volatil-
ity of the cotton market. Still the post-war poverty of the region,
compared to the nation as a whole, is undisputed. At the same
time, the relationships between white and black southerners
were in continuous turmoil, first stirred by the reforms imposed transiently by Reconstruction, and then by the radical
repression that followed in the last two decades of the nineteenth century. By 1905 the South was more urban, more indus-
trialized, and more dependent on the federal government than
it had been sixty years before, but it still remained the most
agricultural and impoverished area of the nation.

The growth of public health in the South took place amidst
the larger currents of southern history. Discussion about the
transportability theory of yellow fever during the 1840s and
1850s, with its overtones of rebellion against northern-held
ideas, took place at the same time as secessionist spirit was gaining in force. The Civil War and Reconstruction created too
chaotic a political environment for public works to thrive, and
this account accordingly jumps fairly quickly from 1859 to
1878. The relatively calm 1880s and 1890s, on the other hand,
brought both revived commerce and its associated tax revenues,
as well as stable governments able to carry out public health
reform measures. It was in this "New South" that newly formed
state boards of health waged their major battles against yellow
fever.

The meaning of yellow fever for southern society was enormous and complex. On the personal level, yellow fever had an
impact out of proportion to its mortality because of its concentration of deaths within the span of a few weeks and the horror
and rapidity of its course. Figure 1 shows that in the city most
frequently afflicted by the disease, New Orleans, there were
only nine years between 1840 and 1905 in which yellow fever
caused more than 10 percent of the deaths. But the disease
could be overwhelmingly destructive, as in 1853, when it accounted for half of the city's mortality. Yellow fever was unpre-
dictable, and its sporadic forays into other southern cities made
many communities that rarely experienced the disease feel
nonetheless vulnerable. As is evident in table 1, yellow fever
could have a devastating impact on a population. Southerners

FIGURE 1

Yellow Fever in New Orleans, 1840–1905
Yellow fever deaths as a percentage of total mortality

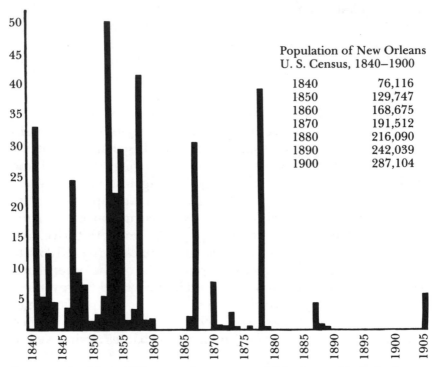

Population of New Orleans U. S. Census, 1840–1900	
1840	76,116
1850	129,747
1860	168,675
1870	191,512
1880	216,090
1890	242,039
1900	287,104

SOURCES: For 1840–1870, mortality reports published sporadically in the *NOMSJ* and *New Orleans Medical News and Hospital Gazette;* Stanford E. Chaillé, "Vital Statistics of New Orleans," *NOMSJ* 23 (1870): 1–31. For 1870–1905, *LSBH Reports;* Gayle Aiken, "The Medical History of New Orleans," in Henry Rightor, ed., *Standard History of New Orleans, Louisiana* (Chicago: The Lewis Publishing Co., 1900), 203–225.

might encounter yellow fever only once in a decade, but still feel panic-stricken at the approach of the yellow fever season, dreading its arrival far more intensely than they feared other diseases that systematically killed their fellow citizens.

Understanding the power of yellow fever to generate public health action requires knowing something about the basic biology and epidemiology of the disease. Yellow fever is caused by an arbovirus carried from victim to victim by blood-sucking *Aedes*

TABLE 1

Mortality in Selected Yellow Fever Epidemics, 1843–1888

City	Year	Population	Yellow Fever Deaths
Mobile, Ala.	1843	11,500	750
	1853	25,000	1,191
Norfolk, Va./Portsmouth, Va.	1855	26,000	2,807
Charleston, S.C.	1858	40,500	717
Galveston, Tex.	1867	22,000	1,150
Savannah, Ga.	1876	20,560	1,594
Memphis, Tenn.	1873	40,220	2,000
	1878	33,600	5,000
Holly Springs, Miss.	1878	3,000	309
Jacksonville, Fla.	1888	21,000	430

SOURCES: Compiled from George Augustin, ed., *History of Yellow Fever* (New Orleans: Searcy and Pfaff, 1909); and L. G. LeBeuf, "Some Notes on the History of Yellow Fever," *NOMSJ* 58 (1905–06): 456–477.

aegypti mosquitoes. Frost kills the mosquito vector, so the disease is only truly indigenous in tropical locales. In the United States the disease was probably imported with each epidemic, which would usually last from July, when the first case appeared, to the first autumn frost. There is a native *Aedes* population still in the South, so that yellow fever can be introduced there by a single case, if that case is bitten. In colder cities such as Boston, yellow fever epidemics result only when enough infected mosquitoes disembark to create the critical numbers needed to sustain spread. This latter scenario happened rarely. The *Aedes aegypti* mosquito breeds in fresh water; it particularly favors cisterns, puddles, buckets, flower pots, and so on—any receptacle capable of holding rainwater. It is accordingly an urban disease, for this particular mosquito disdains swamps and lakes. The disease preferred to rage in hot, crowded cities, with only occasional forays via trains or boats into smaller communities.[1]

Yellow fever is a miserable disease. It can appear in a mild form, causing a flu-like illness that lasts a week or so. The existence of this milder version often confounds attempts to estimate morbidity and mortality rates. Classic yellow fever begins with the abrupt onset of shaking chills, fever, and muscle aches. This is followed by liver failure and jaundice, giving the fever its name. Hepatic congestion combined with systemic dysfunction of the clotting system causes hemorrhage from the gums, nose, and stomach lining. When vomited this digested blood looks black; the Spanish name for yellow fever is "vomito negro." Renal failure, as evidenced by the cessation of urine output, precedes death by one to two days. In fatal cases, death occurs in about a week. Estimates of mortality range from ten to sixty percent of those infected.[2]

Lay accounts of tending yellow fever victims make horrific reading. A letter written by a Memphian to a relative provides a particularly vivid image of this experience. "Lucille died at Ten O'Clock Tuesday night, after such suffering as I hope never again to witness," his letter began. The man nursed the girl, who was probably his niece, continually until her death. "Once or twice my nerve almost failed me, but I managed to stay," he confessed. "The poor girl's screams might be heard for half a square and at times I had to exert my utmost strength to hold her in bed. Jaundice was marked, the skin being a bright yellow hue: tongue and lips dark, cracked and blood oozing from the mouth and nose." That was hard for him to watch, but worse was to follow. "To me the most terrible and terrifying feature was the 'black vomit' which I never before witnessed," he continued. "By Tuesday evening it was as black as ink and would be ejected with terriffic [sic] force. I had my face and hands spattered but had to stand by and hold her. Well it is too terrible to write any more about it."[3] This experience, repeated in thousands of households during the three or four summer months that encompassed the typical epidemic, left memories not easily erased.

Yellow fever chose its victims with evident selection. It was known as the "Stranger's Disease" in antebellum New Orleans. Since childhood cases were often non-fatal and conferred immunity, those who grew up in a town frequented by the disease were not at risk as adults. On the other hand, the immigration of Irish and later Italian laborers into the city brought large numbers of susceptible individuals to fuel epidemics. In cities visited less often, cohorts of natives could grow up innocent of the disease, only to meet it as adults with grave results. There was less blame attached to the victims of yellow fever than to some other diseases of the mid-nineteenth century. Catching yellow fever seemed to depend less on behavioral factors (e.g., personal cleanliness and morality) and more on where one lived, whether one could leave, and how long one had been there. Since filth was felt from early in the nineteenth century to be the principal culprit in breeding yellow fever, the blame for its persistence tended to fall most heavily on those government officials charged with sanitation rather than the unlucky inhabitants of the dirtiest districts.

Those familiar with the major issues of southern history may wonder at the scant mention of blacks in this narrative. It reflects the inattention to the subject by the southern medical literature on the disease. Blacks had significant immunity to yellow fever and malaria, two diseases their genetic pool had known well in Africa. This protection was well enough known in the antebellum period to be used as a justification for slavery; labor under southern conditions killed whites, so blacks were the "natural" choice for the plantations. In the medical literature concerning yellow fever that appeared in the four decades following the Civil War, blacks were largely invisible. Historian Kenneth Kiple's recent review of the historiography of black health reflects this fact. There are abundant studies of the antebellum period and the twentieth century, but only a handful covering the late nineteenth century. Blacks are occasionally mentioned in accounts of epidemics, as in 1878, when blacks were used to police a chaotic Memphis, or, in the same epidemic, when provisions had to be made for poor relief of blacks abandoned by their white employers. Not until the concept of the carrier became current at the turn of the twentieth century were blacks viewed as important figures in the yellow fever drama, and then at the point when yellow fever disappeared.[4]

The other "invisible" population in the nineteenth-century public health story is the rural poor. Southern boards of health, with few exceptions, were perennially underfunded well into the twentieth century. The collection of vital statistics, in particular, lagged well behind the northern states. Physicians and politicians in New Orleans could declare their city healthy, at least between yellow fever epidemics, until reformers published years of damning statistical information showing continual excess mortality. In like fashion, the absence of data concerning the morbidity and mortality of the rural population hid the tolls taken by malnutrition, malaria, hookworm, and other diseases. The impetus for rural public health action in the twentieth century came from federal and philanthropic sources, not southern public health officials. Most southern boards—poor, urban, and caught up with the persistent threat of yellow fever—turned a blind eye to the appalling health conditions of the rural south until well into the twentieth century.

Yellow fever was a profound burden upon southern commerce. It stopped trains and bottled up ports, keeping cotton from the mills and preventing the movement of basic merchandise from distribution points in cities to the countryside. Much of the South's foreign trade consisted in fruit, coffee, and other agricultural commodities that were imported from the tropical regions that frequently hosted yellow fever. A leading topic of public health debate in the nineteenth-century South concerned the strictness of quarantine against these ports and the damage such preventive measures would wreak on trade. Southern ports competed with each other for the lucrative benefits of foreign commerce, which made municipal rivalries a factor in the formulation of quarantine codes. Yellow fever's threat made doing business in the South a risky proposition, for the rigidity of quarantines tended to vary unpredictably with the level of public anxiety, making it difficult to plan long term business strategies. Such a climate of uncertainty discouraged northern investment and slowed the commercial growth of the South.

Aside from the damage done by quarantine, far more serious were the losses incurred by businessmen during the course of an epidemic. Once yellow fever had become firmly entrenched in a town, few inhabitants who had the means to flee to safety remained. Most shops, businesses, and trading houses were closed on account of the absence of both customers and businessmen. This cessation of commercial exchange could last three to four months, from mid-July to early November. Furthermore, the merchant who attempted to ship goods by rail or steamboat to the interior was met by severe hindrances. For example, suspicious armed guards would meet a train, demanding to know if it might carry infection. If the replies given were unsatisfactory, the train might be turned back or else ordered to speed through town as quickly as possible, debarking neither passengers nor freight. Panicky country dwellers sometimes destroyed railroad bridges or tracks in order to prevent the passage of possible yellow fever carriers. Transportation companies in particular, but also merchants in general who routinely shipped cargo northward, lost thousands of dollars as a result of these "shotgun" quarantines. As the stability of southern markets was impaired by the threat of yellow fever, investors were understandably wary of backing southern business ventures.

Yellow fever was a source of great frustration and opprobrium for the South's physicians, for the hundreds of deaths that occurred during an epidemic provided ample testimony to their inability to cure their patients. Driven in part by this insult to their prestige and abilities, southern physicians turned to research on the treatment and etiology of yellow fever to vindicate their profession, producing a prolific literature on the disease during the latter two-thirds of the nineteenth century. Whatever the shortcomings of the medical profession, the public did look to them for those ideas and practices that offered any hope at all for yellow fever's control. While yellow fever contributed to a loss of faith in the practitioner's therapeutic ability, it also somewhat paradoxically elevated the physician to a position of crucial importance to the community, as the one professional who had the most to offer in overcoming the dreaded scourge of the South.

The story of the control of yellow fever in nineteenth-century America coincides intimately with the history of southern public health and the growth of federal responsibility for the prevention of disease. In contrast to the focus of northern boards of health on endemic health problems, quarantine against external diseases was the central function of both southern and national public health agencies in the late nineteenth century, with yellow fever occupying their attention almost exclusively. "While the quarantinable diseases as defined by our regulations are nominally cholera, smallpox, yellow fever, typhus fever, plague, and leprosy, still it is only yellow fever whose shadow ever crosses our path, and is always a source of dread, a constant source of expense, and at once a danger to our people and an onerous burden upon commerce," one federal official commented in 1897.[5] Although yellow fever appeared relatively infrequently after 1875, with extensive epidemics occurring only in the years 1878–79, 1888, 1897–98, and 1905, the southern ports remained on alert by necessity during the summer and fall of every year. Both federal and state authorities maintained expensive quarantine stations that interrupted shipping; physicians nervously examined each possible case of fever; and southerners regularly scheduled vacations in the mountains or the North during "the yellow fever season"—all on the expectation that yellow fever might again appear anywhere in the South that had close communication with the yellow fever–infested ports of Mexico, Cuba, or South America.

It was explicitly to fight yellow fever that southern legislatures by and large created boards of health. Preventing this disease was a central preoccupation of state boards of health in Louisiana, Mississippi, Alabama, Florida, Tennessee, and South Carolina from their inception, mainly in the 1870s, through at least the first decade of the twentieth century. Southern public health officials were primarily quarantine administrators, and yellow fever so absorbed their professional concern that there was little time left for the objectives which northern sanitarians considered so central during the same time period, such as pure food, milk, and water; sewage reform; smallpox vaccination; the collection of vital statistics; or campaigns against tuberculosis, typhoid, diphtheria, and the various ailments of infants. Southern boards did make some movements in these directions, but as long as the shadow of yellow fever loomed over the South, its control remained their primary duty. Many northern boards owed their inauguration to the public health awareness inspired by invasions of cholera, but given the rarity of cholera's presence or threat, northern officials soon had to turn to other activities in order to impress legislators of their permanent value. In contrast, the orientation of southern boards of health remained largely monolithic, turned southerly toward the tropical menace of yellow fever.

This book is not a comprehensive history of southern public health during the period it considers. My thesis, that yellow fever provided the main fuel for the growth of public health in the region, leads me to focus attention on those areas where yellow fever was most active. Thus the antebellum section looks at Charleston, Memphis, Mobile, New Orleans; the 1878 episode involves Tennessee, Mississippi, and Louisiana; the later chapters concentrate on Florida and the gulf coast. State board of health reports from the various southern states support my suspicion that, in states without yellow fever, public health activity was at a low ebb. Charles Chapin's survey of southern boards' status in the early twentieth century bolsters this impression.[6] This is certainly a hypothesis to be tested. It is likely that the growth of interest in rural health issues that distinguishes the next phase of southern public health in the decades following 1905 occurred earlier in some states than others. It would be interesting to explore whether prior preoccupation with yellow fever made a southern board more or less likely to pursue the new rural health agenda. This book leaves unanswered the question of whether the focus on yellow fever ultimately retarded the evolution of domestic sanitation in the South. If there had been no yellow fever, would the South's sanitarians have made any progress at all toward the goals espoused by their northern colleagues? More detailed studies of individual boards of health with extension into the twentieth century might begin to answer such questions, but they are beyond the scope of this effort.

Yellow fever epidemics in the American South have received extensive coverage by historians. On the most basic level, the story of yellow fever makes good copy. A number of studies have recounted the drama in different locales, following in essence the same saga. The first cases appear; physicians and government officials try to hush it up; the disease spreads inexorably; people flee in panic; too little is done too late; hundreds or thousands die; and isolated examples of heroism are identified. Such descriptive accounts fill the basic need of identifying when and where epidemics occurred and how the government responded, and often outline contemporary viewpoints on the disease. The studies of Louisiana by Duffy, Carrigan, and

Gillson; of Memphis by Ellis and Baker; of Philadelphia by Powell; and of Tallahassee by Miller are all examples of this tradition.[7] These detailed works provide essential background to this broader study of southern public health up to 1905. I hope to establish that the consideration of the southern public health experience as a whole reveals trends less evident in these more focused studies, and quite different from the course of public health in the North. Its course was overwhelmingly shaped by one epidemic disease, yellow fever, and it was intimately entwined with the growth of the federal health bureaucracy—a fact underappreciated in the current historiography.[8]

Yellow fever was crucial to the expansion of federal public health involvement in the late nineteenth century, largely because, unlike any other disease that steadily afflicted the country, it was fundamentally a national problem. Analogies likening yellow fever to an invading army, or to an imported commodity such as bananas or coffee, emphasized those characteristics of the disease that made it a national, and not merely a state or regional, calamity. From this perspective, it was an easy step to the conclusion that protection from yellow fever should be in the hands of the federal government, just as military security and international diplomacy were constitutionally reserved for federal jurisdiction. Particularly in the last two decades of the nineteenth century, when public health officials increasingly viewed yellow fever as a product of Cuba, Mexico, and other tropical countries of the Western Hemisphere, the federal government appeared to be the most appropriate power to implement measures necessary to control the disease. This attitude reinforced the American imperialistic perception of Cuba; not only was the United States proclaimed fit to rule the island by right of geography and democratic virtue, but also because it had such a direct stake in the eradication of yellow fever at its perennial source.

Furthermore, once yellow fever had successfully breached the nation's defenses, it was seldom confined within state boundaries. Although other maladies such as smallpox crossed state lines as well, yellow fever's interference with business made it a singularly central concern for the authority that had sovereignty over interstate commerce: the federal government. That national public health agencies were lodged in the Treasury Department during the nineteenth century was not accidental; it was from the right to regulate commerce on both the international and interstate levels that the federal government derived its base of authority for administrating quarantines against yellow fever. This power was vested briefly in the National Board of Health from 1879 to 1884 and then in the Marine Hospital Service, which was renamed the Public Health Service in the early twentieth century. The Marine Hospital Service's expansion of authority, from being merely a bureau in charge of seamen's hospitals to its status as a national department of health, was due heavily to its gradual acquisition of responsibility for coastal quarantine directed against cholera, plague, and most importantly, yellow fever during the last two decades of the nineteenth century.

The period from 1878 to 1907 was a time of conflict between state boards of health and the Marine Hospital Service over the question of who was more competent to control yellow fever. Historian Morton Keller, in a splendid study of American public life in the Gilded Age, has traced the dominant tensions that persisted throughout the era, tensions "between equality and liberty, between the desire for freedom and the need for social order, between dependence on government and hostility to the state, between localism and nationalism."[9] The debate over the control of yellow fever was strongly marked by such tensions, with the public simultaneously demanding maximal protection from yellow fever and resisting any interference with their personal lives, and state governments battling Washington for the privilege of administering public health institutions in the South. States' rights advocates argued that only southern public health officials, who were well versed in yellow fever's behavior and had the greatest stock in the protection of their region, were qualified to devise local public health codes and quarantine regulations. The opposing view doubted that local authorities would be able to resist commercial pressures to favor trade by minimalizing quarantine, and countered that federal agents, administering one uniform code equally applicable to all communities, would be well-trained, impartial, and dedicated to the public welfare. Southerners feared that any national organization might be dominated by the interests of other regions that would approve the suppression of southern commercial growth.

Finally, supporters of local control in public health pointed to the Constitution's reservation of police powers to the states, including, in their appraisal, powers of quarantine. Neither Congress nor the courts were ready by the first decade of the twentieth century to decide conclusively whether the states or the federal government held exclusive rights to the power of quarantine, and instead Congress passed legislation that called for a mixture of state and federal action. Federal lawmakers enacted a series of compromise measures during the 1878–1907 period that allowed the U.S. government to incrementally assume ever-greater quarantine responsibilities, but which never directly wrested such authority from the state boards of health.

It was not until after 1900 that these struggles for political control of yellow fever took place in the context of a sound understanding of the disease's etiology. Prevention of yellow fever during the nineteenth century was guided by a model of disease transmission that accidentally produced results positive enough to sustain its credibility. From the 1840s southern physicians increasingly accepted that yellow fever could be transported, although they were divided on what the nature of this pathogenic traveler was. Still, they felt confident that disinfection and sanitation could slow its spread. By the late 1870s most southern physicians agreed that yellow fever was caused by some sort of germ, and accordingly set out to destroy that germ with chemicals, and to deny it a hospitable environment through municipal sanitation. During the 1880s a quarantine system employed these ideas on a large scale, so that ships, trains, and their contents could be purified with disinfecting gases and ovens, thus heralding a new scientific age in yellow fever prevention. Although the mythical germ was the target, these techniques probably killed many mosquitoes as well. The germ theory of yellow fever offered a simple explanation for the disease, and moreover dictated an apparently effective way to stop it. Legislators were happy to vote funds for such a clear-cut means of control. They might be loath to spend money on vague sanitation plans that promised to deny the germ its needed habitat, but this new system of directly killing off the offenders seemed quite worthy of support.

The new quarantine system originated in Louisiana, and its officials boasted of the international acclaim accorded their model station. The Louisiana officials were understandably dismayed by Walter Reed's announcement in 1900 that yellow fever was spread by mosquitoes. His experiments made their scientific assumptions look foolish and rendered their sophisticated quarantine equipment obsolete. The federal government further robbed southern public health officials of prestige when it stepped in to fight mosquitoes in the last yellow fever epidemic in 1905. The United States Public Health Service men shone so brightly in their battle against mosquitoes that they had little trouble in gaining complete coastal quarantine jurisdiction in 1906.

The southern preoccupation with quarantine and yellow fever did little to further sanitary reform, except in a few instances. Even though throughout the nineteenth century physicians argued that unsanitary conditions abetted yellow fever's spread and aggravated its virulence, by and large they placed the heaviest reliance on quarantine for protection. Most southern public health officials praised sanitation and did what they could with their meager appropriations to promote drainage, the proper disposal of human waste, and clean streets, water, and air. Still, southern cities remained distinctively dirtier than those of the North at the turn of the century. The new quarantine stations built in the 1880s offered apparent security against yellow fever; the few epidemics after 1885 were all traced to illegal vessels smuggling from Cuba and Mexico. Yellow fever prevention seemed to turn on closing these loopholes, rather than cleaning the streets or building sewers. Although it is impossible to know whether miserly southern legislators would have funded any public health initiatives at all in the absence of yellow fever, it can be said that yellow fever contributed little to the growth of public hygiene in the South, for it overshadowed the myriad endemic diseases and conditions that far more commonly brought death to the region's population. When yellow fever departed after

1905, southern public health officials were far behind their northern counterparts in educating their legislators about the need for programs against endemic health problems. Deprived of both yellow fever and quarantine authority, members of southern boards of health had to look elsewhere to find a new foundation for professional identity, esteem, and responsibility.

PURSUING AN ELUSIVE DISEASE: Etiology and the Control of Yellow Fever

Y ellow fever was a central disease in disputes about contagion, the germ theory, and public health action in nineteenth-century America. Since it occurred in discrete epidemics, physicians believed that yellow fever's etiology could be discovered if only the peculiar circumstances of its appearances could be identified. Theories about the disease were intimately tied to public health practice, so much so that the implications of an idea could be as important as the logic behind it in establishing its validity. Believed by most early nineteenth-century physicians to be non-contagious, yellow fever came to be characterized from the 1840s as being at least "transportable." After the Civil War the germ theory was invoked to explain this phenomenon. During the last quarter of the nineteenth century, public health action increasingly focused on the exclusion of the yellow fever germ and its destruction with disinfectants. In 1900 Walter Reed and James Carroll discovered the mosquito vector of yellow fever, providing the basis for a wholly new approach to yellow fever prevention.

Yellow fever appeared sporadically in the United States during the eighteenth century, but awaited the advent of urbanization in order to have its fullest impact. It found a receptive home in Philadelphia in the two decades surrounding the turn of the century, striking with particular devastation in the summer of 1793. America's pre-eminent physician, Benjamin Rush, studied the epidemics and pronounced the disease non-contagious. Believing it to be merely an aggravated form of the autumnal fevers that regularly plagued Philadelphia, Rush blamed the virulence of the epidemics on the city's filthy condition. Three decades later French physician Nicholas Chervin arrived at the same conclusion concerning a yellow fever epidemic in Spain. Science had spoken: yellow fever was not contagious, and quarantine had no place in its prevention.[1]

Impressive evidence was marshalled against contagionism: while thousands fled from a yellow fever–infected city, the disease did not in large measure follow the refugees. The fact that cases which occurred among the emigrants rarely spread further than the victim demonstrated conclusively that yellow fever could not be communicated from one person to another by contact. This was the accepted meaning of contagion, modeled on smallpox and syphilis transmission, and it was clearly inapplicable to yellow fever. Therefore, the disease could only arise from local causes. Importation, according to this argument, was impossible, for if it traveled at all, the disease must be conveyed by human carriers—but was not.[2]

Influenced by Rush and Chervin, from the 1790s to the 1840s southern physicians shared a widespread conviction that yellow fever was non-contagious, and quarantine hence futile,[3] but this was not the case with the populace as a whole. Lacking the greater knowledge of yellow fever's peculiar behavior available to the medical profession, lay southerners found abundant evidence for the communicability of yellow fever from infected persons and things. Quarantine followed a less steady course, and was alternately praised and damned by politicians and newspaper editors in the South, depending upon whether it had appeared efficacious or worthless in the most recent epidemic. While physicians might scoff at the possibility of yellow fever being personally contagious, few lay southerners approached the disease's victims without fear.[4]

Some facts about yellow fever were accepted as common wisdom by the 1840s. The local causes that purportedly generated, or at least nurtured, yellow fever were widely believed to be related to heat, filth, and moisture. In the United States, yellow fever was a disease of late summer and autumn and appeared to be correlated with the degree of nearness to its year-round home, the West Indies. The more frequently a city's summer climate approximated that of the Caribbean, the more likely it was that yellow fever would occur there. Physicians described the "yellow fever zone" as a region with Charleston on its northern edge and Mexico and the West Indies at its heart, within which yellow fever originated. The zone's location might vary from year to year, and had apparently moved southward from the earlier years of the century.[5]

Yellow fever's limitation to cities and towns was a subject of much speculation. Some targeted the miserable overcrowding of poor city dwellers as the central condition around which the other aspects of yellow fever's development clustered.[6] Others argued that it was the presence of abundant animal, as opposed to vegetable, decay that distinguished cities. The miasmata of cities, resulting from dead animals, the by-products of slaughtering and rendering establishments, and piles of unremoved human excrement, seemed distinctively capable of breeding yellow fever.[7] A third etiological factor peculiar to the urban environment was the upturning of soil during construction, leading to the exposure of putrefying matter.[8]

From the 1830s medical researchers both within and outside the South sought to discover the identity of the miasma's disease-causing element. This questioning posture applied both to the miasma of marshy, vegetable origin, and to that indicted in the causation of yellow fever. Some sought to locate organic matter in foul air, and thus attribute the danger to floating microorganisms; others expected to find some poisonous chemical agent, such as hydrogen sulfide, which would explain the deadliness of malaria. Researchers generally looked for a specific component of the air whose presence was consistent with an overabundance of heat, moisture, and rotting substances. For example, John K. Mitchell of Cincinnati published the theory that malaria consisted of different varieties of fungal spores which caused yellow fever, intermittent fever, and cholera.

Josiah C. Nott, on the other hand, argued for the infectious qualities of tiny insects or animalcules that floated in the miasmatic mists.[9]

Accompanying this reexamination of etiological doctrine was an increasing acceptance of the distinct identities of the various fevers. The differences between yellow fever and intermittent fever were particularly stressed; lists of their contrasting signs and symptoms appeared frequently in the medical literature during the 1850s.[10] The association of yellow fever with cities only, its apparent antagonism with malarial diseases and ability to make them temporarily disappear, and the fact that physicians observed many cases of fatal bilious fever that never resembled yellow fever even at the point of death, lent credence to their separate identities. Those physicians such as Rush and his followers who believed that yellow fever was a particularly malignant version of intermittent fever had no difficulty ascribing the exacerbation to poor hygienic conditions or the poverty of the victim.[11] But by the 1840s most southern physicians familiar with yellow fever had come to believe that it was a distinct nosological entity. This decision that yellow fever was a specific disease, with a specific cause of some sort, spurred the search for its etiological agent.

The essential problem in the exploration of the etiology of yellow fever was to separate the cause or causes that were necessary for the development of the disease from those that only contributed to its virulence or spread. For this the case of the town that was only occasionally visited by yellow fever proved the most revealing. "Where the disease is of annual occurrence, it must be difficult if not impossible to point to the sources of its origins," the committee of physicians who investigated the 1855 epidemic in Norfolk began. "It is only where its visits are rare, with long intervals of healthy seasons, that we can hope, by contrasting all the conditions and circumstances of epidemic and healthy years, to discover . . . some local causes which had not previously existed, some unwonted [sic] meteorological conditions, some foreign and imported elements, or a combination of circumstances to furnish an explanation of the occurrence of so extraordinary an epidemic."[12] Not only did theorists who supported a particular theory need to show that in every case their pet cause coincided with the onset of an epidemic, they also had to explain the absence of yellow fever when all causes were apparently present. After one season without yellow fever, a New Orleans medical editor exclaimed, "What a quandary the yellow fever wizards must be in! We have heat and moisture, dead dogs, cats, chickens, etc., all over the streets, and plenty of hungry doctors; yet Yellow Jack will not come. . . . How does the present differ from some of the past, in regard to the *peculiar* conditions?"[13]

During the 1840s southern physicians began to challenge the assumption that yellow fever always originated spontaneously in the towns where it appeared. Works by three southern physicians, Benjamin B. Strobel (1840), John W. Monette (1842), and Wesley M. Carpenter (1844) formed the vanguard of the new tradition supporting the transmissibility of yellow fever. "Now what is meant by transmissibility, is simply this," explained Carpenter, who was professor of materia medica at the Medical College of Louisiana.

Under certain circumstances of temperature, population, &c., the introduction of cases of the disease from abroad; or of the air of other cities, where the disease is prevailing, whether in boxes or the holds of vessels, will tend to generate such a condition in the place, as to give rise to new cases, and finally to an epidemic of the disease. The point which we desire to prove, is, that the disease is transmissible, and consequently importable; and the question as to whether this transmission is by contagion or infection, does not enter into the general problem at all.[14]

Like Carpenter, many authors who wrote on yellow fever in this period struggled to explain the phenomena they had observed. Yellow fever appeared in upriver towns only when an epidemic was active in New Orleans, but most people who traveled from yellow fever centers did not carry it with them. Epidemics apparently had been generated by the arrival of persons, baggage, clothing, or ships from yellow fever areas, yet many such events were innocuous. For most southern physicians in the decade before the Civil War, the evidence indicated that at least in some instances yellow fever had been transported from one infected community to another.

Few southern medical authors adopted Carpenter's insouciant attitude toward the question of contagion. A common ambition of nineteenth-century yellow fever literature was the demonstration that yellow fever was either contagious, i.e., transmitted by personal contact, or infectious, a term of varying definition. One infection theory postulated that the disease was communicable to a limited extent, such that in a close, ill-ventilated room, a companion would receive a sufficiently large dose of the aeriform poison to become diseased. Supporters of the more common, anti-contagionist view of infection denied that yellow fever could be transported by people at all. Instead material goods and trapped air transmitted the germ of yellow fever from a diseased community. Such theorists variously believed that the specific etiological agent, be it termed virus, materies morbus, animalcula, or fungus, could be transported by physical means and released into a new location, where it would reproduce under the proper conditions of filth, moisture, and heat. This idea was not inconsistent with the notion that yellow fever could develop spontaneously in, say, New Orleans or Mobile. Whatever the germ's nature, it might well be resident in some American cities and require only a particular match of meteorological and hygienic conditions to develop.[15]

One center of the debate over transmissibility of yellow fever in the 1840s was rural Louisiana and Mississippi. The editor of the *New-Orleans Medical Journal* noted in 1844, "We find that a good many of our oldest and most respectable physicians have changed their original opinions in regard especially to the transportability of Yellow Fever."[16] Two physicians of Rodney, Mississippi, for example, published their conclusion that yellow fever had been imported into their town from New Orleans in that same year, revealing the self-conscious break with authority that these lower Mississippi Valley physicians experienced. "It is a difficult matter to combat old and received opinions," they wrote. "We are aware that the views we have expressed are counter to those of many, perhaps a majority of our professional brethren. These convictions, however, have been forced on us from observation and reflection, in opposition to early imbibed impressions, and views of those in whose opinions we were thoroughly indoctrinated."[17] In a discussion about a much-contested 1844 epidemic in Woodville, Mississippi, by the Louisiana Medico-Chirurgical Society, both the local origin and transmission theories were presented, although all agreed that they were anti-contagionists and opposed to the idea of personal contagion.[18] By 1854 a Jefferson County, Mississippi, physician could report that while "the practitioners of this section, with one exception, have heretofore been non-contagionists—local origin men—now, with one exception, they are all the other way."[19]

The events of 1853 provided ample data for the transportability controversy, as well as furnishing scenes of such horror as to give the debate added passion. The epidemic began in New Orleans, whence it spread to the cities and towns of Louisiana, Mississippi, and Alabama. At its peak during the month of August more than two hundred people a day were dying in New Orleans. Grave diggers could not keep up. In one particularly graphic instance, "the coffins were deposited on the ground by the cartmen, who then left." After two days in the hot Louisiana sun, the swollen corpses burst their coffins. "Attracted by the unusually violent and offensive effluvia, several citizens in the neighborhood visited the spot . . . [where] the ghastly, reeking bodies . . . might be seen, whilst the odor was almost overpowering."[20] The impact of the epidemic was all the more powerful in that the previous years had seen fairly mild visitations. Those watching the epidemic spread out of New Orleans toward their communities had little doubt that the disease could and did travel.

New Orleans remained a bulwark of anti-contagionist thought throughout this period. The majority of New Orleans physicians were convinced that yellow fever spontaneously originated in New Orleans. In the city, yellow fever often first appeared simultaneously in widely scattered locations, belying the notion of a chain of communication, and was always worst in the filthiest quarters of town. The well-publicized committee report on the disastrous 1853 epidemic in New Orleans argued persuasively that the city was replete with noxious exhalations, heat, and humidity, so that there was no need to postulate some obscure imported cause. Even in New Orleans, however, the profession had come to believe by the 1850s that while not personally contagious, yellow fever could be transported. "The fact of transportability as a property belonging to this disease, no one now disputes," concluded the 1853 committee. "If it were ever doubtful, the current events of the past summer (1853) must be admitted as finally settling it."[21] Yellow fever had not been imported into the city, where it was an indigenous resident, but it had certainly been the city's most significant export in 1853.

The idea of the portability of yellow fever also became popular in the Atlantic coast southern cities during the 1840s and 1850s. Two prominent Charleston physicians, Samuel Henry Dickson and P. C. Gaillard, argued for the contagiousness of yellow fever in an appropriately noxious atmosphere. Editors of medical journals in Charleston and Augusta also promoted the concept that yellow fever could be imported.[22] After some years of respite the east coast cities of Savannah, Charleston, Augusta, and Norfolk were ravaged by severe epidemics of yellow fever in the mid-1850s that converted many physicians to the new doctrine.[23] Physicians studying these epidemics were impressed by the fact that the earliest cases could all be traced to ships arriving from yellow fever–infested Caribbean ports.[24] The events of these 1850s epidemics had an impact beyond the South. "Many of this assembly are doubtless now, for the first time, led to the conviction that the scourge is an imported disease—a conviction imposed on their judgment by the pestilential ravages of 1856, 1857, and 1858," declared a New York physician addressing a northern sanitary conference in 1859. "Let Norfolk and Memphis, and Charleston and Savannah speak."[25]

By the 1850s, the majority of southern medical authors no longer believed that yellow fever always arose locally, and had come to admit the possibility of transporting yellow fever. This transformation is difficult to explain. Erwin Ackerknecht has argued that the evidence for both contagionism and anticontagionism was so evenly divided at mid-century that no physician could decide on the basis of the facts alone. Rather, political inclinations dictated medical theory, with liberals supporting anti-contagionism and conservatives contagionism. This pattern does not emerge among southern physicians during the 1850s.[26] A more useful approach is to realize that even if they all had similar access to the medical evidence relating to yellow fever, physicians at different locations in the South actually saw the phenomena of yellow fever differently. The Atlantic coast cities so ravaged by yellow fever in the 1850s were like the interior towns of Mississippi and Louisiana in that yellow fever was not an annual visitor; thus the epidemics made it possible to determine the essential elements in the development of yellow fever by contrasting the characteristics of epidemic and non-epidemic years. In most cases such evidence resulted in the judgment that yellow fever had been imported into the town. The opportunity to treat the rare occurrence of yellow fever as a sort of laboratory experiment, with non-epidemic years as the control, seems more than any other factor to have critically influenced many southern physicians' decision to accept the transmissibility of yellow fever.

The concept of the transportability of yellow fever was to have a decided impact on the shape of southern public health, but it was not until the last two decades of the nineteenth century, when research on other diseases had provided the germ theory of yellow fever with a solid (if analogical) basis, that this influence was fully realized. By maintaining that both germ and environment were key elements in the development of yellow fever, the theory allowed for reconciliation between the advocates of sanitation and the proponents of quarantine. It proclaimed that both were useful and worthy of pursuit. Yet it would be an oversimplification to see this theory as a comprehensive, unified doctrine, recognized as such at the time; rather, it should be considered a group of assumptions that physicians had come to share, though not precluding strong differences about the implications or elaboration of those assumptions. Too many issues, such as the nature of the germ and its mode of transport, were still unresolved, and the appropriate significance to be assigned to germ or environment in the prevention of yellow fever had yet to be settled.

With transportability no longer seriously at issue by the mid-1850s, quarantine became a central topic for debate. The fact that yellow fever could be imported did not refute the possibility that it could also develop spontaneously from local causes, the same causes that acted in the West Indies, where it was indisputably indigenous. Prominent physicians in New Orleans and Mobile, such as E. D. Fenner and George A. Ketchum, grudgingly admitted that to quarantine seriously filthy ships was perhaps a wise practice. They remained convinced, though, that the major source of yellow fever was to be found at home, in the unsanitary condition of their cities.[27] Quarantines were useless for the prevention of yellow fever not because they were founded on a faulty theory, but because it was foolish to try to exclude an already established local inhabitant. Physicians in towns less frequently visited by yellow fever were more likely to believe that the main line of defense against the disease was quarantine. Thus C. B. Guthrie of Memphis, who accepted the impropriety of quarantine for Mobile and New Orleans, concurrently believed that a quarantine system was necessary for the protection of communities outside of the semi-tropical region where yellow fever developed spontaneously.[28] The public health controversies of the 1850s revolved around the questions of whether quarantine was relevant at all to the protection of southern communities, and, if it could prevent the introduction of yellow fever, to whom or what the inhibition of passage should be directed.

While the idea that yellow fever could be transported brought a renaissance of interest in quarantine, it also brought a newly critical attitude toward its function and operation. Those who believed that people carried yellow fever within their bodies continued to advocate human isolation. Others, who thought the danger lay primarily in the emanations of people as transmitted to their clothing and belongings, argued that a thorough cleansing of the patient and his material accompaniments was sufficient to limit the personal spread of yellow fever. The more dominant view demarcated human beings as non-carriers of yellow fever, and focused instead on physical objects, such as ships, clothing, and baggage. This theory was approved, for example, at a series of Quarantine and Sanitary Conventions held in Philadelphia, New York, and Boston from 1857 to 1860. By a vote of eighty-five to six the 1859 convention, composed almost entirely of physicians and businessmen from the Northeast, renounced the theory of personal contagion but approved the quarantine of material goods. Rejecting the old system of mere detention, this convention and many reform-minded southerners argued for the disinfection of ships, baggage, and passengers. Approved disinfectants were agents known to halt fermentation and extinguish foul putrefactive odors, such as chloride of lime, steam, or the gas evolved from burning sulphur.[29] A variety of conflicting quarantine programs were thus postulated to meet the indications of the new faith in yellow fever's portability.

Events during the Civil War added new information to the sanitary debates. New Orleans suffered no yellow fever epidemics during the federal occupation from 1862 to 1865, and those outbreaks that did occur, in North Carolina and Key West, were isolated. General Benjamin F. Butler, the federal officer in charge of occupied New Orleans, was given almost universal credit for excluding yellow fever from the city; he employed armies of men to clean the streets and enforced a strict quarantine against yellow fever ports, to the point of risking an international incident with the Spanish government. Although some southern physicians doubted that Butler's tyrannical ways had saved New Orleans, other observers pointed to the Civil War experience as evidence for the power of modern sanitary science to protect a population. As strategems for controlling yellow fever, both quarantine and sanitation emerged from the war with higher prestige, as did the reputation of the federal government as a force for the prevention of epidemic disease. The recurrence of yellow fever epidemics from 1867 to 1876, with especially serious epidemics in 1867, 1871, 1873, and 1876, heightened by contrast the apparent success of the Civil War years.[30]

Theoretical knowledge about yellow fever had expanded but had not dramatically changed since the antebellum period. Before the war the southern medical community had been divided over the issue of what was carried by a ship that transported yellow fever, with the majority arguing for something organic and a minority maintaining that an inanimate gaseous poison was the danger. By the 1870s, however, most southern medical authors agreed that the causative agent of yellow fever was a living germ of microscopic proportions. The transportability theory of the Old South became the germ theory of yellow fever in the last quarter of the nineteenth century. A few physicians still contended that yellow fever could arise spontaneously out of filth—the theory that transportability had largely replaced in the mid-fifties—but for the most part southern physicians were agreed that yellow fever developed from a specific transportable poison, not a concurrence of filth, heat, moisture, or other non-specific factors. By the 1870s European authorities had independently advocated the transportability doctrine, and their conversion no doubt solidified American medical opinion.[31]

The yellow fever epidemic of 1878 ended the dispute over the transportability theory. As will be described in later chapters, this epidemic was unusual in its ferocity and distribution. Beginning in New Orleans, it traveled on the newly rebuilt railroads and revitalized river transports to over a hundred communities in the South and Midwest. Residents of small towns such as Gallipolis, Ohio, and Paris, Tennessee, who had never before worried much about the disease, watched as natives died of yellow fever, usually those who lived in close proximity to railroad stations. One rural Mississippi physician, who had watched the fever moving ever closer on the railroad lines, described it in a letter to his wife as "the most terrible fever that ever invaded any country before." He believed it to be unusually severe, and noted, "I do not know of a single recovery so far."[32] Further letters document, one by one, the deaths of his fellow physicians. The letters end in mid-September. Throughout the South the tracks of the invader could be traced. The germ theory of yellow fever provided the most convincing explanation of this behavior, and the permeation of yellow fever throughout the Mississippi Valley in 1878 clearly heightened the theory's prestige.[33]

One prominent issue in the 1850s that remained unresolved in 1880 was the question of whether yellow fever was indigenous to any part of the South. Could the germ of yellow fever become a "naturalized citizen" of any southern city, or did it at least have the capacity to hibernate after a particularly malignant epidemic and then incite disease the following summer without again being imported? "An overwhelming majority of the profession believe that the disease is not indigenous in any part of the United States," one physician told the American Public Health Association in 1877, "unless, perhaps, in the semi-tropical climate of our Gulf Coast, in regard to which there may be some doubt."[34] Those that believed that the germ could survive the winter reasoned that if preserved in vomit-soaked bedclothes or the putrid (but warm) cellar of a formerly infected house, the germ might well escape the exposure to frost which usually destroyed its malignancy. The question was no longer whether yellow fever could arise spontaneously from filth; rather the debates over the indigenous nature of yellow fever in the late nineteenth century concerned the germ's chances of finding an environment hospitable enough to sustain it until warm weather returned.

It was in New Orleans that the issue of indigenousness had the greatest significance and aroused the greatest passion. Yellow fever had beset the city so frequently that during the 1870s it was considered the most likely American city to be permanently harboring yellow fever. "It is the opinion of a large majority of the physicians of New Orleans, perhaps nine-tenths of the whole number, that yellow fever is not indigenous there, and that every new epidemic outbreak of it is due to a new importation," noted Jerome Cochran of the Alabama State Board of Health in 1880. "But there remains a very respectable minority of her physicians . . . [who believe] that it has become acclimated and naturalized so that domestic cases occur every year, springing from germs that live through the winter in sheltered places, and that are awakened to malignant activity on the approach of summer."[35] Nevertheless, the endemicity question in New Orleans seemed conclusively settled by the turn of the century, since with the exception of three epidemics in the late 1890s, the city suffered no epidemics for almost two decades.

By the mid-1890s, fears that yellow fever might establish a permanent foothold in the United States were focused almost entirely on the southernmost tip of Florida, where recurring epidemics of yellow fever in Key West led to speculation that the island's near-tropical climate and unsanitary condition had provided an ideal year-round home for the yellow fever germ. Permanent residency aside, the belief that the yellow fever germ could survive at least one winter to spark a recrudescence the following summer was still widely held. In order to prevent such an occurrence, public health officials recommended the thorough sanitation of a town following an epidemic, including the disinfection of all materials soiled by contact with the yellow fever patient and the general cleansing of the town's streets and privies.[36]

The belief in the germ theory of yellow fever, which matured in the 1870s and was largely unquestioned in the 1880s, developed not so much from the discovery of new information about yellow fever but from the evidence accumulated by medical researchers about other diseases. Germ theorists of the 1850s had asserted that only such a theory could explain the behavior of yellow fever, especially its ability to develop into a wide scale epidemic after the introduction of only one source. In their view, such proliferation indicated the rapid reproduction of some living thing. Germ theorists in the 1870s and 1880s were forced to rely on similar arguments, but in addition they could point to the demonstration of microbial causes for other diseases and proclaim that it was only a matter of time before the agent of yellow fever would likewise be found. The recurring discoveries of yellow fever germs in the 1880s and 1890s bolstered this faith.[37]

The concept of the germ was an amorphous one in the 1870s. Although medical authorities could agree on the evidence for its existence, they were not in accord as to its exact nature. The germ's base definition was, in the words of one medical editor, "something which is capable of growth and propagation outside the living human body."[38] Naturally such a creature had to be microscopic as well, to qualify for germ status. The biological order thought most likely to contain the yellow fever germ during the 1870s was the fungi, since its preference for warm, moist climates accorded well with the distribution of yellow fever. The bacteria replaced the fungi during the 1880s and 1890s, as microbiologists discovered more and more bacterial causes for other diseases. It is interesting to note the emphasis on outside development here. Although researchers believed that the external support system was filth, and not an animal vector, the essential notion of survival outside the human body was present.

Any proposed germ had to conform to several accepted criteria. Physicians embraced the germ theory of yellow fever largely because it proved so useful in explaining the epidemiology of the disease, especially its portability. A microorganism identified by a researcher as the specific causative agent in yellow fever was plausible to the extent that it preserved this explanatory power. There were many puzzling facts about yellow fever that physicians hoped the discovery of the yellow fever germ would clarify. "It is generally admitted," wrote the president of the Louisiana Board of Health in 1875 when describing the peculiar behavior of yellow fever, "that the chief danger to a city lies in the transportation of yellow fever poison by holds of ships, cargoes and baggage, and that the disease is rarely, if ever, propagated from person to person."[39] That the yellow fever germ could travel in material objects few denied; any claimant to identity with the yellow fever germ should be capable of doing likewise. The issue of whether yellow fever was directly contagious, however, remained cloudy through the end of the century. Most public health officials acted as if they assumed diseased persons were dangerous, at least to those around them. Whether the peril arose from one-to-one contagion or the patients' personal effects, isolation of yellow fever patients and the disinfection of any material objects accompanying them were standard public health procedures during the last two decades of the nineteenth century. Any germ theorist who could explain the exact place of the patient in the transmission of yellow fever and the ability of the germ to thrive in an environment exterior to the patient through the elaboration of his germ's lifecycle or behavior had excellent evidence to offer in the verification of his discovery.

Most late nineteenth-century physicians believed that the germ of yellow fever entered the body through the respiratory tract. The wafting of the yellow fever germ through the air accounted for the disease's ability to jump from house to house in the absence of communication between the occupants, and also made understandable the outbreak of an epidemic at several points in a city simultaneously. An adjunct to the idea that the yellow fever germ was an aeriform poison was the assumption that air particularly heavy with unhealthy vapors, such as emanations from garbage heaps or mounds of putrefying filth, provided the most hospitable environment for the germ. Many public health practitioners argued that the germ could not survive in a clean atmosphere. Explaining the supportive qualities of dirty air was another task for the proponent of a neophyte yellow fever germ.[40]

Perhaps the most significant characteristic of yellow fever with which any proposed germ had to be consistent was the disease's well-marked geographic selectivity. The existence of a yellow fever zone was undisputed, however physicians might wrangle over its boundaries. The disease clearly preferred hot, humid, and filthy locations. The germ could flourish outside of its normal habitat, as the experiences of Philadelphia and New York demonstrated, but only under extraordinary conditions of filth and heat. One Cincinnati physician made a typical argument, that for an epidemic of yellow fever to develop in his city, it was "not only necessary to bring it [yellow fever] here, but, so to speak, to care for it in its incipiency, and afford it the congenial soil of bad hygienic surroundings, in order to develop it into an epidemic form."[41] Any microorganism proposed as the yellow fever culprit that was not subject to damage by extremes of cold, or that was widely prevalent outside of the yellow fever zone, was not likely to achieve medical acceptance.[42]

The study of yellow fever in the laboratory during the 1870s and 1880s marked a new approach to medical research on the disease, and challenged the information garnered by early researchers who relied on a quite different method. The yellow fever authorities who had been studying the disease in the South since the early years of the century were natural historians, whose technique consisted in closely observing the disease—carefully noting its apparent origin, symptoms, response to therapy, duration in individuals and the community, association with temperature, humidity, and filth, and other characteristics. Some writers on yellow fever, such as Stanford Chaillé and Joseph Jones of New Orleans and Cochran of Alabama, were major public health figures who produced an abundant literature on the disease. But many others were physicians who experienced a particular epidemic and chose to describe its course, perhaps as their only foray into medical publication. By the 1880s there existed a large body of literature from which physicians could cull facts about yellow fever's epidemiology, pathology, and treatment. Medical researchers studied and described yellow fever in much the same way that biologists characterized an animal species through field research. To prove a new theory about yellow fever within the natural history framework, a researcher rarely relied on tests or experiments; instead, he or she was constrained to demonstrate the ways in which the new idea more powerfully explained the natural history of yellow fever and did not contradict accepted knowledge about the disease. Thus during the late nineteenth century a proposed yellow fever germ had not only to meet the requirements of laboratory science in establishing its validity, but also the dictates of the natural historian of yellow fever.[43]

The triumphant discoveries of the bacteriological laboratories of Europe were well known to American physicians of the 1880s and have been extensively documented by historians.[44] For every major success, such as Koch's establishment of the tubercle and anthrax bacilli or Klebs's and Loeffler's work on diphtheria, there was a multitude of research efforts that did not yield the correct causative agent. The frequent announcement and then retraction of microorganic etiological breakthroughs created skepticism about the claims of bacteriologists. In an address before the New York Academy of Medicine in 1884, its president, Abraham Jacobi, lamented the "bacteriomania" that had swept the medical profession. While praising the careful research and conservative attitude of "Robert Koch and his peers," Jacobi feared that too often Koch's followers were given to sloppy technique and over-enthusiasm for their own discoveries. And American physicians were too quick to believe every announcement. "The practitioners, either general or special, have readily accepted the new gospel with but few exceptions," Jacobi reported. "The new theories that infectious and zymotic diseases have each their own bacillus, are so pleasant and promised to be so fruitful that it required some courage to critically resist the flood."[45] Jacobi was not alone in his call for moderation. One medical editor expressed similar cynicism after experiencing the pattern of rapid discoveries and refutations common to the 1880s and 1890s. "We have earnestly endeavored to keep up with the times and avoid the reproach of 'old-fogy-ism,' " he declared in 1897. "Each year we have proclaimed the bacterial causation of various diseases, and laboriously retracted it all in the next session's lectures."[46]

A number of yellow fever microbes were proposed and discarded during the last three decades of the nineteenth century. Those of Domingos Freire and Giuseppe Sanarelli were the most famous of the many contenders. Since the cause of yellow fever is viral, those researchers who were considered successful were describing fungal or bacterial contaminants. Further complications arose from the fact that yellow fever cannot be transmitted to the usual laboratory animals; only monkeys share susceptibility with humans. So researchers most likely confused cases of sepsis in their experimental rodents with yellow fever. Army physician George Sternberg, one of America's first microbiologists, was the most prominent critic of these various yellow fever germs. In 1890 he published a landmark study discrediting all the yellow fever germs proposed to date, including Freire's.[47] Appointed Surgeon General in 1893, Sternberg promoted research on yellow fever and other infectious diseases within the army. When Sanarelli announced his yellow fever germ in 1897, Sternberg asked Walter Reed and James Carroll to investigate the new discovery. Their resulting papers prompted a vigorous debate that Sanarelli eventually lost. Reed and Carroll then faced two choices, either to pursue further bacteriological explorations seeking the yellow fever germ, or to test the theory proposed in 1881 by Dr. Carlos Finlay of Cuba, that yellow fever was transmitted by the mosquito.[48]

"First, it seemed probable that it could be decided in a few weeks," recalled James Carroll, when listing the reasons why the commission chose to study the mosquito's role in yellow fever's transmission.

Second, there were many points of similarity between the two diseases, malaria and yellow fever, in regard to seasonal prevalence, favorable locality, manner of extension, etc.; third, the lapse of an interval of several weeks between primary and secondary cases pointed to the existence of an intermediate host; the prompt subsidence of an epidemic upon the occurrence of severe frosts corresponded with the effect of the latter upon the mosquito, and the same insect was suggested by the peculiar manner in which the disease appeared to jump from house to house, even when the inhabitants, did not communicate with one another.[49]

Carroll's comments illustrate the several factors classically accepted as influencing the Reed commission's decisions: the suggestive impact of Ronald Ross's work on malaria, epidemiological evidence on the chronological course of yellow fever, and the peculiar behavior of yellow fever in its mode of communication within a community. It was thus from the natural history of yellow fever, and not from laboratory research, that the most successful nineteenth-century researchers on the etiology of yellow fever acquired their clues.[50]

Carroll's comments also highlight the importance of recent work done in 1898 on the epidemiology of yellow fever. Henry Rose Carter, a Marine Hospital Service officer, established the time interval between the point at which the first cases of yellow fever appeared in a community and the second wave. By looking at two small towns in Mississippi, he calculated that it took two weeks for the second cases to appear after the first had been introduced from outside the towns. This implied that the disease organism spent that time in an outside host, or that the disease had a prolonged incubation period. Carter's work stands as one of the classics of tropical epidemiology.[51]

Carlos Finlay had argued since 1881 that yellow fever was spread by mosquitoes; why did it take almost two decades for his theory to be accepted? In part, because the theory had no company. With the exception of the exotic filariasis, during the 1880s there had been no analogous suggestion of an insect vector for another disease. This would change in the coming decade. In 1893 American bacteriologist Theobald Smith announced the transmission of the plasmodium of Texas cattle fever by ticks. Ross demonstrated that malaria was transmitted by mosquitoes in 1897, and other researchers had conclusively established the connection for man by 1899. So the idea that insects could transmit disease was current in the 1890s. The precedent of Ross and Smith no doubt made Finlay's suggestion seem much more relevant in 1899.[52]

In a perceptive article, Nancy Stepan has asserted that social and political factors are more important in explaining the delay than strictly scientific ones. She maintains that the unwillingness of the American government to sponsor research on yellow fever, coupled with the Army's complacent attitude toward the disease, made yellow fever a problem of low priority. The Army had previously relied on depopulation of camps as a mode of controlling yellow fever; according to Stepan, once Cuba had been occupied this no longer remained a viable means of fighting the disease and a new solution had to be found. Furthermore, the relative scarcity of yellow fever in the United States in the nearly two decades since Finlay's first publication on the mosquito had meant that interest in the disease among American researchers was minimal. It was not, as some historians had argued, that Finlay's work was inherently unscientific or unconvincing, Stepan concludes, but rather that factors external to science caused the delay.[53]

Stepan's explanation is cogent, but incomplete. Certainly the factors she cites were important, although she has overestimated the American satisfaction with contemporary yellow fever methods for dealing with yellow fever epidemics. Events chronicled in the last two chapters of this work demonstrate that public health officials attempting to limit the epidemics that occurred during the last two decades of the nineteenth century actively sought some technique other than depopulation. Another way to interpret the impact of rare yellow fever epidemics is to see that the disease's absence not only dampened interest in research, it also denied researchers opportunities for studying the disease.

It is exceedingly difficult to say with certainty why an event did not happen, why an idea was not pursued. But in the case of the mosquito vector of yellow fever, suggestive explanations that depend on the content of the science involved can be offered. Physicians did not feel particularly constrained to account for the ability of the yellow fever germ to reside outside the body for considerable periods. There was no need to postulate an insect vector when filth appeared to supply such a suitable habitat. Finlay not only championed the mosquito as the yellow fever vector; he also claimed discovery of the germ that the mosquito was transmitting. Sternberg included that discovery among the many that he dismissed in his 1890 report on yellow fever bacteriology. Finlay's emphasis during the late 1880s and 1890s was on the value of the mosquito for deliberately inoculating patients with a milder yellow fever than they would acquire naturally. Sternberg challenged the logic of Finlay's argument in 1891 with an analysis based on the physiology and anatomy of the mosquito, which Sternberg believed precluded the transmission of any microbe. Thus the most respected yellow fever researcher in the United States had rejected Finlay's claims as ungrounded. It is likely that Finlay's views were lumped together, in the minds of many American physicians, with all the other pseudo-discoveries of the day.[54]

The American occupation of Havana was certainly important for bringing together American researchers with the immediate problem of yellow fever. But at least as important were the two demonstrations of insect vectors for other diseases that had occurred during the decade. The slight interest in Finlay's work before 1893 is not very surprising, but after the elaboration of the epidemiology of Texas cattle fever by Theobald Smith, it becomes somewhat harder to understand. Like yellow fever, the cattle disease was limited to a southern climate, although the disease could be transmitted outside of its natural zone. The diseases were analogous enough that one physician suggested in 1898 that perhaps, as in the relationship of cowpox to smallpox, the preventive inoculation developed to protect cows from Texas fever might in addition protect humans from yellow fever.[55]

But the disease that was viewed as most analogous to yellow fever, and which even at times mimicked it, was malaria. Although malaria was by and large a disease of rural districts, endemic to large parts of the United States and usually much less fatal than yellow fever, the epidemiology of the two diseases was strikingly similar in many respects. This information, gathered within the natural history tradition of epidemiological research, was probably the most important factor in causing Reed and Carroll to draw the analogy between malaria and yellow fever, and to consider Finlay's theory worth testing. Carroll said Finlay's hypothesis was selected "because of the numerous points of resemblance between yellow fever and malaria, which was known to be conveyed by the mosquito. Both diseases are air-borne; both are contracted mostly at night; both jump from house to house in a mysterious way; both prevail in the season when mosquitoes are numerous, and infections cease to occur upon the appearance of a sharp frost."[56] This list of characteristics supporting the idea that malaria was transmitted by mosquitoes had recently been elaborated in an 1899 article in the *Johns Hopkins Hospital Reports,* which reviewed the present status of the role of insects in disease. Although the author of the article dismissed the possibility that mosquitoes spread yellow fever, one familiar with the natural history of the disease, as Reed and Carroll surely were by 1899, might perhaps have been struck by the fact that the epidemiological arguments cited as evidence for the transmission of malaria by mosquitoes could with equal force be applied to yellow fever.[57]

François Delaporte has published a rather different interpretation of the events surrounding the discovery of the mosquito vector theory of yellow fever. He sees a direct and unacknowledged line from Patrick Manson's work on filariasis to Finlay's hypothesis. Furthermore, he feels that since Finlay saw the mosquito as merely a vessel, like a hypodermic syringe, and not as an intermediate host crucial to the organism's life cycle, his work's influence on Reed was less than Ross's. Delaporte argues that the most significant influence on Reed and his colleagues was Ross's description of the mosquito as a true intermediate host, which made the Reed commission able to see the significance of Carter's work on the interval between primary and secondary cases. He goes on to claim, on rather thin evidence, that this connection was pointed out to the Americans by a visiting commission from Liverpool. Be that as it may, one is still left without firm knowledge of who guessed what when, and why. Delaporte explores in fascinating detail the ways in which the claims for the priority of the mosquito have become matters of national pride, especially for Cuban historians. Suffice it to say here that Finlay, Ross, Carter, Manson, and Smith probably all contributed to the fund of knowledge from which the American commission drew their working hypothesis.[58]

The simple but brilliant experiments by which Reed and his co-workers established the mosquito vector are well known.

To test the fomite theory of transmission, they isolated army volunteers in one hut with bedding, clothing, and other items drenched in the ejecta of yellow fever patients. Other men were housed in clean surroundings, and merely exposed to the bites of mosquitoes who had recently fed upon a yellow fever patient. The first group, although undoubtedly miserable, stayed healthy, while many of second sickened with yellow fever. Reed never tested the possibility of direct personal contagion; it was generally assumed that if the yellow fever patient somehow gave off the yellow fever germ, it would be found in those items traditionally accused of spreading the disease. Reed's experiments appeared to demonstrate that those objects were harmless.[59]

The path to discovery followed by Reed illustrates the practice common to disease investigations of the time, the process of reasoning by analogy. For at least two decades physicians had accepted the germ theory of yellow fever at least in part because so many other diseases had been shown to have microorganic causes. Similarly, researchers in the 1880s had postulated that the yellow fever germ might be like that of cholera or typhoid, and spread from alimentary tract to alimentary tract through the water supply. Others argued that it might, like the diphtheria bacillus, enter through the respiratory system and poison the body with toxins. Reed's guess, that yellow fever was transmitted in the same way as malaria, was not necessarily any more inspired—it just happened to be correct. After the mosquito vector for both diseases had been established, yellow fever researchers attempted to extend the analogical relationship between the diseases by searching for a plasmodial parasite for yellow fever (and, consistent with earlier research patterns, such an organism was actually discovered).[60]

The process by which Reed and his followers attempted to convince the medical world of the validity of the mosquito doctrine demonstrates the power of the natural history approach for explaining yellow fever etiology. Proponents of the mosquito theory knew that it was not enough merely to recount the experimental procedure followed and the conclusive results obtained. They had to show that the theory was in accord with the accepted body of knowledge culled from former yellow fever epidemics.

Carroll and William Crawford Gorgas, whose work in eradicating yellow fever first in Havana and later in Panama had proven the practical merit of the mosquito doctrine, especially emphasized how well the mosquito theory explained the facts of yellow fever's natural history.[61] Opponents to the theory also utilized historical arguments. New Orleans physician Charles Faget, for example, denied that "the mosquito craze" held any truth at all. "With the authority of all past observers, I will state: this pretended fact is an error of observation, because, if true, it would contradict the well-established fact of the non-contagiousness of yellow fever."[62] Surely there were and had been ample mosquitoes in hospitals, ready to transmit yellow fever to hospital attendants; yet they rarely contracted yellow fever. With pun intended he scoffed, "This mosquito theory rests on a reed!"[63]

Perhaps the most important phenomenon that the mosquito theory had to explain was the obvious success achieved by American public health officials during the last two decades of the nineteenth century in the control of yellow fever. Most public health officials believed that their work had not been in vain, for yellow fever had disappeared from most of the country, and become increasingly rare where it still occurred. They sought to discover why their misguided efforts had been fruitful, not to ridicule past practices. The drainage of cities, which accompanied sanitary reform efforts, was the most commonly cited factor in the elimination of yellow fever during the last half of the nineteenth century. By reducing mosquito breeding areas, the insect population was correspondingly thinned and the chances of disease transmission greatly lowered. In regard to the actions of Baltimore, Boston, and Philadelphia against yellow fever early in the nineteenth century, the president of the Orleans Parish Medical Society remarked in 1905, "They immediately devoted themselves to cleaning up and widening their streets, constructing parks, establishing running water and splendid drainage and sewerage systems. Unconsciously, they had destroyed the hosts of transmission without knowing in what way they had done so."[64] The disappearance of yellow fever from the Atlantic coastal cities north of Georgia by the late nineteenth century, an event physicians linked inexorably to their improved sanitary condition, was used by both sides in the debates over the mosquito theory.[65]

Acceptance of the Reed commission's work came rapidly. Although Reed's group had failed to find the parasite of yellow fever and demonstrate its stages in the lifecycle of the mosquito, as had been done for malaria, this was not a major strike against the mosquito theory. At the meeting of the American Public Health Association in 1902, the American Medical Association in 1903, and a quarantine conference of delegates from southern states in 1905, the conclusions were the same—almost unanimous support for the mosquito as the sole carrier of yellow fever.[66]

Reed's work revived interest in finding the yellow fever germ. Several mosquito-borne bacilli were proposed and then disproven.[67] As early as 1898, Frederick Novy had suggested, "It is more than likely that the germ of yellow fever, as well as those of smallpox, measles, hydrophobia, etc., belongs to a group of organisms, smaller than our bacteria, and as yet unknown, awaiting discovery. The recent work of Roux and Nocard on the microbe of pleuropneumonia already proves the existence of organisms smaller than the 'infinitely small' bacteria."[68] In that same year reports appeared from the German microbiologists Friedrich Loeffler and Paul Frosch that the cause of hoof and mouth disease, an affliction of cattle, was submicroscopic in nature. After learning of their findings, William Welch suggested to Reed and Carroll that the germ of yellow fever might be similar in size. In 1901 Reed and Carroll took up this question, and discovered that filtrate acquired by passing blood from yellow fever patients through porcelain filters did indeed cause yellow fever when injected into humans. It remained for a host of researchers, working in the late twenties and early thirties, to demonstrate with finality the viral identity of the long-sought yellow fever germ, and to develop a vaccine to guard humans from its ravages.[69]

What difference did these continuing disputations about the etiology of yellow fever make for those public health officials charged with protecting their communities from yellow fever? To answer this question it is necessary to look at how etiological theory was used to justify public health practice. From the 1870s, the sheet anchor of yellow fever prophylaxis was the germ theory. Public health measures were all concentrated on excluding, starving, or killing the yellow fever germ. Public health workers employed disinfectants to destroy the germ on clothing, bedding, the surfaces of houses, streets, ships, and in privies. Although physicians often questioned the value of particular disinfectants, and researchers sought to discover the most potent germicide that was at the same time safe and practical, by and large the efficacy of disinfectants in the prevention of yellow fever was unquestioned.

Disinfection was central to new quarantine procedures, which, although conceived before the Civil War, were only fully implemented in the 1880s. The new system, termed revolutionary by its foremost proselytizer, Joseph Holt of the Louisiana State Board of Health, involved the cleansing of ships that had arrived from yellow fever ports and their subsequent purification with disinfectant substances. The contents of the ship, including personal items carried by passengers, were disinfected as well. Costly new quarantine stations were erected, which included equipment for filling a ship's hold full of sulphurous acid gas and large disinfecting ovens that raised clothing and bedding to 250 degrees. Passengers were observed for a short period (usually 5–10 days if they came from a yellow fever port); if no signs of disease developed they were released. To this procedure the assumption of a germ target was central. This was the most crucial contribution of etiological theory to public health efforts against yellow fever during the late nineteenth century. Public health officials regarded this new system as thoroughly scientific, and derided the old method of mere detention as barbarous.[70]

The new system combined sanitation and detention, the two methods of yellow fever control advocated by opposing sides in earlier years. The idea that yellow fever was spread by a germ supported both the use of disinfectants to kill imported organisms and general sanitation to render cities less receptive to the germ. Through the end of the century physicians continued to believe that the yellow fever germ survived and propagated in filth. Yellow fever's threat bolstered sanitary drives in cities oppressed by the disease, and was instrumental, for example, in the provision of sewers for Memphis in 1879–1880. Yet the revolutionary quarantine, which promised to remove yellow fever as a factor altogether, at the same time removed a powerful impetus for public sanitation. As the presence of yellow fever in the South lessened toward the end of the century, so did the usefulness of yellow fever as a goad for sanitary reform.

Southerners accepted the dual approach to yellow fever's etiology—seeing both the germ and its soil as important—more uniformly than did northern sanitarians. The most outspoken dissenter was George Waring, whose posts included New York City street commisioner in the 1890s. His career was intricately interwoven with the control of yellow fever. He designed the Memphis sewer system that revolutionized the city's hygiene in 1879, and died of yellow fever after carrying out a sanitary survey of Havana in 1898. Waring believed that filth alone caused yellow fever, and worried that attention to a particular germ would detract from the essential need for urban sanitation. His Memphis sewers were famous, credited for keeping yellow fever out of the city permanently. It is perhaps fortunate that he died before it was demonstrated that the thorough cleaning of Havana his survey recommended had no effect at all on yellow fever. His dismay at anti-mosquito tactics that slighted basic sanitation can only be imagined.[71]

Because the main steps in the control of yellow fever employed by southerners in the 1880s and 1890s relied solely upon the existence of a germ, but not upon knowledge about its specific identity, public health practice remained aloof from the controversies surrounding each new yellow fever microorganism. This is not to say that a genuine discovery might not have been extremely valuable to the prevention of the disease, but during the last two decades of the century public health officials did not alter their procedures on account of the stirring announcements of even the most widely accepted germ, the one proposed by Sanarelli. Physicians did hope that finding the true yellow fever germ would lead to more accurate methods of diagnosis, the production of a vaccine, or even a cure, but none of the germs postulated from 1880 to 1900 fulfilled these expectations. Southern public health officials were often among the

American physicians most actively concerned with the yellow fever germ disputes, but until Reed's work on the mosquito, their interest grew out of the perceived potential of the new discoveries rather than from implications for extant public health practices. The multiple identifications of yellow fever germs could bolster, but in no way challenge, confidence in the contemporary techniques for controlling yellow fever.

The discovery of the mosquito vector did, on the other hand, strike at the very roots of public health practice. An analysis of the acceptance of the theory by southern public health authorities appears in chapter four; suffice it to say here that the new knowledge about the transmission of yellow fever required a fundamental restructuring of public health procedures and called into question the principle underlying the germicidal techniques so central to yellow fever prophylaxis. But before 1900 the medical research on yellow fever, inspired by the exciting successes of bacteriological investigations of other diseases, only affected public health practice by deepening the conviction held by southern public health professionals that yellow fever was caused by some germ. On this principle they based their operations. Although there were innovations in the control of yellow fever during this period, they were not the result of theoretical changes, but rather of the application of the germ theory already established by 1880.

2

YELLOW FEVER, THE SOUTH, AND THE NATION, 1840–1880

Yellow fever unmistakably dominated public health thought and activity in the nineteenth-century South, and an analysis of southern efforts to comprehend and control this disease offers the most promising means of understanding the public health endeavor in this region. The public health awareness that evolved in the South during the 1840s and 1850s displayed the distinctive features that were to mark southern public health efforts well into the twentieth century. Like the North and West, the South suffered from cholera, typhoid, and intermittent fevers, but it was yellow fever that distinguished it from the rest of the nation as a region where life and health were particularly endangered. The challenge of yellow fever gave quarantine a prominence in southern public health efforts not evident elsewhere in the country. While southern physicians sought to control the disease with the usual public health tools of statistics and hygiene, it was in the management of quarantine that they found their principal role. During the 1870s state boards of health were founded in the South with the mandate to fight yellow fever. When the disease devastated the South in 1878, the inadequacies of these boards seemed evident. The epidemic consequently spurred the evolution of federal public health institutions and set the stage for competing local and national interests to dispute the distribution of public health responsibility over yellow fever.

By the 1840s both northern critics and southern jeremiahs were depicting the South as the unhealthiest region of the United States. Southerners, and especially southern physicians, became increasingly concerned with the high mortality levels and the prevalence of deadly disease in their region. From the colonial period Americans of both regions had acknowledged morbid differences between North and South, but during the 1840s and 1850s a new anxiety about regional disparities marked the writings of medical Southerners. This consciousness was largely occasioned by the retreat of yellow fever from northern cities, and the concomitant rise in both the frequency and malignancy of yellow fever in the South.

The emerging awareness of the distinction yellow fever conferred in the two decades before the Civil War coincided chronologically with the public health movements of the American Northeast, England, and France.[1] Southern physicians concerned with public health shared with their reform-minded colleagues elsewhere the belief that disease was the result of physical, often artificial causes, and could be overcome if governmental power were directed against its sources. There can be little doubt that the promotion of urban sanitation in the South was on the whole less energetic than in the Northeast or in Europe. But there are few insights to be gained into the inner workings of southern public health by a systematic comparison of public health in the South and North, seeking to establish the extent of southern inferiority or parity. After all, the South did differ from the North socially, economically, intellectually, demographically and, not least of all, epidemiologically, and the simple fact that these differences altered public health activity is hardly surprising. Instead, in order to understand public health in the antebellum South it is important to scrutinize the choices and decisions of Southerners concerned with public health against the backdrop of the southern disease environment.

As it was in the seaport and inland commercial cities and towns of the South where yellow fever flourished, antebellum public health activity concentrated on the urban setting. All boards of health established in the Old South were civic in scope, even the so-called Louisiana State Board of Health (1855), which in reality was a New Orleans board. Although city authorities appointed boards of health to battle yellow fever in Norfolk (1800), New Orleans (1804), Charleston (1808), Natchez (1841), and Mobile (1841), such organizations generally had no continuous existence, and became active only when an epidemic threatened. The boards typically were charged with enforcing quarantine codes that dated from the colonial or territorial periods, and frequently received broad sanitary responsibilities as well.[2] Medical members of the boards of health, and the port physicians whose task it was to inspect ships in quarantine, became the South's first public health officials. But their influence was for the most part overshadowed by a larger body of physicians, otherwise prominent in the southern medical community, who appointed themselves guardians of the public welfare and spokesmen for the need for public health reform.

Southerners did not ignore the other major epidemic of the period, cholera, but it figured much less prominently in discussions about public health. The cholera epidemic of the 1830s, which proved so deadly to the Northeast, touched much of the South lightly. The epidemic that spanned the years 1848–1855 was more serious in its impact, especially in and around New Orleans, but since the disease struck heavily in the Midwest as well, it did not peculiarly stigmatize the South. Cholera provided the principal inspiration for public health activity only in southern cities such as Richmond, Nashville, and Memphis, which were rarely or not at all subject to yellow fever. In response to the threat of cholera the editors of medical journals in these cities promoted civic sanitation and personal hygiene, and temporary boards of health were appointed. Cholera motivated public health action in some southern cities, but it was yellow fever that by and large fostered the South's reform activity.[3]

In each year in the two decades before the Civil War, there was at least one major yellow fever epidemic in some southern maritime city. New Orleans, Mobile, Pensacola, Savannah, Charleston, and Norfolk were ravaged with varying frequency during these twenty years, as were numerous inland towns in their shadows. "Yellow Fever," wrote the editor of the *New-Orleans Medical Journal* in its 1844 inaugural volume, "is the *great disease* of our City and region."[4] The disease was becoming an uncomfortably familiar part of the southern landscape. As southern medical authors repeatedly reminded their readers, Boston, New York, and Philadelphia had been free from yellow fever for at least twenty-five years by 1850, although severe epidemics had attacked the latter two during the first three decades of the nation's history. It was an indictment of southern civilization that a disease which had been conquered in the North was not only becoming more common but also deadlier and more widespread in the 1850s.

During the early settlement of the South, physicians had regarded the country, and not the city, as the region's most unhealthy place to live. The country fever, which appeared under a variety of labels—bilious, congestive, remittent, intermittent or periodic—was generally attributed to the bad air hovering over hot swampy lowlands of the South. Although exemption from malaria had made urban areas relatively more salubrious than the country for a time, as southern communities such as Norfolk, Charleston, Mobile, and New Orleans developed during the early nineteenth century, this advantage disappeared. By the 1840s many southern cities had experienced rapid population growth fueled in part by European immigration. Census figures show a four to tenfold increase in the urban populations of, for example, Alabama, Georgia, and Louisiana from 1830 to 1860.[5] The disproportionately small numbers of immigrants coming to the South, in contrast to the other regions of America, nevertheless made a significant contribution to the South's urban population.

As was the case in other American cities, urbanization and immigration brought housing and water shortages, and rendered municipal systems for sewage and waste removal inadequate. To the South, these processes also seemed to bring yellow fever, a disease often linked to the urban phenomena of overcrowding, putrefying organic matter, and the excavation of soil for construction. Mobile physician Josiah Clark Nott believed that yellow fever inexorably followed the erection of cities on the southern seaboard. "When the forest is first levelled and a town commenced, intermittents and remittents spring up," he recounted. "As the population increases, the town spreads, and draining and paving are introduced, yellow fever, the mighty monarch of the South, who scorns the rude field and forest, plants his sceptre in the centre, and drives all other fevers to the outskirts."[6]

In the assessment of alarmed Southerners writing in the 1840s and 1850s, yellow fever was greatly damaging their region's interests. Inhibiting immigration and investment, and hence the growth and prosperity of the cities in which it flourished, yellow fever was also very expensive to the South in more direct ways. One physician estimated that yellow fever had cost New Orleans ten and a half million dollars annually in loss of labor and capital from 1846 to 1851.[7] In Florida, the yellow fever epidemic of 1841 nearly delayed its admission to the Union by reducing the territory's population.[8] On a deeper, but less frequently articulated level, epidemics threatened the security of the southern slave-holding community by weakening the defenses against a black uprising. Whites fleeing yellow fever often left household slaves under minimal supervision, while free negroes were thrown out of work with the absence of their employers. A Louisiana physician's diary reveals that the scenario of a slave revolt was not entirely unrealistic. In 1833, he recorded that during one yellow fever epidemic, "the slaves took advantage of the sickness at Alexandria & the absence of many planters & formed a plan of insurrection which was discovered 2 or 3 days before the massacre."[9] The South's wealth, prosperity, and security were all imperiled by the repeated yellow fever epidemics of the antebellum period.

Southern physicians recognized that their efforts to control yellow fever rested upon their knowledge of its etiology, a subject about which little was known with certainty. Accordingly, all southern physicians who witnessed a yellow fever epidemic were encouraged to carefully observe and record information about it. Studies of yellow fever were pursued with new vigor and purpose during the 1840s and 1850s. Such data would purportedly shed new light on the origins of yellow fever, support etiological theory with the certainty of facts, and end the harmful squabbling that had so diminished the profession in the public's estimation.[10] Yellow fever research was part of the broader southern medical renaissance called for by Erasmus Darwin Fenner in the opening pages of his *Southern Medical Reports*. He urged physicians to investigate southern diseases by regarding the topography, climate, demography, and peculiar symptoms characteristic of their practices. Southern physicians alone could study southern diseases and discover the knowledge necessary for the salvation of their professional and regional integrity.[11]

Another tack followed by urban southern physicians concerned with public health was to advocate the collection of vital statistics, the registration of births, marriages, and deaths. In part, the statisticians sought to show that except for yellow fever, southern cities were fundamentally healthy; the apparent high mortality said nothing about the quality of life of the acclimated resident. Since yellow fever was the only serious danger and it was confined predominantly to what Nott called the "unwashed democracy," the better sort had little to fear in a southern city.[12] He argued for the longevity of the "better class" of people, those most likely to buy life insurance, and concluded that rates for Southerners should not be higher than those in the rest of the country.[13] Nott's explanation of the high southern mortality figures as an aberration caused by the vicious poverty of the transient population was a common one. In Norfolk, the Irish slums were burned by an angry mob that blamed that town's yellow fever epidemic on the condition of "the dirty Irish."[14]

Other southern physicians, who recognized the genuine unhealthiness of southern cities and were concerned about the toll from both yellow fever and the region's more deadly endemic diseases, sought in vital statistics one pathway to the improvement of public health. Following the lead of northern, British, and French hygienists, southern sanitarians such as Edward Hall Barton and Fenner of Louisiana and P. C. Gaillard and Thomas Simons of Charleston held that in order to control the disorder of death and disease that characterized the urban South, statistical evidence had to be gathered which would demonstrate its extent and guide its amelioration.[15] Accordingly, the

New Orleans Board of Health urged in its 1849 report the need
for both vital statistics and accompanying sanitary surveys, arguing that if "a city or country is ignorant of the diseases fatal to its
population, if it does not know the age at death, sex, color,
length of residence, occupation, and in what part of the city,
death took place; it must be ignorant of one of its most important duties." Such knowledge was necessary to inform public
health action and gauge its effectiveness. The report concluded
that "all laws intended to benefit the sanitary condition without
a previous knowledge of *what that sanitary condition is*, are defi-
cient in the basis of all wise legislation and trifle with common
sense."[16]

Southern legislators were for the most part unconvinced that
vital statistics were of any value in the alleviation of the South's
diseased condition. Only in South Carolina (1853), Virginia
(1853), and Kentucky (1853) was statewide registration of vital
statistics required in the antebellum South. Some mortality data
based on interment and hospital records were available in certain cities, but it appears that only Charleston (from 1842) had a
registration plan that included births and marriages as well. In
Louisiana, agitation for the registration of vital statistics surfaced again and again in the 1850s, but to no avail.[17]

Students of southern health statistics hoped that their research would vindicate the healthiness of their unfairly ma-
ligned localities. Instead, they were appalled by their findings.
"The *motive* which led me to the investigation of our Vital Statistics," a Memphis physician confessed in 1851, "was the conviction . . . that Memphis is one of the healthiest places on the
Mississippi river; and that a comparison of our sanitary condition with other places . . . would conclusively establish the truth
of this opinion."[18] Instead he found a mortality rate nearly equal
to New Orleans, and higher than all other cities in the country.[19]
In like manner, J. C. Simonds began his statistical research on
New Orleans planning "to convince the world, by an array of
unquestionable statistical details and impregnable arguments,
that . . . our city was not the Golgotha which it was every where
represented to be." Unhappily, he concluded, "So far as I have
been able to obtain complete data, New-Orleans has manifestly
been the most unhealthy city in the civilized world."[20] Other

southern cities were also considered unhealthy, if to a lesser degree. Mobile was healthier than Memphis, and Charleston more so than New Orleans, but the figures that could be collected indicated to contemporaries the clearly superior health in northern cities.[21]

Critics of the statistical studies displaying the South's unhealthiness went beyond refutation to impugn the patriotism and personal morals of Southerners who defamed their cities' reputations and damaged their commerce. But it would serve no purpose, statistical advocates responded, to conceal their cities' condition, for the facts were well appreciated abroad.[22] Public health reformers called for an end to dishonesty, a recognition of the South's unhealthiness, and a campaign to resolve the South's health problems. Statistical studies demonstrating the high, non-yellow fever–related mortality of southern cities did not by themselves create a sense of crisis, but coupled with the continual return of yellow fever to the region, they contributed to the overall sense among southern medical reformers that action had to be taken to remedy the South's unhealthy situation.

Bolstered by the teachings of European hygienists, southern physicians committed to the elevation of public health had few doubts about the surety of one avenue to that end. The public health agenda was clear. Sewers were needed to carry away human wastes; the streets should be paved and efficiently cleaned; pure water for drinking and bathing should be supplied cheaply to the populace; stagnant water must not be allowed to stand in the city to generate noxious air; privies should be regulated; and the selling of putrid food must be forbidden.[23]

Southern sanitary reformers could draw upon European authorities for documented evidence when they claimed that hygienic improvements would advance the general health of the population. But if lawmakers were to be goaded into action, public health expenditures would have to be for measures indubitably effective against yellow fever, the one disease that aroused the sensibilities of the electorate. Yet the 1840s and 1850s were not years of theoretical consensus about yellow fever prophylaxis. The growth in awareness of the South's unhealthy condition during this period was paralleled by an increasing tendency on the part of southern physicians to question the etiology of yellow fever and offer new explanations for it. The doctrine of transportability emerged in the South in just these years, and offered mixed messages for public health action.

The idea that yellow fever could be transported had obvious implications for quarantine as a method of keeping yellow fever out. Its acceptance was accompanied by a resurgence of popularity of quarantine in the South. The most visible manifestation of this trend was the creation of a board of health for Louisiana in 1855 whose officers were "to be *selected in reference to their known zeal in favor of a Quarantine system.*"[24] The quarantine law prescribed that if the ship were particularly foul or if there had been pestilential fever on board, the captain of the vessel was to be compelled to "land the sick at the Quarantine ground, [and] to fumigate and cleanse all such vessels."[25] The first Louisiana quarantine administrator believed that the effluvia emanating from the sick were a source of danger, as were the air and articles about them. He did not deny the indigenousness of yellow fever to New Orleans, but reasoned that if one cause of the disease could be eliminated, it would be all the better for the city.[26]

Many New Orleans physicians pronounced the new quarantine system a failure when yellow fever reappeared in 1857, 1858, and 1859. The experiment had been fairly tried, they declared, and had proven to be a decided mistake. Quarantine was not and could not be the answer to the city's unhealthy condition if sanitary imperatives went unheeded.[27] Even contagionists like Gaillard of Charleston stressed that the crucial element in an epidemic was not the imported spark but the receptivity of the urban environment, which could be rendered nonflammable by civic hygiene.[28] The repetition of yellow fever epidemics in the 1840s and 1850s brought strident demands that the South's cities be drained and cleaned. As ephemeral boards of health were created and then disappeared during these years in New Orleans, each new incarnation brought appeals from Fenner, Barton, and other physicians for the promotion of the sanitary agenda. Likewise, in Charleston, Knoxville, Mobile, Savannah, and Norfolk, public health advocates called for improved urban sanitation.

The South's hygienic reformers met with some success. Charleston was judged to be notably better drained, paved, and cleaned by the 1850s; in New Orleans the street cleaning contract was wrested from a corrupt monopoly and brought under municipal control.[29] But such positive results were not typical. The very repetition of the litany of sanitary deficiencies indicates the general lack of action on the issue. This failure is evident in an 1860 review of the *Annual Report of the State of Louisiana Board of Health*. The reviewer first quoted the report as saying, "Its (the Board's) labors then and subsequently have been unavailing to inspire our city fathers with a sense of their importance . . . and the utter destitution of the city in every essential of sanitary regulation necessary to health, or even to decency and self-respect." He then went on in his own words to conclude: "Pretty strong language, and appropriate; yet calculated to have as little effect on political eyes and ears as a morning mist or a schoolboy's pop-gun. New Orleans is the filthiest hole in the land, except New York City. . . . Our city fathers wade through the filth to reach their seats in the hall, and they thus become accustomed to it."[30] Similarly, reformers in Savannah, Charleston, and Mobile continued to chide their legislators for ignoring urban filth, and held forth cleanliness as the path that would elevate the South's salubrity. But sanitarians, foiled by the lack of agreement concerning the precise relevance of filth to yellow fever, could not convince their parsimonious lawmakers that such measures would save the South.

The research that the awareness of the Old South's health crisis sparked led not to the consensus necessary to inform practice and arouse legislative action, the objective envisioned by the proselytizers of yellow fever studies, but rather to a multitude of contending theories that weakened the chances for effective public health reform. At times these opposing theories crystallized along urban-rural or coastal-inland patterns, only to shift again in a continuous kaleidoscope of combinations. Although yellow fever's transmissibility was widely accepted, it left undecided the species of quarantine required, and the degree to which filth contributed to the origin and growth of yellow fever. No physician publicly condemned the intrinsic value of sanitation; at issue was whether the scarce public health dollar should be spent on street cleaning or quarantines, if it could be found at all. Sanitarians who sought to gain legitimacy for their efforts by tying them to the imperative of preventing yellow fever failed to persuade legislators that sanitation could eradicate the disease. The squabbling among quarantine theorists about appropriate procedure undermined attempts to improve quarantine, and allowed critics to ridicule it as a remedy based on uncertain speculations. By the eve of the Civil War, Southerners had been for the most part unsuccessful in combatting their region's epidemiological reputation and reality.

The Civil War and its aftermath distracted attention and funds from southern physicians' efforts to promote public health. In the 1870s, however, recovery was evident in the formation of numerous state and local boards of health in the South, and the simultaneous generation of a small group of public health professionals. Southern states and cities established boards of health largely to deal with one problem, repeated invasions of yellow fever, the control of which remained the chief focus of public health discourse and action until the twentieth century. In response to southern demands for national intervention following the devastating yellow fever epidemic that spread throughout the Mississippi Valley in 1878, Congress created the National Board of Health to prevent the importation of epidemic disease. During its brief career, the National Board elicited reactions from southern public health authorities that illustrate clearly the elements of public health professional identity in the South during the late nineteenth century.

The growth of state boards of health in the 1870s was a national, not regional phenomenon. Inspired by the example of the New York City Metropolitan Board (1866) and the Massachusetts State Board (1869), sanitarians from all parts of the country promoted the establishment of state boards of health from the early 1870s. This sentiment was in part reflected in, and then promulgated by, the American Public Health Association, founded in New York in 1872. While in that year there were only three state boards of health in America, by 1879 seventeen were in existence. Of these, nine were in the South, where epidemics of yellow fever and cholera provided the main energies for their formation. The most vigorous boards were those in states most threatened by yellow fever. For example, state boards of health were founded in Virginia (1872) and Georgia (1875) but languished for lack of epidemics and funds. The state boards of Mississippi (1877) and Tennessee (1877), belated products of movements initiated after the 1873 yellow fever epidemic, received no financial backing from their respective states until the return of yellow fever in 1878 sufficiently alarmed their legislators. Two other southern state boards, those of Kentucky and South Carolina, were direct products of the panic generated by the 1878 epidemic. In Alabama, Jerome Cochran included a state committee of health within the constitution of the state's medical society (1875), and then convinced the state government to support it. The Louisiana State Board continued to serve in the capacity of quarantine agency and board of health for the city of New Orleans during the 1870s.[31]

The newly minted southern boards lacked not only money but power as well. The law creating the North Carolina State Board of Health in 1876 was typical in that it called for the board to "take cognizance of the interests of health and life among the citizens of the state," "make sanitary investigations and inquiries," and be the "medical advisors of the state." While the concern was especially focused on collecting data concerning epidemics, no powers to fight epidemics were created, nor was money made available to fund even the research called for. In describing his board's impotence to counter the 1878 yellow fever epidemic, President C. A. Rice of Mississippi noted that "for want of proper legislation, we have been unable to institute measures that might . . . have averted the destruction of our people last year (1878) by yellow fever." He went on to explain that "under the present laws we stand as an advisory board only, without power to establish quarantine or law to enforce it, with no appropriation to put it into operation, and none to sustain it."[32] It took the dramatic scenes of the 1878 epidemic to create the legislative will to empower the state boards of health as something more than paper organizations. Yet because of that environment, the resulting charge to the public health official would be very specifically shaped around how he was to respond to the problem of yellow fever epidemics.

The professional identity of southern public health workers pivoted upon their roles as the guardians of their states or municipalities. This protective function extended inseparably to both health and commerce, a dual role that caused most southern legislatures to add businessmen to their boards of health. The public health official's primary legal responsibility was the administration of quarantine. More so than in the North, the need for quarantine protection, especially against yellow fever, was the main impetus driving the creation and continuation of southern boards of health.[33] A related function was the dissemination of accurate information about the presence or threat of epidemic disease. Quarantine authority frequently led to contradictory impulses emanating from the two-sided nature of the public health official's role; a strict quarantine, for example, might well exclude yellow fever and preserve the health of the populace, but only at the cost of commercial stagnation or ruin. The southern public health professional's delicate task was the defense of his locality's total prosperity, both in commerce and in health, through the sensitive enforcement of quarantine.

Sanitation continued to be of only secondary importance in the battle against yellow fever. Although many public health officials in the South strongly favored incorporating sanitation into their protective duties, they were typically hard-pressed to convince legislators to fund permanent sanitary reform. By the 1870s most physicians agreed that both quarantine and sanitation were effective in limiting yellow fever, and that, yellow fever aside, the general health of the population would be improved by hygienic measures. But southern legislators replied that their weak financial condition allowed for only immediately necessary programs, and also that sanitary work was done well by private, charitable organizations. Southern politicians adhered to laissez-faire policies in regard to social reform, and even to a certain extent equated schemes for improving the lot of the poor with the much-hated Reconstruction programs for assisting blacks. As a consequence sanitation was at best pursued haphazardly, with only the imminent invasion of disease leading to even transient cleanup campaigns. Long-term solutions such as sewers, pure water, paving, and drainage demanded large outlays of funds, often engendered political wrangling and graft, and required a commitment to government intervention not yet prevalent among southern lawmakers.[34]

The responses to an 1870s survey of physicians interested in public health indicate a broad recognition among southerners of these impediments to reform. "There is a strong disposition on the part of medical men of the State to have health laws enacted; but, at present, our impoverished condition and political state render such enactments impossible," replied one physician of Charleston, South Carolina, in the common southern fashion. "I despair of the State, in its present Africanized condition, spending money to improve health. Two-thirds of our Legislature would think such money thrown away."[35] It was difficult to justify the need for sanitary reform, and in the southern states of Reconstruction, harder to find the necessary funds even when politicians had been converted to the sanitary gospel. Although in the late 1870s southern sanitary reformers succeeded in pushing board of health bills through the newly redeemed southern legislatures, the funding provided was by and large meager, and allowed for scant progress toward cleaner cities. Thus sanitation remained a personal aspiration of southern public health authorities, but they were able to devote minimal attention to it in the actual performance of their professional duties.[36]

In addition to the responsibilities imposed by their own locality, southern public health officials were also subject to expectations from outside their jurisdiction. On the regional level, inland states insisted that the Gulf states' authorities be accurate and timely in their reports concerning yellow fever, and rigid in their maintenance of quarantine. Bitter denunciations were leveled against officials who were lax in these duties, for such weakness left the interior regions defenseless. Similar charges emerged from intra-state public health disputes as well. The local official felt no legal compulsion to abide by these outside demands, and when faced with the choice of safeguarding his own locale or giving priority to the needs of other states or communities, he had no doubt about where his professional responsibility lay.[37]

Members of southern boards of health were drawn from the medical and business community. Some boards were composed entirely of physicians, such as those of Alabama, Kentucky, and Mississippi; others had specific spots reserved for laymen, as in Louisiana and Tennessee. Given the minimal funding for the boards, their members had to support themselves by other means, usually medical practice and teaching. The boards' presidents who figure most prominently in this narrative were literate men with a strong interest in epidemic disease. Several of them, most notably Joseph Jones, Jerome Cochran, and Joseph Porter, had written works on yellow fever prior to their appointments, achieving local academic fame that presumably contributed to their election as well as their desire for the job. The boards were all closely tied to their respective state allopathic medical societies. Accordingly, sectarians were largely excluded. The boards' leaders were clearly drawn from the medical elite; much less can be said about those men whose names appear on the rosters but who never authored papers or reports.[38] To my knowledge, no women or blacks served on southern state boards of health up to 1905.

As rapid rail transportation erased the geographic isolation previously guaranteed to inland states, southern public health officials in the 1870s became increasingly aware that in order to fight yellow fever effectively greater cooperation was necessary. Voluntary associations of southern boards of health sought to strengthen the determination of quarantine administrators and to infuse a new spirit of trust into the relationships between inland and coastal regions. The major expression of this impulse was the Sanitary Council of the Mississippi Valley, created by public health officials and concerned citizens from states bordering the Mississippi and Ohio Rivers who were vulnerable to the importation of yellow fever by river traffic.

The Louisiana State Board of Health was viewed by the other southern and midwestern boards as the main impediment to regional harmony and safety. In their view, public health officials in New Orleans, the frequent port of entry for yellow fever, were notoriously prone to conceal the presence of epidemics, with the result that the disease was rarely contained within the city. According to one Tennessee sanitarian, New Orleans was "a standing menace to the country along the Mississippi River for several hundred miles north of her, for at least three months of the year."[39] The New Orleans newspapers were charged with abetting the Louisiana officials in their attempts to hide the existence of yellow fever. "The press of New Orleans," a northern medical scientist reported to a Memphis newspaper, "seems to consider it a duty to conceal, as long as possible, facts relating to early cases of yellow fever, and I am credibly informed that in certain instances—notably in 1876—it has gone so far as to falsify the official mortuary reports furnished for publication over the signature of the Sec'y of the Board of Health."[40]

Louisiana authorities denied these allegations of dishonesty and pledged to communicate faithfully the most preliminary evidence of infestation, but in the inevitable panic accompanying the appearance of yellow fever such promises were easily ignored. No voluntary organization, however free to pass resolutions, could compel compliance to the regional will. "Such an organization [as the Sanitary Council of the Mississippi Valley]," admitted even its secretary, John Henry Rauch of Illinois, "must necessarily rely upon the moral influence it can exert and upon the good faith of its individual members."[41] The failure of regional obligation to overcome local jealousies was made strongly apparent by the yellow fever epidemic of 1878, which spurred extensive public health activity in the southern states, and led to the organization of the Sanitary Council.[42]

The 1878 epidemic was distinctive in its severity. The report of the Tennessee Board of Health for that year vividly depicted that state's experience:

1878 will be long remembered by the people of Tennessee as a year especially marked as one of disaster and death. The yellow fever was brought up the Mississippi River and fastened its deadly fangs upon the Western Division of our State, carrying dismay and death into almost every household. It did not stop here, but traveling with dread fatality on the lines of the railroad and river, it swept into the mountain city of Chattanooga, and into the various towns and cities of Kentucky. Nor were its ravages confined, as heretofore, to towns, but it scattered through all the villages and farms of West Tennessee, with a virulence and fatality heretofore unknown in the annals of this dread pestilential fever.[43]

Mississippi suffered a similar fate, and the disease spread as far north as the midwestern states of Indiana, Illinois, and Ohio. The Surgeon General of the Marine Hospital Service estimated that twenty thousand deaths resulted from one hundred thousand cases in one hundred cities throughout the Mississippi and Ohio Valleys.[44]

No prior yellow fever epidemic had so displayed the inadequacy of the existing public health system to protect southern lives and commerce. It is not clear why the 1878 epidemic was so virulent nor why it spread so efficiently, though certainly the growth of railroad lines played a part. Be that as it may, any reader of the newspapers from New Orleans and Memphis could see that something very unusual was happening. The disease traveled doggedly up railroad lines, marching progressively outward from the urban centers. In town after town people began to panic. Whatever the local and state governments were doing, it was not working. Men met by torchlight, angry and afraid. Some groups resolved to tear up train tracks, vowing to keep "yellow jack" out even if it meant isolating the town from needed supplies. Others formed armed bands to meet trains, forcing them to keep moving. Their shotguns spoke eloquently, and the trains moved as ordered. Unfortunates fleeing infected cities on foot were denied shelter, often at gunpoint, and many died of exposure and starvation. States, attempting to restore order, initiated quarantines at their borders, completely disrupting rail travel. Commerce was destroyed, with no measurable impact on the rising death toll. The dramatic images of panic and death so harshly impressed upon the national consciousness by the events of 1878 generated a nationwide sentiment in favor of federal enforcement of a strong quarantine against yellow fever.[45]

In the wake of the 1878 epidemic, southern public health professionals were briefly unified in their conception of the South's need for drastic public health reform. The extensive diffusion of yellow fever and its attendant mortality were clear signs that the current southern strategy for disease control was not working. These officials shared a common sense of frustration and helplessness over their incapacity to remedy the inadequacies of local quarantines, and over legislatures that would not or could not pay for badly needed hygienic measures. During 1879 most towns in the Mississippi Valley made progress in cleaning streets, disinfecting privies, and burning the clothes and bedding of yellow fever patients. Such efforts were limited, however, by municipal impoverishment resulting in part from the inability of families weakened by the events of 1878 to pay their taxes.[46] Aware of their impotence in the face of such economic and political realities, southern public health authorities were willing to relegate elements of their protective role to the federal government, hoping to gain in return the protection of their localities from yellow fever.[47]

The broad public demand for the exclusion of yellow fever put intense pressure on Congress for some form of national quarantine. This idea was not new in 1878, but did reach a peak of acclamation in that year. A national health agency had been proposed in Congress as early as 1871, and was promoted actively by the American Medical Association and the American Public Health Association in following years. Plans for the national agency included quarantine among its duties, and interest in a national quarantine grew with the publication of a report by Harvey E. Brown, an Army surgeon, demonstrating the South's weak quarantine defenses. After the yellow fever epidemics of 1871, Congress resolved, "Experience has proved that the present system of quarantine on the Southern and Gulf coasts is inefficient to prevent the ravages of yellow fever in the cities and towns of that section," and requested that the Army make an investigation of the matter.[48] Brown's report unequivocally urged for a national quarantine to bring uniformity and efficiency to the South's quarantine administration.

John M. Woodworth, who in his position as head of the Marine Hospital Service from 1871 had reorganized the Service and improved the quality of its officers and activities, held aspirations of transforming his service into a national health bureau. He took up Brown's conclusions and pushed for Marine Hospital Service supervision of a national quarantine. Opposing his ambitions were the leading figures of the American Public Health Association—James Lawrence Cabell, Henry Ingersoll Bowditch, John Shaw Billings, John Rauch and Elisha

Harris—who sought instead an independent national board. Although Woodworth won a temporary victory in 1878, when Congress granted limited quarantine powers to the Marine Hospital Service, by 1879 measures were before Congress to create a separate national health board.[49]

The arguments of one congressional spokesman for what became known as the "yellow fever bill" bore the imprint of Brown's ideas, with additional force imparted by the history of the previous year's epidemic. "The experience of the past has taught us that no seaport town having any commerce will ever adopt and adhere to any quarantine regulation which will interfere to any great extent with their commercial interest, and especially is this so of southern ports of entry," stated Casey Young, the representative from Memphis.[50] He maintained that only a national quarantine, administered by a national board of health, could effectively exclude yellow fever. The federal government's constitutional right to regulate commerce was the justification that the legislative supporters of the bill used to establish the legality of the measure, and the manifest need for national defense against a foreign invader provided the underlying animus for their cause.

Opponents of the bill, refusing to accept the commerce clause argument, countered that the bill was unconstitutional, that a national quarantine would not provide enough flexibility to deal with the idiosyncrasies of local conditions, and that it would take quarantine out of the hands of those local authorities who were most knowledgeable on the subject. The main thrust of the opposition was the violation of states' rights inherent in such federally imposed uniformity. An odd coalition of northeastern congressmen, acting under orders from their states' well-paid quarantine officials, and a few southerners rallied around the doctrine of the inherent right of the states to administer quarantine. After one "yellow fever bill" was defeated in the House, a Memphis newspaper was caustic in its criticism of these southern traitors: "The banana interests, the interests of the more Northern ports, where yellow fever is less feared, and the tender consciences of the Southern nincompoops who fall down once a day and worship the glimmering of the ghost of state rights abstractions, combined, and the all-important measure fell to the ground."[51] However a much weaker bill did pass, creating the National Board of Health in March 1879.[52]

The constituting act of the National Board of Health stipulated that it was to advise state and local boards, obtain and publish pertinent health information, conduct special inquiries into public health questions, and draw up plans for a permanent national health organization. On 2 June 1879 further congressional action expanded the powers of the board to include the provision of monetary support to state and municipal boards where necessary to prevent the importation and spread of disease, and also gave the board the authority to assume quarantine powers when states failed in their protective duties. The board's appropriation was limited to four years, so that without additional legislation it would expire in 1883.[53]

The newly appointed National Board, composed of such prominent members of the American Public Health Association as Billings, Bowditch, and Cabell, translated these vague instructions into four main lines of attack against yellow fever. First, in order to transform the complex and discordant state and local quarantines into a unified system, the board promulgated a set of regulations that prescribed quarantine procedures. They then set as a condition for the receipt of financial support that local and state boards adopt the new regulations. Their second step, fundamental to the success of these rules, was stationing a network of National Board inspectors at the various localities of the South most susceptible to yellow fever. The inspector's announcement that a city was "dangerously infected" with yellow fever would trigger the implementation of the board's quarantine regulations with regard to that city. Third, in an area where yellow fever actively existed, the board was to provide the appropriate local boards with funds to shore up their efforts in controlling the disease, which could include quarantine, sanitation, or disinfection and isolation of infected patients. Finally, they decided to set up quarantine stations on the Gulf of Mexico, on the Atlantic Coast, and on the Mississippi River.

It was up to the states to accept or reject the bills of health issued by these stations; agreeing to do so meant, in effect, turning over their quarantine responsibilities to the National

Board.[54] There was considerable confusion among state and local boards over the limitations of the National Board's powers. The National Board could not intervene until local boards had submitted itemized requests for funds. This was necessary, according to the National Board, to satisfy Congress that the money was well spent, but it seemed callous to many officials fighting the yellow fever epidemic of 1879 that so much paperwork was required before desperately needed monies could be released.[55]

The National Board of Health was not successful in sustaining public and congressional support. One of its major faults was ineptitude at public relations; another source of weakness was its constant competition for power and money with the Marine Hospital Service. Congress, never thoroughly convinced that national action was necessary, reacted to fading public enthusiasm with increasingly parsimonious appropriations for the National Board. After the nation experienced three years of relative freedom from yellow fever, Congress saw little urgency for the continuation of the national public health experiment, and allowed the original legislation to expire without providing further funds in 1883.[56]

The fact that contemporary medical science indicated no single, well-justified direction for a campaign against yellow fever made the National Board's position uncertain. By 1878 there was general medical accord on the existence of yellow fever as a specific disease caused by a specific poison. Whether that poison was animalcular, fungal, or chemical, or whether it infected an American locality only after importation or was a permanent inhabitant, were still strongly argued questions.[57] The National Board's policies represented the prevailing trends in disease etiology and prevention, but the Board was by no means in possession of an undisputed, unified truth about yellow fever.

The National Board's members were united, however, in their commitment to hygienic reform. Although they might differ about the specifics of epidemic disease control, there was no doubt in their minds that cleaner cities meant healthier cities. They sought to prevent disease in the aggregate, not necessarily one particular malady. It followed that the preeminent task of public health reformers was to sanitize the urban environment. The National Board's president, James Cabell of the University of Virginia, typically formulated the goals of state medicine as the promotion of pure air and water, vital statistics, improved drainage and sewerage, and general sanitation. Yellow fever and other quarantine-related diseases were largely peripheral to this central focus on hygiene, which preoccupied Cabell and other national sanitarians, who were far more concerned during the 1870s with endemic health problems and the high urban mortality that continued in the absence of sporadic epidemics.[58]

Under the auspices of the American Public Health Association, these sanitarians had lobbied for a national board of health whose purpose would be the general elevation of public health in the United States. Instead, Congress handed them a national quarantine agency, with the provision that sanitation reform was reserved for state and local boards of health. Still, the board's members attempted to accomplish what they could toward hygienic reform within the limits imposed by Congress, thus trying at once to be a national hygienic agency and a national yellow fever prevention bureau. They carried out or encouraged sanitary surveys, for example, and sponsored studies on several diseases and methods of testing water purity. John Shaw Billings, the National Board's vice-president, warned that unless the public could be educated to see the value of the sort of national sanitary board that he and his colleagues had fought for, even the limited beginning toward such a body would be aborted as the perception of crisis that had brought it into existence faded.[59] The Boston sanitarian Henry Ingersoll Bowditch reiterated this feeling when he wrote Billings after the National Board's creation: *"What we want now is to get a firm basis for national sanitation."*[60] In a letter to Bowditch, Thomas J. Turner, the board's secretary, encapsulated the credo to which he and his fellow sanitarians subscribed: "I believe with you Dr. that cleanliness is next to Godliness—personal & then civic and so on all the way to National Cleanliness."[61] But Billings's prophecy was fulfilled: without yellow fever the American people saw little need for a national board of health.

As a group these sanitarians also shared a faith in the universality of hygienic law and a concomitant vision of health reform carried out on a national scale. Their fundamental duty was to teach the American people that filth and disease were inevitably linked, that there could be no escape from the judgment decreed by natural law. Bowditch, along with his fellow National Board members, extended this allegiance to the universality of hygienic law to the matter of quarantine by calling for a national, and even international, quarantine code to be uniformly applicable to all ports.[62] The overriding nationalistic philosophy of these sanitarians dictated a clear course for public health reform based on the one, universal sanitary truth. This gospel was to clash sharply with the localistic, protectionist policies of southern boards of health.

Although the National Board warned southerners not to ignore sanitation while hiding behind the ephemeral safety of quarantine, the board expended the chief thrust of its energies upon the problem of developing a self-consciously modern and scientific method of quarantine to replace the archaic system that merely detained ships for a given period of time or denied them entry altogether.[63] The National Board rejected "the extreme of enacting ordinances prohibiting all intercourse with infected places," which they characterized as "a return to the barbarous and inhuman quarantine system of the dark ages, [that] practically ignores all the discoveries of science, as to the nature of infectious and contagious diseases, and the methods by which they may be controlled and exterminated."[64] The board was convinced, however, that since the experience of 1878 had shown conclusively that yellow fever could be transported, some limitations on travel were necessary to contain the disease.

The quarantine system evolved by the National Board entailed the inspection of passengers for evidence of disease and the disinfection of cargoes, baggage, and mail. Disinfection, if it merely involved splashing strong chemicals on filth, was no substitute for cleanliness. But board members felt that following the cleansing of a ship or railroad car with fumigation and disinfection added an extra measure of safety to the procedure. The power of disinfectants to destroy the yellow fever poison was the subject of considerable controversy during the 1870s, and the issue had no clear resolution.[65] They were attempting to kill a germ whose existence could only be assumed, and whose death could not be certified. The board was in the uncomfortable position of needing to formulate an official federal policy for quarantine practice when there was only circumstantial evidence that any form of quarantine or purification had proven effective.

In spite of theoretical uncertainties, the National Board did succeed in evolving a fairly consistent plan for fighting yellow fever. In one of their earliest publications the National Board's members laid down their assumptions about the disease upon which preventive measures were to be based. "It is prudent to assume that the essential cause of yellow fever is what may for conciseness be called a 'germ,' " stated the board's Circular #6 of 28 July 1879, "that is, something which is capable of growth and propagation outside the living human body; that this germ flourishes especially in decaying organic matter or filth, and that disinfection must have reference both to the germ, and to that in or on which it flourishes."[66] All of the board's actions against yellow fever stemmed from these premises. An infected town was cleansed to destroy the habitat of the germ, and disinfected to kill it directly. Vessels were expected likewise to be clean and, if coming from an infected area, disinfected. National Board inspectors gathered information about whether a locality was infected or was in a state that encouraged the propagation of the yellow fever germ.

The National Board's team of inspectors, who were physicians chosen for their interest in public health from both the North and the South, traveled throughout the areas afflicted by yellow fever in 1878 during the spring of 1879, and reported back to Washington about the sanitary status of the communities they visited. This information served as a basis for National Board financial contributions to the local authorities, and as a foundation upon which to build preventive control efforts should yellow fever again erupt. The National Board inspectors also kept watch for signs of yellow fever that might have escaped or been concealed by local officials, and advised local authorities on the best ways to combat yellow fever. The board's activities were largely limited to the lower Mississippi Valley, where yellow fever had been so severe in 1878.[67]

Two instances of the National Board of Health's participation in epidemic disease control, the cases of Tennessee and Louisiana, provide particularly useful contexts for evaluating the anxieties and commitments that were bound up with the southern public health professional's role and identity. National Board intervention in Tennessee and Louisiana called forth markedly different responses from local public health officials. Tennessee officials strongly favored federal involvement, for it enhanced their own professional power by providing the means necessary for their programs of sanitary reform and yellow fever eradication. Quite to the contrary, in Louisiana, the president of the State Board of Health believed that the National Board's interference would strip his office of authority and disrupt its function, imperiling both the commerce and health of Louisiana. Neither state board shared the nationalistic perception of the federal board; but instead each gauged the value of the National Board's assistance by the standard of their own particular local needs.

In Tennessee, the primary location of the National Board of Health's work was the city of Memphis, which had suffered severely from yellow fever epidemics in 1873 and 1878. Sensitive to the special vulnerability of Memphis to river- and rail-borne yellow fever, Tennessee officials were vocal proponents of the National Board's river and railroad inspection services, which guarded the Mississippi Valley. They saw in this assertion of federal authority the fulfillment of one aspect of their professional responsibility which they were powerless to effect alone, namely, the protection of the city from the invasion of yellow fever. Although these officials regarded hygienic reform as even more crucial to the control of epidemic disease, the city's near-bankrupt condition prohibited the implementation of permanent sanitary measures. Thus when yellow fever reappeared in 1879, the local board appealed to the National Board of Health for money and counsel. The National Board promptly supplied financial assistance, facilitating local sanitation and disinfection, and enabling the state board to isolate Memphis from the surrounding countryside.[68]

Advice was also readily forthcoming. Billings met with state and local officials at McKenzie, Tennessee, a small town about

110 miles northeast of Memphis, to map out a strategy for combatting the epidemic and to lay plans for further federal assistance. According to the president of the Memphis Board of Health, the National Board's greatest contribution was a measure decided upon at that conference, the sanitary survey of the city which the National Board directed during the last two months of 1879. The survey generated a series of recommendations that included the installation of a modern sewer system, proper drainage, street paving, and the improvement of water quality. Armed with this federal agenda for reform, Memphis authorities were able to convince the state legislature early in 1880 to levy a special tax to fund the measures. By the following summer the city's sanitary revolution was largely underway, and public health officials manifested a new confidence and pride in their identity as the preservers of municipal health and welfare. The sewer system installed under the watchful eye of George Waring became a model for the nation. They openly credited the National Board as the wellspring of the hygienic reform impulse in the state, and remained steadfast in their support of the National Board for the duration of its career.[69]

On the other hand, the Louisiana State Board of Health was actively hostile toward the National Board of Health from its inception. This antagonism centered most intensely around Joseph Jones, who was appointed president of the Louisiana board early in 1880. He approached his duties with a crusading zeal to affirm the board's reliability and legitimacy in the eyes of the country. Jones saw himself as eminently qualified to fulfill the two main obligations of his role: providing trustworthy information on the threat of yellow fever, and maintaining the state's quarantine in such a way as to protect health while not endangering trade. The National Board of Health, in Jones's view, refused to assist him in these efforts, and instead sought to damage the state by ruining her reputation and commerce. Jones and the National Board's members did not differ on how yellow fever was to be prevented, but rather on whose implementation of mutually accepted methods would be the most effective with the least damage to local commerce. From his self-styled valiant struggle against the Yankee imperialists, Jones emerged victorious, staving off an impending invasion of his professional space by the national power.[70]

Neither the National Board nor the rest of the Mississippi Valley shared Jones's confidence in the reliability of the Louisiana State Board of Health. The National Board made it blatantly obvious that the Louisiana State Board of Health was not to be trusted, and Jones quite naturally resented such an open allegation of dishonesty. When in the spring of 1881 the National Board requested that one of the board's inspectors be allowed to attend all state board of health meetings, and another to reside at the Louisiana quarantine station during the summer months, Jones angrily refused. The Louisiana State Board portrayed the National Board as "an inquisitorial system of espionage and detention," whose local inspector, Stanford Chaillé, they particularly held up for condemnation.[71]

Jones believed his worse fears were justified when in July of that year the inspector at the quarantine station publicly warned masters of ships coming from yellow fever–infected Rio de Janeiro that their vessels would have to undergo disinfection before they would be allowed to enter New Orleans. The inspector said no more than the truth, but it was not his position to make such an announcement. Jones told Chaillé, during an angry meeting recorded in Chaillé's diary, that the station inspector "had meddled with matters outside his duty, was little more than a detective, . . . had no business to advise as to Rio vessels and interfere with our coffee trade, etc., etc."[72] The National Board was, in other words, controlling commerce in Louisiana, yet was invested with none of the constraints inherent in the state board's accountability to local commercial interests. The National Board, for its part, claimed that its associates merely reported the truth, and that its reputation for not concealing facts about yellow fever had gained it the confidence of public health officials throughout the Mississippi Valley, bringing stability to the region. The New Orleans business community was initially ambivalent about the quarantine, but came to be supportive of the National Board's efforts. While Jones claimed to be acting in their interest, commercial leaders turned instead to the stability offered by the federal government, as will be discussed later.

The National Board offended Jones even more deeply when it proposed that the Louisiana State Board send all infected vessels to the National Board's quarantine station at Ship Island, off the coast of Mississippi. The Ship Island station was to secure the Gulf coast from New Orleans to Pensacola, providing isolation and disinfection for infected ships and crews. The National Board felt that the Louisiana quarantine station could not adequately protect the Mississippi Valley from yellow fever; its location permitted free communication with the people of the surrounding area, and the hospital and other facilities were poorly maintained and in dilapidated condition. More damning was the lack of onshore housing for healthy crews and passengers during detention, so that there was strong incentive for them to evade the quarantine guards and travel overland to New Orleans, thereby escaping the unpleasant and unhealthy environment of the ship.[73] A. N. Bell, who inspected the station on the National Board's behalf in 1879, reported with contempt of the station's hospital, "It is now very filthy, and rapidly going to wreck. . . . Throughout the wards festoons of old cobwebs filled with broken fragments of wall and dead flies ornament the walls and cover the windows. . . . [The] floors are covered with accumulations of filth, stained with blood and the sprinklings of carbolic acid."[74] The National Board believed that the Louisiana facility was not worth maintaining, and rejected outright Jones's counterproposition that federal funds be expended for rehabilitating the Louisiana stations and not for Ship Island.

Jones's strident defense of the quality of the local quarantine station, renovated under his administration, was fueled by his perception that the National Board's designs struck at the very core of his professional status. Should the State Board relegate quarantine authority to the federal government, he and his fellow board members agreed,

we should at once, to be consistent, abolish our State board with its well-equipped and costly quarantine establishments in the Mississippi River; . . . we should abandon the fulfillment of our sworn and sacred duties, that of protecting ourselves, the lives of our people, the interests of our commerce, not confiding to others, however great and powerful they may be, that sacred obligation. Commerce once destroyed, as it would surely be by the enforcement of this strange and unnatural quarantine which is sought to be imposed upon us, we might as well abandon all our rights, powers, and duties, for Louisiana would no longer need any protection. It would be entirely ruined, and would soon disappear from the family of States.[75]

This lucid expression of the anxieties generated by the possibility of federal involvement indicates plainly that for Jones, the National Board served only as a hindrance to the performance of his professional duties. The National Board was pictured as a power-hungry monster that sought to devour the state board, and even Louisiana itself, in order to sustain its own existence. Only steadfast opposition, not cooperation, could be the appropriate response to this federal encroachment upon professional public health autonomy.[76]

In analyzing the conflict between the Louisiana and National Boards of Health, some measure of the vehemence involved must be attributed to the personality of Joseph Jones. Intolerant of the slightest criticism, Jones was highly sensitive to any intimations that his work was not entirely satisfactory. His opposition to the National Board may have arisen in part from seeing his appointment as an inspector for the National Board rescinded due to a shortage of funds, and then in the wake of this insult being requested to inspect a nearby Louisiana town.[77] After a tense conversation with Jones, Chaillé wrote in his diary: "[I am] thoroughly convinced of Jones's lack of policy or sound sense. With all his zeal and industry he is impracticable, most captious, and pig-headed."[78] In keeping with his personal history of being a confederate surgeon and ardent secessionist, Jones likened the National Board to a northern conqueror, and refused to be swayed from his self-image as sole warrior protecting New Orleans from destruction.[79]

The reaction of Jones to the National Board of Health was not purely idiosyncratic, however. There were other municipal and state boards of health, both within and outside the South, that found the interference of the National Board in local affairs intolerable. An alliance including public health officials of Louisiana, Georgia, Alabama, New Jersey, and New York coalesced around the imperative of protecting the nation's seaports from domination by the National Board of Health. Jerome Cochran, head of the Alabama Board of Health, shared Jones's perception of the role of the local public health official. Every community had the right and responsibility to protect itself, claimed the Alabama board in a memorial to Congress, and it was "neither wise nor prudent for us to intrust the administration of quarantine to the hands of any other health authorities than those who are of our own appointment and directly responsible to our own people." A proper quarantine had to be molded to the particular needs of the locality, the memorial argued, and, in regard to quarantine, "the State can not afford to allow this large grant of power, so nearly affecting the welfare of our people, to be placed in the hands of the National Board of Health, or of any other agent of the federal government."[80] Spouting rhetoric about respect for states' rights and the dangers of centralizing power under the control of Washington bureaucrats, the coalition urged Congress to incorporate state representatives into the National Board. When this failed, they contributed to the ultimate demise of the board through lobbying efforts.[81]

The recommendation that some form of national advisory sanitary council be composed of representatives from each state board was common, even among otherwise strong supporters of the National Board's design and function.[82] It was the professional duty of each public health official to maintain the equilibrium between public health and commercial prosperity that was most beneficial to his locality; yet the National Board of Health's rude imposition of a uniform quarantine code rendered such local flexibility impossible and eliminated this aspect of the local professional's role. The nationalistic attitude of the federal board was irreconcilably at odds with the localistic orientation of coastal public health authorities, both in the North and South.

The southern practice of seeking federal funds while avoiding federal supervision was not limited to public health administration. The South was in a peculiar position in the 1880s. After years of federal domination, the southern states had again achieved home rule, but found themselves with massive internal problems and empty treasuries. They welcomed interventionist federal legislation when it meant money for internal improvements, such as bills that provided funds to control flood waters and improve navigation on the Mississippi River. Yet southern politicians wanted federal funds without paying the price of diminished local control. They bridled at the suspicious attitude with which northerners often viewed their actions, whether in education, voter registration, or public health administration. Southerners wanted no part of snooping federal investigators overseeing their performance.

Although the National Board devoted the bulk of its administrative energies to the problems of yellow fever and southern public health, the tensions inherent in the clash between local and federal authority were not limited either to the South or to yellow fever.[83] But the history of the National Board cannot productively be viewed apart from either. The efforts of sanitarians to establish a national board of health in the 1870s succeeded only because the threat of yellow fever made such a step appear mandatory. Even with this impetus congressional funding was scant, and its support was fickle when the immediate danger of yellow fever subsided. But beyond the importance of yellow fever for understanding the history of this first experiment in national public health, the singular prevalence of yellow fever in the South and the National Board's energetic campaign against it combine to provide a particularly useful context for displaying the ambitions and priorities of public health officials in that region.

The preoccupation of southern public health officials with the protection of their localities precluded the development of true regional or national identity among southern public health workers. Instead, a tendency toward polarization characterized the relationships among public health officials in the South, as elsewhere in the country, which pitted inland areas against the coastal regions. The temporary consensus which followed the 1878 epidemic disintegrated as the implications of federal intervention became apparent. A board's reaction was predicated not upon its identification as a southern entity, but upon its perception of the utility of national assistance for the attainment of its parochial goals. Public health officials of interior states and municipalities generally found that the National

Board's activities substantially bolstered their inadequate defenses against yellow fever, and thus welcomed federal involvement as shoring up their professional functions. Southern coastal authorities mostly viewed the National Board in negative terms, for its work appeared to nullify, rather than strengthen, their ability to perform their professional duties. So even though the South shared a common enemy in yellow fever, there was far from a solid South on the issue of national public health involvement. Just as no true sense of sectional identity could develop among southern public health authorities because of their allegiance to their own communities, so too these officials could not accept the experiment in nationalized public health that threatened to violate their local interests for the sake of regional and national well-being. The members of the National Board largely failed in their attempt to convey the broader conception of state medicine to their southern colleagues. Since their identity was rooted in the defense of their communities, rather than in the improvement of health as an end in itself, southern public health authorities could not fully join in the nationalistic sanitary religion proselytized by the National Board of Health.

·········3·····························

DISEASE, DISORDER, AND
DEFICIT: The Business Malaise

T he late 1870s and early 1880s were critical
years in the history of southern public health not only for the
emergence of professional public health action on a large scale,
but also for the appearance of unprecedented mercantile involvement in public health affairs. In the two cities most affected by the yellow fever epidemic of 1878, Memphis and New
Orleans, businessmen became newly alert to the commercial
implications of yellow fever and the disease's attendant preventive measures. In an effort to overcome the commercial hazards
of yellow fever, businessmen established sanitary organizations
with the intent of shaping public health directives to favor commercial interests. These new organizations took on immediate
responsibility for cleansing their city's streets and otherwise exe-
cuting sanitary reform as one path toward the elimination of
yellow fever. Also new was the strong support expressed by the
mercantile sanitary associations for federal intervention in the
control of yellow fever, a solid sentiment in favor of national
rather than the despised local or state quarantines. This chapter
explores the foundation of this burst of commercial public
health initiative, examining first the business environment of

the post-Reconstruction South within which public health concern matured, and then the ways that businessmen in both cities met the reality of yellow fever and the preventive measures instituted against the disease by public health authorities.

In general it is difficult to directly assess the influence that commercial interests had on public health policy in the nineteenth-century South. Financial persuasion and outright bribery no doubt occurred, but such transactions are only rarely revealed to historical scrutiny. New Orleans public health spokesmen like Jones frequently lauded the protection of commerce in their writings; it is hard to know how much their advocacy grew from actual lobbying pressure as opposed to honest civic spirit. It is clear that when a figure became unpopular enough, his job was taken by someone else, although the exact means of the transition is usually murky. It is this lack of detail about the day-to-day interaction of commerce and health in the urban South that makes the opportunity to scrutinize the mercantile sanitary organizations all the more valuable.

Any attempt to describe the influence that southern businessmen had on the course of public health efforts immediately runs into the problem of defining the population being studied. Businessmen were not a unified group, all feeling the same way at the same time. Local merchants might have very different priorities than railroad company representatives. Merchants in Memphis supported the National Board's efforts when it meant protecting them from New Orleans, but cried out when Memphis itself was quarantined and the cotton trade stopped. In the discussion that follows it will be evident that when commercial groups formed an official opinion, it was only after much debate. Still, the views of the majority, as expressed by their representative organizations, can be tracked. The terms "businessmen," "commercial interests," and so on are convenient labels to describe this majority opinion, but are artificial in that they gloss over the frequent variance in views. Also, while the term "businessmen" might be assailed for its exclusion of women, it accurately represents the leadership of the business community that I describe.

The commercial environments of Memphis and New Orleans in the late 1870s and early 1880s exhibited many features common to other southern cities. By the end of the 1870s, the South was emerging from both the turmoil of Reconstruction and from the nationwide depression that railroad speculation had precipitated. Local government expenditures during the Reconstruction era had left both cities with a legacy of crippling debt. The city of Memphis had declared bankruptcy, repudiated its debts, and abandoned its city charter by the end of 1878; New Orleans did not repay its municipal debt until 1895. The prospects for any reform projects that depended upon city or state financing in this period were dim. The taxpayer, and more particularly the businessman, had to furnish money for public works in special tax levies or by direct contribution if funding was to be forthcoming at all. The southern states, with the nation's most impoverished people and governments, faced the most threatening epidemic disease of the period bereft of the financial means to support reform.[1]

The late 1870s were, at the same time, years of revived hope in the South. After the recall of federal troops in 1877, southern governments were again in the hands of the Democrats, the political party to which most white southerners owed allegiance and trust. Historian C. Vann Woodward has characterized the redeemer governments as by and large composed of affluent, middle class Democrats who approved of business and industry and sought to promote the South's commercial growth.[2] Accompanying the so-called redemption of southern statehouses was a visible upswing in business activity toward the end of the decade. In 1879 cotton exports in New Orleans were finally nearing the levels typical of the antebellum period; the rehabilitation of the sugar industry was complete by 1880. After a decade of default, receivership, and consolidation, the region's railroads again began to show a profit.[3] From the 1870s businessmen and newspaper editors spoke more and more often about the "New South," a South of industry and commerce, a South that was to grow especially from the development of textile manufacturing. Southern commercial leaders eagerly sought the influx of northern and European capital into their straitened economy. This drive was most apparent in the industrial areas of Alabama and the Piedmont, but was fervently encouraged in New Orleans and Memphis as well. Businessmen in both communities were newly optimistic that their cities might again rise to commercial prominence, attract immigrants, industry, and investment, and recoup the financial losses that the destruction and stagnation of war and Reconstruction had inflicted.[4]

At the same time that American business was moving out of the depression of the 1870s and southerners were learning again the virtues of home rule, business involvement in politics grew markedly in all regions and levels of government. On the national level, beginning in the late 1870s, politicians with backgrounds in commerce were elected to Congress and became cabinet officers in significant numbers for the first time in the nation's history. Railroads increasingly pressured politicians to pass legislation in their favor.[5] In the South, mercantile contributions to the new regimes that took power following Reconstruction were frequent and overt. One student of Alabama's business history has found, for example, that from a sample of 186 businessmen prominent in the state from 1865 to 1900, nearly half were active in politics, either as office holders or party stalwarts.[6]

In both New Orleans and Memphis, businessmen became active in politics in the 1870s and sought to gain control of Democratic municipal governments, which they viewed as profligate, taxation-happy, and corrupt. Business leaders seized power in Memphis following the 1878 epidemic, when the municipal government was reorganized. Although less successful in acquiring dominance in New Orleans, members of the commercial community did launch an effective reform party to counter the powerful Democratic "ring" that ruled the city. Belying Woodward's depiction of redeemers as "New South" proselytizers, the Democratic party that had assumed power after the ouster of carpetbag rule was governed largely by working-class interests, with the Irish heavily represented among its politicians and ward bosses. The explicitly business-oriented reformers did succeed in electing their candidate as mayor in 1880. Even though the new mayor could effect little of the promised reform due to the inadequate city budget, the commercial party remained a force in city politics through the end of the century.[7] This political activism developed in part out of a sense that through government action the business climate could be made more salubrious, and also in part from a fear of regulation and onerous taxation by the government. The railroads were particularly beset by public opposition to their rate scales, and felt the need to prevent oppressive government regulation. In a like manner, businessmen taking part in southern politics were motivated to a certain extent by the desire to elevate their cities' commercial advantage by improving its health, and at the same time sought to direct public health efforts along avenues not inimical to business interests.[8]

Prior to the late 1870s, the participation of southern businessmen in the amelioration of epidemic crises had largely taken the form of relief work, not sanitary improvements. From the early years of the nineteenth century business leaders had been at the forefront of charitable enterprises organized during epidemics to provide medical care for the indigent, and food, clothing, and supplies for those left destitute by the circumstances surrounding the disease, such as the absence of employers. The most persistent and widespread philanthropy, the Howard Association, was established in New Orleans by a group of "young gentlemen" in 1842 and developed chapters throughout the South, continuing in existence until 1905. Their work, however, was often limited to the sick patient, for whom they provided a physician's attention, as well as sustenance and nursing. They neither cared for the unemployed citizen nor for the convalescent (but as yet non-wage-earning) yellow fever victim who could not support his or her family. Other relief organizations attempted to fill this gap by furnishing more general welfare services. The Howards's money could not be spent on sanitary or other preventive efforts, either. Unlike the aim of providing assistance to the victims of an epidemic, the ambition of cleansing southern cities by means of private philanthropic efforts was new in 1879. It was premised, as were the other charitable activities sponsored by business groups, largely upon recognition of the inadequacy of existing government agencies to provide services desperately needed by the community.[9]

More so than any other southern city, New Orleans in the 1870s possessed a community of businessmen who were beginning to form associations in order to advance the interests of their own particular trades and to further the general prosperity of the city. The extent of activity in part reflected the size of New Orleans; as the most populous southern city, it consequently had the density of commercial activity requisite for the sustenance of such organizations. The Chamber of Commerce, founded before the Civil War, became newly active in the 1870s. But businessmen realized that organizations more specifically focused on the peculiar needs of their own occupations were necessary. In 1871 the Cotton Exchange was established, with the purpose of providing cotton merchants with space in which to carry out transactions, adjudicating controversies between members, generating rules for the transactions of the cotton trade, and decreasing the risks incident on the trade by acquiring and disseminating information about cotton prices and production. A final explicit function of the Exchange was the general promotion of the business and trade interests of New Orleans and the expansion of the cotton industry.[10] Other merchants followed the cotton dealers' example. Several attempts were made during the 1870s to organize a produce exchange, and these were finally successful in 1880. Navigation companies, importers and exporters, founded the Maritime Association to promote their concerns that same year. In 1877 the cane growers organized the Louisiana Sugar Planters Association in New Orleans, with the dual purposes of increasing knowledge about the sugar manufacturing process and of securing favorable federal tariff legislation.[11]

The creation of these varied trade associations was one expression of the anxiety New Orleans businessmen felt about the position of commerce in their city vis-à-vis that of cities elsewhere in the nation. New Orleans had significantly declined as a commercial center since the years before the Civil War. Prior to the extension of the railroads into the Midwest, the produce of that region had principally flowed down the Mississippi to the port of New Orleans. But with the construction of railroads, by 1880 the bulk of that produce was following an iron path to the eastern ports, primarily New York, and bypassing New Orleans altogether. Although by 1883 the amount of cotton exported from New Orleans had again achieved the level of 1859, its percentage of the cotton market had fallen from twenty-five to three percent. A similar phenomenon plagued the grain and livestock trades.[12]

A separate source hampered the city's import trade, especially in tropical fruits and other produce from Latin America.
According to distressed New Orleans merchants, fruit dealers
were avoiding New Orleans and sailing directly to New York in
order to escape the onerous quarantine regulations of the southern port. Furthermore, the internal trade by which New Orleans sought to supply towns inland was threatened by those
communities' fear of yellow fever, and the possibility that quarantines or the fever itself might interrupt lines of supply. A
planter in Mississippi might well reason that it would be better
to order his corn or merchandise from St. Louis than to engage
the risks of trade with New Orleans. Businessmen were con-
scious of these combined factors impeding the commercial progress of New Orleans, and organized in part to find ways to
overcome them. The spirit was strong to remove obstacles to
the city's commerce, and return the city to its once prosperous
and central place in the American economy.[13]

The practice of quarantine was one visible target for those
seeking to assign guilt for New Orleans' weak economic position. In addition to closing the port during one third of the year
and consequently diverting trade elsewhere, Louisiana's quarantine was also directly costly to ship owners; quarantine fees
acted as a tax on trade not necessarily imposed by other ports.
The ports of Mobile and Galveston, made accessible during the
1870s to their hinterlands by railroads that robbed New Orleans
of its unique position as port for the South and Southwest, were
in open competition with New Orleans for the South's business.
Not only might these ports impose a weaker quarantine than
New Orleans, but they also could quarantine New Orleans itself,
so that goods from that city would be bottled up with fewer
trade outlets.

The grounding of these so-called "commercial quarantines"
in economic rivalry was often quite blatant, as when one of the
cities continued its quarantine barriers against New Orleans
weeks longer than other ports in similar danger (while, perhaps, allowing free access to ships from diseased tropical ports),
or else refused to rescind its quarantine even when yellow fever's absence from New Orleans had been conclusively demonstrated. During the 1870s Galveston repeatedly quarantined

New Orleans on the barest whisper of a yellow fever rumor, much to the benefit of the shipping lines which serviced the Texas city. Rather than ship his cotton first to New Orleans and from there to England or New York, a merchant in Galveston would instead be forced to ship directly to New York, bypassing New Orleans, even if the shipping charges for the Galveston-New York route were higher. In a similar fashion, the planter in Mississippi faced with the choice of selling his cotton through New Orleans or Mobile might well choose the latter option if quarantines isolating New Orleans promised a marketing delay. Commercial and political spokesmen acknowledged that quarantines might be erected from a genuine fear of infection, but New Orleans businessmen repeatedly charged throughout the 1870s that quarantines issued against their city were commercially motivated. They further asserted that the health authorities of New Orleans, to secure the overall well-being of the city, had to be sensitive to the competitive environment within which the city's commerce was conducted.[14]

Again and again in the 1870s New Orleans businessmen called for a rational, sensible quarantine. The words "rational" or "sensible" had different meanings to different businessmen, and understanding the complexity of their usage is preliminary to comprehending the commercial attitude toward quarantine. It would be easy to caricature the commercial community as composed of men heartlessly unconcerned with the health of their city's inhabitants and untouched by the suffering occasioned by an epidemic. Certainly, it was a common enough portrait sketched by contemporary critics outside of New Orleans. Some businessmen unquestionably fit into the mold, such as W. C. Raymond, who was quoted by the *Picayune* in the fall of 1878 as proclaiming himself "in favor of no quarantine and taking our chances."[15] Yet by and large the merchants of New Orleans sought the minimally obstructive quarantine, which would allow them to carry on their business and work to overcome the many detriments to the prosperity of the city.

Quarantine rules appeared understandably arbitrary and unsystematic to the New Orleans businessman of the 1870s. Medical science was certainly not unified on the protective value of twenty versus five or ten days as a quarantine period, and those establishing the board of health's rules would often double the quarantine period in an effort to increase rigor without supporting their action by any medical knowledge beyond their own common sense. Under the detention method, passengers were off-loaded to detention quarters at the quarantine station, and the ship sat at anchor. Many sanitarians had been arguing since the 1850s that mere detention was ineffective, and that what was needed instead was a thorough disinfection and cleansing of the ship and its contents. This doctrine had considerable appeal for the business community, as it promised to curtail the quarantine period and ease the obstruction to commerce. In 1876 pressure from businessmen successfully convinced the state legislature to allow the state board of health to lower the detention period, and the board of health in power in the first half of the decade was active in exploring disinfectant methods. But in the person of Samuel Choppin, who became president of the Louisiana State Board of Health in 1877, the business community found a staunch advocate of detention quarantines. Choppin, after the 1878 epidemic, went so far as to recommend that New Orleans maintain complete non-intercourse with yellow fever ports during the summer months as the only way to ensure the safety of the city. Such a prophylactic solution clearly could not meet the requirements of the ambitious commercial community.[16]

During the 1870s the Louisiana quarantine lacked both regularity and a clear scientific basis, and by responding to commercial pressure, the board lent credence to the business community's belief that there was little that was objective, immutable, and scientific about the board's actions. In April 1878, for example, the physician in charge of the main Louisiana quarantine station fumigated a banana cargo from a yellow fever port with sulfurous acid gas. The bananas turned black and brought a much lower price at auction than comparable green fruit. The ship master and fruit company involved sued the board of health for damages. Although Choppin concluded from a cursory examination that the fruit was palatable, an independent auditor judged the shipment to have lost half its value. As a result of this suit, Choppin ordered the quarantine physician to allow fruiters to be unloaded before their holds were subjected to fumigation. Merchants were pleased that the fruit trade was not to be totally destroyed, but could hardly have avoided being impressed with how quickly the danger of imported fruit for the transmission of yellow fever was dissipated by a civil suit. Respect for the board of health and the sanctity of its rulings was certainly diminished as a result.[17]

The year 1878 was pivotal in piquing the business community's awareness of the impact of public health matters on commercial life. By comparing imports, exports, and manufactures in that year to the healthy years immediately before and after it, New Orleans sanitarian Stanford Emerson Chaillé estimated that more than one and a quarter million dollars was lost to New Orleans commerce in 1878. During the 1878 epidemic the commerce of New Orleans ceased for almost three months, with little traffic entering or leaving the city and most of its prosperous consumers absent. The Congressional Board of Experts that studied the 1878 epidemic put the loss figure much higher, by including in their estimate sums spent for relief efforts, the economic value of the lives lost, crop spoilage, and the value of diverted labor.[18]

The record of the 1878 epidemic was dismal for those seeking to attract investment capital to the city. Northern financiers suffered large losses as a result of the epidemic, a lesson they were not soon to forget. "As was recently stated by one of the largest Bankers in the United States," reported Elisha Harris, a New York sanitarian and associate of the National Board of Health, in a letter to T. J. Turner, "the health of the Southern States cannot suffer a visitation of yellow fever or any great epidemic without a loss of millions, at once, in the Banking and Commercial interests that are centered in the City of New York."[19] Never before had any epidemic moved so widely into the South, and never had so much money been lost as a result. Businessmen who had seen epidemics as inconveniences before, and targeted quarantine as the villain, began to think that the true evil to be fought was yellow fever itself.

The apparent tendency of the 1878 epidemic to spread to every community having contact with a yellow fever center, in contrast to the fever's rather more localized behavior in previous years, created a new problem for the New Orleans merchant.

In the place of just a few maritime quarantines inhibiting the flow of trade, literally hundreds appeared in 1878, as every hamlet on a train or boat route sought to protect itself by total isolation from New Orleans and other fever spots. In 1870 the interference with trains by inland quarantines would have been only mildly felt, since there were few roads in working order, and trackage was limited. But after a decade of railroad building that connected New Orleans in all directions to new markets, the devastation of her trade with the interior was a serious matter. Businessmen even began to debate whether the interior trade might not be of more value to the city than the much-vaunted trade with tropical ports liable to yellow fever; subsequently, however, non-intercourse with tropical countries during the yellow fever season began to appear a reasonable solution after all.[20] The fever of 1878 spread so effectively because of the railroad network that enabled passengers and mosquitoes to travel quickly into the rural communities of Mississippi, Louisiana, and Tennessee, and it was that same network's fledgling patterns of trade that were to be sorely damaged by the local inland quarantines of 1878.

In late November 1878 a large group of businessmen met in New Orleans to discuss the impact of that year's epidemic on commerce and to formulate a plan of action. The meeting was attended by members of the Chamber of Commerce, Cotton and Produce Exchanges, and, according to one newspaper account, "leading merchants, lawyers, bank and insurance presidents, [and] manufacturers." A few days earlier a small number of businessmen had assembled, and their report was read at the massive meeting which resulted from the same concerns which prompted their original deliberations. "The City of New Orleans has found itself, at the close of the late epidemic, under circumstances of peculiar and unprecedented commercial embarrassment," the report began. The report's cosigners, who included in their ranks the last editor of *De Bow's Review* as well as prominent commercial leaders, then pointed out the system of artificial trade lines created by the railroads which carried imports and exports of the West directly to and from the East, denying New Orleans the trade that was "naturally due exclusively to her merchants" by the right of their location at the mouth of the Mississippi. During the recent epidemic, while New Orleans was embargoed, the east-west rail lines remained unaffected and flourishing, and by the end of the epidemic the city's customers had learned to acquire commodities from other sources.

The report went on to complain petulantly that interior quarantines were mostly commercial in nature, and the net result disastrous to the city: "It would be useless to do more than estimate in general terms the immense loss resulting from . . . the withdrawal of capital, the cessation of industry, the exclusion of trade and travel and the disorganization of purposes and of businesses which commercial ostracism, with general illness and anxiety, have occasioned." The ultimate outcome of interior quarantine and that imposed by their own state board, if they continued in the future, would be to establish New Orleans "as a leper among cities, with which it will be forbidden to conduct the operations of trade or exchange the offices of a common humanity for a period of at least one third of each year."[21]

By framing the quarantine explosion of the interior areas almost solely in terms of commercial competition, and illustrating how damaging the Louisiana quarantine was to the city's commercial interests, this report could conclude that the local quarantine should be abolished, and call upon the federal government to step in and prevent local communities from obstructing interstate trade. While the report's authors were skeptical of the possibility of changing state quarantine, they were hopeful that the federal government might enact a quarantine law that would at least subject every port to the same restrictions, and operate to prevent the interior chaos characteristic of 1878.[22]

Some businessmen, at any rate, believed that the ambitions of the November committee with regard to quarantine were wrong-headed and doomed to failure. At the meeting one merchant reminded the group how strongly the interior communities blamed New Orleans for admitting the disease, and expressed doubt that any federal legislation would be forthcoming that would weaken the nation's defenses against yellow fever or a community's right to protect itself. Yellow fever had to be kept out of the city; nothing else would truly serve commercial inter-

ders also saw themselves as wrestling with a Demo-
' as corrupt as their city streets, and vowed to clean
city's government and environment.[27]
rleans physician who was a member of the Associa-
further reason why its efforts were necessary. The
usted the state board, which had stressed quarantine
nse of sanitation in the past, and were unwilling to
axes increased to support such an inactive agency.[28]
d the Association's members feel that the municipal
could not do the work effectively, they believed that
usiness experience they were better qualified to get
e. Businessman Edward Fenner, the vice president of
tion and its most prolific proselytizer, claimed that
ence of the past has taught them [businessmen] that
porations cannot be depended upon for that prompt
ed action which enables men trained in the severe
usiness affairs to execute large undertakings with
d dispatch."[29] In the years since its founding the state
spent large sums of money on sanitary enterprises,
e board's composition varied with the fortunes of
s, and many such projects were designed largely to
y for political favorites, little had resulted from this
e. Businessmen, argued Fenner, were much better
b bring such work to completion.[30]
ociation took on a variety of sanitary tasks and
rmoniously in its first months with the state board of
aid the wages for ten new board of health sanitary
bought garbage scows and carts for the city, had
s cemeteries covered over with fresh dirt, provided
ctant to the poor for use in privies, and established a
stem to clean the streets. In addition, the Association
the creation of a board of public works, advocated a
latrine with a removable pail that could be covered
ed weekly by municipal collectors, and later, after
success of the Memphis system, supported the estab-
sewer lines for New Orleans. Another major area of
the abatement of nuisances, such as yards filled with
garbage or a situation where an establishment's
e overflowing into the street. The Association kept

ests. Another meeting o
echoed these sentiments
tine, this gathering reso
yellow fever and perhaj
unnecessary. Opposition
was no less strong, but th
thing had to be done or
would destroy the city's t
noyance of quarantine ha

In late March 1879, a
businessmen appeared in
ing the community of the
tary Association of New C
to one account, grew out
absolute necessity for in
form," subjects that were
of our thoughtful and in
public press and at open
Association had several th
in the phrase of one of its
cents to the millionaire's t

The organization mark
volvement in southern p
crying quarantine and o
rational and suited to con
the cleansing of the city,
any soil in which to grow.
public health authorities
successful if thoroughly i
the only conceivable path
yellow fever, and the dis
both. The Association's lea
city government lacked tl
reformation. Garbage wen
ing with filth; the city's
tunity for water and air
Orleans below sea level m
Yet the city's coffers wer
shackled with a debt that

Business lea
cratic "ring
up both the

A New C
tion cited a
people distr
at the expe
have their
Not only di
authorities
with their
the job don
the Associa
"the experi
political con
and sustain
school of
economy a
board had
but since t
state politic
make mon
expenditur
equipped t

The Ass
worked ha
health. It
inspectors,
malodorou
free disinfe
flushing sy
lobbied for
new sort o
and empti
seeing the
lishment o
activity wa
putrefying
privies we

records of complaints by citizens, sent an inspector to the scene, and then assisted the board of health in putting pressure upon the implicated miscreant.[31]

A National Board inspector who visited New Orleans in the summer of 1879, only a few months after the Association's work had begun, was impressed with the results. "I found everywhere a marked improvement as compared with my previous visit in the Spring; gutters were being flushed, streets cleaned, and the results of a thorough and general policing were evident at every hand." He observed two hundred men employed by the Association at work filling in stagnant ponds along the river bank, a project of such magnitude as to convince him of the depth of the Association's commitment to public health reform. "It is safe to say that for the past two and a half months more attention has been paid to sanitary sciences and sanitary matters in the city of New Orleans than in any other city in the United States; so far as municipal sanitation goes there is so much of present accomplishment and promise for the future as to leave little to be desired." He attributed this happy state of affairs entirely to the energetic performance of the Auxiliary Sanitary Association.[32] It is difficult to assess the actual influence of the Association upon the condition of New Orleans. While it is likely that they made a significant difference through some of their projects, such as establishing pumps to flush and hence clean certain major streets, they could do little to remedy the fundamental sanitary problems of the city—the inadequacy of its water, sewage, and drainage systems.

The economic motivations of the participants in the Association were explicit and clear. Their motto was "Public Health Is Public Wealth," and the letter which called the group together proclaimed "Health is capital for a man. It is also capital for a community."[33] The business sector, struggling to emerge from the depression of the 1870s and the blight of 1878, feared that their prosperity would be continually drained by epidemic disease. "When a menacing plague is ever hanging over a city, like a sword suspended above the head of Damocles, confidence vanishes, capital, timid and sensitive, is withdrawn, and business languishes and dies," wrote Fenner in explaining the Association's origin.[34] Unlike the charitable contributions directed toward providing drugs for the sick or clothing for those left indigent by an epidemic, this was philanthropy tinged with a spirit of investment that promised tangible returns. After yellow fever had not appeared in New Orleans to any significant extent during 1879 and 1880, the Association took the credit for having exterminated the disease by their sanitary accomplishments. "We are satisfied with the investment of our money as a business enterprise," commented one Association spokesman in 1879, "and we fully recommend other communities to take stock liberally in works of public and private sanitation."[35]

The founding members of the Auxiliary Sanitary Association were of the city's commercial and social elite, many of them the same people who supported the reform party in politics and led other commercial associations in the city. The president of the Cotton Exchange was an active member, as was one of the men instrumental in the movement for a produce exchange during the 1870s. Leading railroad, insurance, produce, and cotton men made considerable contributions to the Association's activities and treasury. The Association's membership list was also replete with the names of men who had been elected to the prestigious social clubs of the city. One-eighth of the exclusive Boston Club's 1879 roll signed the Association's first declaration of principles; around one-third of the Association's members were included in either the Boston or Pickwick Clubs. Both their place in society and in the business world had led these men to expect the assumption of leadership in New Orleans. Their position at the apogee of the social and business communities gave them the courage both to take on the financially extensive burdens of urban sanitation ($30,000 was appropriated at one meeting for street flushing alone) but also to persist in challenging the appointed authorities of the board of health when they believed that the Association's stance was in the best interests of the city of New Orleans.[36]

While carrying out sanitary reform projects, members of the Auxiliary Sanitary Association did not forget the thornier and more emotional issue of quarantine. Their opposition to unreasonable quarantine was heightened in the spring of 1879 by the erratic and ill-functioning quarantine regulations then in force. President Choppin of the Louisiana State Board of Health was ill during the late spring, when the quarantine edict went into effect, and no quorum could be assembled for board meetings. In order to exempt their ships from the twenty-day quarantine required, ship agents took a petition around to the individual board members for signature, a system open to confusion and corruption. One National Board inspector, John Rauch of Illinois, found in the summer of 1879 "much dissatisfaction with the quarantine regulations . . . among the shipping and mercantile interests." This antagonism had led to effective pressure on the board to reduce the quarantine period from twenty to ten days, which, in contrast to the longer period, Choppin claimed could and would be strictly enforced. Although Rauch had earlier garnered a pledge from the Auxiliary Sanitary Association that it would not interfere with the Louisiana quarantine, Choppin told him that "the Association was among the most strenuous opponents of quarantine." "This, I subsequently learned," Rauch continued, "could not apply to the Association in its official action, although many of its members were bitter in their denunciation of the system as presently pursued."[37]

"A quarantine is their abomination," related another National Board inspector who met with Association members that same summer. "At war with every interest in New Orleans, destroying commerce, and preventing the City from being one of the grandest on the Continent. It keeps out ships, and merchants, and capital and dont [sic] keep out yellow fever," he reported. "This view is not advocated alone by merchants and businessmen and tradespeople, but by a large number of the best medical men in New Orleans."[38] The years of wrangling over what form of quarantine to enforce and the blatant use of quarantines as commercial weapons had left a legacy of distrust toward the practice and the board itself. The Association sought to educate the people to beware the false security of quarantine, and to create "a more lively public sentiment in favor of *cleanliness* and public *sanitation*."[39]

One aspect of the Louisiana quarantine which businessmen found particularly galling was the practice of making ship owners pay for quarantine services. Merchants commonly expressed the belief that the state board, which relied heavily on quarantine fees for its funding, was leaching money from the shipping

trade in order to fill its own treasury. This was one factor leading businessmen to support a national quarantine, for which
they presumably would not have to pay. Gustavus Devron, a
physician who worked with the Association, predicted that such
a nationally administered quarantine would become " 'A work
of Humanity,' not one [of] 'fee making and extortion['] as now
considered by the majority of those who are at present compelled to fill the empty coffers of the Board of Health of the
State of Louisiana."[40] The Morgan Steamship and Railroad
Line, a major Louisiana company that carried a large portion of
the trade between Texas and Louisiana, even challenged in
court the Louisiana board's right to collect quarantine fees. The
company's lawyers argued that such fees were a levy on interstate and foreign commerce, and as such violated the Constitution. Morgan had earlier won suits against Galveston and
Mobile based on the same interstate commerce argument, but
his company lost in the Louisiana courts in 1884 and in the
United States Supreme Court in 1886.[41]

Their varied complaints about quarantine and its administration by the Louisiana state board, coupled with their recognition that yellow fever, and not just quarantine, was a factor
constraining the commercial growth of New Orleans, made the
members of the Auxiliary Sanitary Association strongly receptive to the idea of a national quarantine, and subsequently to
the activities of the National Board of Health. The Association
heartily approved of the National Board's aspirations for a truly
national, uniform quarantine, as such a system would eradicate
the preferential treatment tendered some cities by their government's indifference to epidemic disease. Charles Whitney, president of the Association and manager of the Morgan, Louisiana,
and Texas Railroad and Steamship Company, emphasized the
desirability of uniform regulations that could emanate only
from a disinterested national power. "We hope and trust," he
urged in a letter to A. N. Bell of November 1879,

that the next Congress will invest in the National Board . . . the authority and power to enforce a thorough and definite system of regulations, which will not only govern all alike, but deprive each individual
port or town of the right to exercise these absolute powers, which as

the experience of the past two seasons has illustrated, have often been used to encourage other ties and interests than those appertaining to the health of their communities. Hence, it seems clear, that, to avoid the clashing of such interests, the only possible relief, attainable, is to place the power with those who are likely to remain free from, and above the influence of all individual or local interests.[42]

A National quarantine would thus protect trade by keeping out disease and preventing commercial rivalry from disrupting traffic.

Association members no doubt believed that a quarantine decided upon by the National Board of Health would be shaped according to the best prevailing precepts of medical science about yellow fever prophylaxis. The National Board had publicly advocated a quarantine of disinfection rather than extensive detention, and a system of bills of health issued at foreign ports that could greatly ease a ship's passage through domestic quarantine. With such a quarantine system in place merchants expected more constancy in quarantine regulations, a dependability upon which they could plan and rely, and welcome relief from the ever-changing state board of health requirements.[43]

One of the more compelling reasons for the Auxiliary Sanitary Association to advocate the National Board's cause was the recognition that only a national agency could win the confidence of the interior communities. After 1878 little further was heard of the idea that the National Board would force a community to accept goods from a yellow fever site, although something of that solution was contained in Whitney's letter. The dominant view was that the National Board should do everything in its power to make the interior feel safe and protected, so that trade would be unimpeded by yellow fever rumors or the presence of yellow fever itself. "The National Board of Health is a fact, and it must be accepted as the concurrent sentiment of the people of the whole country," Fenner told a meeting of the Association on 8 November 1879. "No measure will have a greater tendency to allay the apprehension felt in rural districts than the knowledge that hereafter the government will impose such well considered regulations at every point as absolutely to prevent the introduction of disease while inflicting upon commerce the least amount of injury."[44] Given the choices facing the business community in regard to yellow fever and the commercial fate of the city, the National Board offered the least painful route to the restoration of peaceful and trusting relations with markets and sources of raw materials in the interior, while affording far less annoyance than the activities of the state board of health.

A major obstacle to the creation of a mood of regional trust and the improvement of New Orleans' public health reputation was the stubborn attitude of Joseph Jones, whose ascension to the presidency of the Louisiana State Board of Health in 1880 marked the end of the overtly amicable relations that had existed between the Association and the state board of health under Choppin. Jones saw no reason why his board's integrity should be doubted, and refused to make any concessions to the fears of communities outside of New Orleans about his board's incompetence. Thus when the Sanitary Council of the Mississippi Valley argued in resolutions passed in December 1880 that the state board allow one National Board appointee to reside at the main Louisiana quarantine station and another to attend all meetings of and have full access to the information gathered by the state board, Jones used every tool at his disposal to oppose both appointments.[45] Jones's recalcitrance roused the Association to endorse the Sanitary Council's resolutions with the rationale that this fairly innocuous action of allowing impartial inspection would do much to restore confidence in the board. "It is evident that only by compliance with this request that unreasonable apprehensions of danger can be anticipated and premature and unnecessary restrictions upon commercial and personal intercourse with New Orleans be prevented," proclaimed the Association's resolutions.[46] The Chamber of Commerce and the Cotton Exchange also endorsed the proposals, and a petition signed by 800 of "the most respectable firms and citizens of New Orleans" appealed to the state board to acquiesce to the Sanitary Council's request.[47] Jones did finally yield on the issue, in time to take up a new battle with the same configuration of opponents—the National Board, Sanitary Council, and the Auxiliary Sanitary Association—over the issue of Ship Island quarantine.

If Jones at times believed that there was a conspiracy against him and the performance of his professional duty, there was some basis for suspicion. The National Board, the Sanitary Council, the American Public Health Association, and the Auxiliary Sanitary Association were by no means independent bodies that all happened to come to the same conclusions about sanitary and quarantine reform. Their leaderships were intimately intermeshed, and their purposes often parallel. C. B. White, who was sanitary director of the Association from 1879 to 1880, was elected president of the American Public Health Association in 1880. Gustavus Devron, a physician very active in the Auxiliary Sanitary Association from its formation, became president of the Sanitary Council by 1883. Charles Whitney, the Association's first president, represented the Morgan company in its fight against the Louisiana Board of Health's quarantine laws, and the Association's letterhead address was "Room #4 over Morgan's R.R. Office, Corner of Natchez and Magazine Streets." The American Public Health Association took credit for creating the National Board of Health, and its officers and those of the National Board were heavily integrated during the four years of the board's existence.[48]

The National Board was less openly tied to the Sanitary Council, but the connection was nonetheless strong. National Board inspectors held prominent positions within the Council, which generally seconded the National Board's proposals. R. W. Mitchell, a National Board member residing in Memphis, claimed in an 1881 letter to J. L. Cabell that he had controlled the Sanitary Council since its first meeting. "From its inception every important movement of the Council had been instigated or directed by the resident of the Board at Memphis." According to Mitchell, the resolutions of December 1880, which the New Orleans commercial community so publicly endorsed, were written by him, handed quietly to the chairman of the Council's meeting in New Orleans, and subsequently passed.[49] Samuel M. Bemiss and Stanford E. Chaillé, a National Board member and inspector, respectively, and both of New Orleans, continually praised the Auxiliary Sanitary Association's work in their writings, and Chaillé (together with his wife) was a subscribing member. The New Orleans business community may well have been comfortable with these intertwining loyalties, an arrangement that was in their view the best for local commerce, but they were plainly manipulated by those promoting the interests of the National Board of Health.[50]

The Auxiliary Sanitary Association survived the demise of the National Board of Health, but with the end of Jones's administration in 1884 it no longer maintained a high profile. The new president of the board of health, Joseph Holt, had worked closely with the association on its sanitary projects, before he assumed state office. Instead of opposing the sanitary association's members, he harnessed their energy to make major changes in the state's quarantine system. Holt succeeded in acquiring funds to build a new quarantine station for Louisiana, which included apparatus for thoroughly disinfecting a vessel in ways impossible before. His system, which he called "maritime sanitation" to distinguish it from the hated quarantine, required much shorter detention for vessels, and proved much more satisfactory to the business community than the system previously in force.[51]

Holt's scientific quarantine is an interesting example of the power of a new technology to create support for public health reform. When physicians were divided over quarantine versus sanitation, and the efficacy of neither appeared clear-cut, politicians were reluctant to fund large public health projects. Reform in any direction was stunted, and failed efforts at street cleaning or isolation were hailed loudly by those protecting the taxpayer's pocketbook from wasteful expenditures. Only when the disease was on the threshold did politicians vote paltry funds to bar the door. The spurts of privately funded sanitation after 1878 were anomalies in the overall apathy toward public hygiene. This changed in the 1880s. The concept of disinfection offered the possibility of a truly protective quarantine that was at the same time limited and relatively cheap. Businessmen compared the alternatives between commerce-disrupting epidemics and disinfecting quarantine stations, and chose the latter. Here was a technique that anyone could understand: acid gas would kill disease causing germs and purify the ship or train, allowing it to continue on its journey in a few days. The city was safe; the cargo was safe. Fruit was given special treatment that avoided destroying its value. Funds for such quarantine stations appeared repeatedly in state and federal budgets in the 1880s and 1890s. They probably did a fair job of killing mosquitoes, which may account for their good record of success.[52]

Over time, the new system also generated considerable confidence in communities outside of New Orleans, for yellow fever did not return to the city until 1897. No longer was New Orleans the great entrepôt for yellow fever, and her commercial prospects improved accordingly. With such a reasonable quarantine in place, the business community had much less to oppose, much less need for a strident voice in the management of public health affairs. Businessmen continued to urge the Board of Health to lower quarantine fees, which decreased during the period from 1884 and 1905, and their support for a national quarantine remained strong. This was in part a reflection of the persevering hope that quarantine fees might be eradicated altogether. More important was the realization that however well-protected Louisiana might be by her quarantine stations, other states, especially Florida and Mississippi, were not so secure. Particularly after the epidemics of 1888, 1897–1899, and 1905, all of which entered through one of these two states, New Orleans businessmen passed resolutions asking the federal government to take charge of quarantine and prevent the disruption that yellow fever brought to southern commerce.[53]

Business involvement in sanitary reform became gradually less necessary as well. After 1895, when the city again had funds at its disposal, the abortive efforts for sewerage, water supply, and drainage reform undertaken in the previous fifteen years began to bear fruit. Although progress was slow, by 1907 the city had a working system of municipal utilities to provide sewer, water, and drainage services, obviating the need for further philanthropic management. The Auxiliary Sanitary Association had served an interim function while the city government caught up with the problems of urbanization and modern sanitation. Also in 1907, the federal government took over control of the Louisiana quarantine system. The crisis that had brought the Auxiliary Sanitary Association into existence was finally resolved by the maturation of government services and federal control of coastal quarantine.[54]

Businessmen in Memphis, the other major city devastated by the 1878 yellow fever epidemic, were also roused to extensive involvement in public health affairs, although their efforts lacked the enduring organizational structure and extent of their New Orleans counterparts. While their city's population did not approach that of New Orleans, merchants in Memphis likewise harbored ambitions of their city becoming a great industrial and commercial metropolis. The *Daily Appeal*, one of the city's main newspapers, was a constant advocate of promoting "our efforts to make Memphis a great trade center."[55] Like other southern journalists, the paper's editors lamented the lack of cotton manufacturing in the heart of such a rich cotton-producing region. "Whenever the South manufactures the cotton which it produces—brings the looms to the cotton instead of transporting the cotton to the mills of Europe and the Northern States, and succeeds in turning the tide of emigration to the South, we will become the most prosperous people on the globe," an 1880 editorial proclaimed with the resonance of New South rhetoric.[56] In calling for sanitary reform after the 1878 epidemic, the editors explicitly linked economic growth and disease with the maxims "good hygiene makes business good" and "a good sanitary condition . . . is one of the best advertisements a city can have."[57] The drive to improve Memphis's business environment made it a particularly likely locus for sanitary reform. The city was in desperate straits after 1878, with some pundits claiming that no city should stand on the site at all, that Memphis should be burned to the ground and that its people should move elsewhere. Especially after the return of yellow fever in 1879, Memphis's case seemed hopeless to many. From such gloom arose the mercantile drive to rejuvenate the city with sanitary reform that would exclude disease from their midst.

The Memphis commercial community, like that of New Orleans, viewed sanitary projects as the key to the city's revival. Mimicking their Louisiana counterparts, Memphis businessmen established their own Auxiliary Sanitary Association in the spring of 1879. Yet Memphians managed to reach a legislative solution far earlier than did the citizens of New Orleans, for the state taxes, which paid for the Memphis sewer system, provided the means for overcoming one major impediment to urban cleanliness. The explanation for this success in securing government assumption of sanitation lay in part in the smaller size of Memphis, and the consequent diminished extent of the problem, but also in the deeper destruction of Memphis by yellow fever. The very familiarity of New Orleans's citizenry with yellow fever made it harder to gain approval for the taxation that would underwrite public works projects; in Memphis, on the other hand, yellow fever was a relatively rare caller, all the more terrible for its infrequent but decimating visits. Memphians were willing to pay almost any price to stop the disease, for the very survival of the city was at stake. Furthermore, as historian John Ellis has pointed out, Memphis businessmen were far more successful in directing their municipal government than businessmen in New Orleans, and so had less need for voluntary association action.[58]

Memphis businessmen also felt great antipathy toward quarantine when it was leveled against their community. They naturally joined their state and local public health officials in approving quarantines against New Orleans that protected Memphis, but they shared with Louisianans a distaste for apparently unreasonable quarantines that shackled their own trade. In Memphis, the main quarantine dispute of the period concerned not time of detention, but rather what sort of goods could carry the yellow fever germ. The problems of inland quarantine became acute during the Memphis yellow fever epidemic of 1879, when the state health authorities attempted to seal off Memphis, and discussions over what could be transported safely into and out of the city grew quite heated. Yet Memphis merchants, like those of New Orleans, welcomed the National Board of Health, for they believed that the measures inaugurated by the board offered the best hope for ensuring the smooth flow of commerce in the region and of excluding yellow fever.

Even before the epidemic of 1878 had overwhelmed Memphis, the city's businessmen were concerned about sanitary reform, but it was not until August 1878 that this interest ripened into public action.[59] By then enough cases of yellow fever had occurred to make it apparent that an epidemic was imminent if not already ongoing. Representatives from the city government met with a large group of business and community leaders to discuss what emergency measures could be taken to ward off the disease. One Memphis physician argued for the cleansing and disinfection of the streets and privies as an urgent necessity. Someone else at the meeting then suggested that the amply funded Howard Association should take on the project, but its president rose to say that the association's charter did not allow money to be spent for any purpose other than caring for the sick. Another voice called upon the city government, through the board of health, to fulfill the city's sanitary requirements. Why should the merchants pay for it? In response, the city's mayor ruefully pointed out that a municipal contribution of $800 toward the sanitary work was all that could be spared. The gathering consequently resolved that private donations would have to remedy the deficit, and $2,000 was collected on the spot to assist the board of health's efforts.[60] Soon after this meeting the bulk of the city's prosperous citizens abandoned Memphis, the city government broke down, and the board of health ceased functioning, leaving most sanitary projects undone.[61]

Those businessmen who remained in Memphis during the 1878 epidemic organized charitable committees to assist the needy. The Howards took care of the sick, losing many of their members to the disease in the process. Other relief committees with varying functions were formed, such as one described by a Memphis commission merchant in a letter to a Cincinnati group raising funds for the disease-stricken South. The members of his citizens relief committee, he wrote, "with only a few dollars in their treasury," attend to the needs of the city's sick and indigent, take care of the orphans, and guard the property of its residents. He went on to stress the integrity and deserving nature of the work. "The Citizens [Committee] are composed of all of our leading merchants, and I say to you with my personal knowledge [they] are doing more good than the Howards and all other societies."[62]

In the spring of 1879 Memphis merchants again attempted to effect sanitary reform, now inspired by the horrors and losses of the 1878 epidemic.[63] In May 1879, National Board member R. W. Mitchell addressed a combined meeting of the Cotton Exchange and the Chamber of Commerce at which he recommended the formation of an Auxiliary Sanitary Association. "Its object shall be to assist the local authorities in the improve-

ment of the sanitary condition of the city, the diffusion of information on sanitary subjects and to educate the people to a
proper appreciation of the importance of a strict obedience to
sanitary and hygienic laws," he proposed.[64] The businessmen
present organized the Association that day, and by the first
week in June the new organization had purchased disinfectants,
garbage carts, and draft animals for the city board of health.
The Association began a full-scale campaign to identify and
eliminate the fever-producing receptacles of filth; on 12 June it
published a list in the Memphis newspapers of obstreperous
landowners who refused to clean up their property. At a series
of meetings in July the Association's members discussed the
problems of drainage, sewerage, and water supply that afflicted
Memphis, although they took no action.[65] The president of the
Memphis Board of Health, G. B. Thornton, could claim that by
the end of June, "a great deal of sanitary work has been done
during the past four months, and a better sanitary system is
now in force than ever before."[66] In his report for that year
Thornton concluded that "the Association exhibited commend-
able zeal and rendered material assistance at a time when the
city government was most embarrassed for means."[67] The return of yellow fever in 1879 again disrupted sanitary work and
scattered the Association's members.

Yellow fever's recurrence in spite of the extensive accomplishments of the municipal board of health and the Sanitary
Association made it evident that more substantial reform was
demanded. The most obvious source of filth was the privy
system, which saturated the soil with human waste, contaminated the water supply, and poisoned the air. Reformers especially targeted the Bayou Gayoso, a large open sewer that ran
through some of the worst and most diseased sections of the
city. They fastened upon the construction of a new sewer system as the solution to the yellow fever dilemma.[68]

Yet there was not money available in the city's budget. The city
had repudiated its debt and given up its charter in 1878, and by
1879 existed only as a taxing district administered by commission-
ers with a very limited treasury. Having reneged on its debts, the
city could hardly hope to borrow money, and its population and
property had been impoverished by two successive epidemic

years. Still, support for the sewerage plans was strong among the mercantile community. During the 1879 epidemic one hundred Memphis citizens in exile in St. Louis resolved that the prevention of yellow fever by the establishment of a sewer system was worth paying any sort of taxes.[69] A newspaper reporter who interviewed more than twenty leading merchants in downtown Memphis late in 1879 found over three-quarters of them determined to bear the expense if only the new sewers would truly solve the city's public health problems. Such desperate enthusiasm was no doubt instrumental in effecting the legislative passage of a special tax and the subsequent installation of the model sewer system.[70]

That the anti-quarantine animus among Memphis businessmen remained spirited was evidenced by the events of the 1879 yellow fever epidemic. In that year the Tennessee State Board of Health, with the assistance of the National Board, quarantined Memphis in order to protect the state and the region by surrounding the city with a line of pickets that controlled both the ingress and egress of persons and property. The board required railroad passengers and cargoes to undergo disinfection and change trains a few miles outside of the fever district, and they also disinfected mail and other outgoing items. One particularly unpopular provision of the state board's rules, Rule #6 on its list of instructions to pickets, was, "Neither lint cotton nor seed cotton will be permitted to enter Memphis during the epidemic."[71] James Dease Plunket, president of the state board of health, argued that cotton could be a dangerous carrier of the yellow fever germ (or sporad), and that once processed amidst the infectious filth of Memphis, the cotton might set off an epidemic at its final destination. Further, the cotton trade brought large numbers of people into the city.[72] Another member of the state board said, in defense of the rule, that he had discovered full agreement with the board's position among planters and other citizens of Memphis. According to his report to the National Board, for which he served as an inspector, these sources "express the belief very generally that this cotton business had more to do with spreading the fever throughout the country around Memphis last year [1878] than all other means combined."[73] Both the National Board and the Memphis Board of Health approved of the character of the state's quarantine.

The action of the state board aroused fierce opposition within the Memphis business community. Both daily newspapers were harsh in their criticism of "Sporad Plunket's" rule, which they saw in part as motivated by the desire of Nashville merchants to ruin the commerce of Memphis. The only member of the state board from Memphis was inactive, and the city was defenseless against what one paper called the "remorseless tyranny" of the Nashville-oriented board.[74] The height of ridicule against Plunket appeared in the *Daily Avalanche*, which published a poem in his honor entitled "Spore Hunting":

> I've got some yaller fever germ,
> If you'll admit of such a term;
> Caught in various, sundry, divers places,
> After many of the hardest kind of races;
>   (And I killed him so dead as never vas.)
>
> .   .   .   .
>
> I found a gray one up a tree,
> But he was too much for me;
> I filled him full of lime,
> And gave him Bolic Acid all the time;
>   (But he wouldn't die worth a cent.)
>
> Then I sent for Dr. Plunket,
> And on his long legs plunked it;
> Doctor, here's the place to show your skill,
> If you know the way a yaller spore to kill;
>   (I'll kill him, he says, so dead as never vas.)
>
> He says, "I'll isolate this tree,
> And I'll be d—d if he
> Don't die with ennui;
> If not, you may shoot me;
>   (I'll kill him so dead as never vas.)"[75]

In more sober language, the Shelby County Medical Society, the local medical society for Memphis, likewise considered the State Board's quarantine to be ill-considered and ineffective.[76]

The most violent protest came from a group of merchants headed by the owner of the largest cotton gin in Memphis, who went to court to block the enforcement of Rule #6. His brief asserted that the state did not have the right to destroy, in effect, the commerce of Memphis. The group collected over two hundred signatures of business firm representatives on a petition protesting the rule.[77] Since the appointed judge was in Wisconsin, the merchants convinced the local bar association to elect an interim judge favorable to their cause, who then issued an injunction against the rule. The state board's lawyers appealed the decision to the Shelby County Chancery Court, which declared that the state had the right to make such a rule to protect her citizens, was not thereby damaging trade, and that the interim judge's appointment had no validity. The state had won, but a residue of ill will toward the state authorities was left among the business community of Memphis.[78]

Heightened by the apparent favoritism of the state board of health and by the accomplishment of federally backed sanitary reform in 1880, the popularity of the National Board of Health within Memphis business circles waxed brightly in 1880, in spite of the National Board's approbation of the infamous Rule #6. Spokesmen for Memphis merchants portrayed the National Board's inspection rules as fair, uniform, impartial, and effective in controlling yellow fever. During the summers of 1879 and 1880 the National Board had, they believed, successfully squelched panic in the wake of yellow fever rumors and had run its inspection service in such a fashion as to allow the transportation industry to operate at near normal levels. According to the Memphis Cotton Exchange, the National Board's efficiency was due in large measure to the confidence its announcements and actions were able to command throughout the Mississippi Valley.[79] In one widely publicized instance during the summer of 1880, the towboat *Raven* arrived in Vicksburg with suspicious cases of fever on board. "These cases fortunately turned out to be dengue, or 'break bone' fever," said one physician addressing the Cotton Exchange, "but the symptoms were sufficiently alarming to have created a panic and started shotgun quarantines in the absence of the confidence felt in the action of the National

Board of Health, speedily followed by its authoritative announcement of the harmless nature of the sickness."[80] It was
the preservation of the feeling of security, and the consequent
smooth flow of commercial traffic, which caused the Exchange
to endorse the work of the National Board of Health.

In contrast to the divergence of public health officials in Memphis and New Orleans on the subject of national control of
quarantine, businessmen in the two cities displayed remarkable
unanimity in their approval of federal quarantine initiatives.
One reason for this similarity no doubt lay in the businessman's
growing tendency to be concerned with the region as a whole,
to realize that if the flow of trade was interrupted at one point
in the Mississippi Valley, the repercussions would be felt beyond
that one locality. As the rehabilitation of the southern railway
system accelerated in the 1870s, New Orleans and Memphis
were linked much closer to interregional markets and sources
of raw material, especially cotton, the chief commercial commodity of both cities.

Railroad historian Maury Klein has targeted 1880 as the year
after which a marked shift in perception took place among
southern railroad men. From thinking in terms of one city and
its immediate hinterland as their area of responsibility, they
now looked to the vast network of railroad lines stretching from
one corner of the country to the other.[81] A similar transition
characterized the way merchants in New Orleans and Memphis
came to view the movement of their manufactured goods, cotton, or fruit shipments. As their markets expanded, their sense
of functioning within island communities—a mindset that Progressive era historian Robert Wiebe has seen dominant in the
early postwar years—dissipated; instead businessmen in the
two cities began to grasp the reality of interregional trade and
commercial dependence.[82] This tendency to think in terms of
commercial intercourse unfettered by state boundaries made
them more inclined to seek a regional public health code.

Managers of transportation companies—often men in, but
not of, the South—spoke with similar accord in regard to the
usefulness of the National Board of Health's efforts for regional public health protection. The presence of such men as
outspoken leaders in the business communities of New Orleans

and Memphis helped to promote a view of regional prosperity and the extensive interdependence of the cities within the South. Whether located in New Orleans, Memphis, or other major railroad cities in the South, railroad and steamship company men shared a common concern that the trains or boats of their employers run on time and fulfill commitments to their customers. By 1880, only a minority of southern railroads were administered by men with close affiliations to the South, and therefore their public health perspective was even less likely to be structured according to geographic constraints. Charles Whitney, for example, whose participation in the Auxiliary Sanitary Association was extensive, was born in New York State, and came to New Orleans to manage his father-in-law Charles Morgan's transportation company soon after the Civil War. Likewise, James Clarke, the manager and later president of the Illinois Central Railroad, which controlled a route from New Orleans to Chicago by the late 1870s, spent part of his career in New Orleans, but his roots and inclination clearly lay with his home base in Chicago. Control of southern railroads had passed out of the hands of southerners in the two decades after the Civil War, so that by 1885 the main roads were largely owned by financiers on the East Coast. That their minions should have been inclined to promote the cities served by the roads (and thereby increase the carrying trade) is not surprising; that they should simultaneously have been concerned with the prosperity of the road as a whole system and the movement of goods throughout the region is equally comprehensible.[83]

The epidemics of 1878 and 1879 were devastating to the southern railroad industry. The depression of the 1870s had fallen particularly heavily on the southern roads, and the occurrence of these epidemics just when recovery had begun was an unfortunate blow to already tottering companies. After the crash of 1873, the financial underpinnings of many southern roads collapsed, and by 1876 nearly half of them were in default.[84] Many roads subsequently came under the control of northern companies, with massive consolidation as one result. The Louisville and Nashville, which retained its southern management until the mid-1880s, followed the strategy of other companies by expanding considerably in the 1870s, buying defunct roads and constructing new track in an earnest attempt to regain profitability through expansion. It was still struggling to demonstrate the economic wisdom of its growth initiatives when the 1878 epidemic brought many of its trains, especially those in Tennessee and Mississippi, to a standstill. The company estimated direct losses at $300,000, a figure that represented one-sixth of its net earnings for that year. In addition, the L & N ran special relief trains carrying emergency supplies and personnel into Memphis and other stricken localities free of charge. Yellow fever's recurrence in 1879 again lessened the company's profit margin.[85] In the climate of intense rate competition and looming regulation that surrounded railroad management in the late 1870s, disease threatened to prove the determinant of profit or loss.[86]

Agents of railroad and steamship companies were vocal supporters of the National Board of Health's river and railroad inspection service, for such a system was their guarantee against the interruption of traffic caused by local quarantines. Under this system, ships and trains were inspected at certain checkpoints, given clean bills of health or detained for observation and possibly purification, and then issued certificates which instructed local public health officials to let them pass unmolested. R. W. Mitchell, the Memphis member of the National Board, solicited from transportation company executives information on how the National Board's system had affected their companies. In one typical response, M. Burke, the general superintendent of the Mississippi and Tennessee Railroad, stressed his company's approval of the plan. "I know in a general way," he wrote in November 1880, "as I suppose all railroad men south of St. Louis and west of Chattanooga know, that the confidence felt through the Mississippi Valley in the supervision and certificate system of the National Board of Health has been of signal benefit in preventing panic and local quarantine on several occasions last summer." He went on to single out the case of the ship *Excelsior*, which had possible cases of yellow fever on board. The Louisiana Board of Health had hushed it up, but the National Board's inspector in New Orleans broadcast a warning about the ship and its cargo. Burke pointed out that since the incident occurred near the anniversary of the outbreak of yellow fever in 1879, it would have been expected that if it were not for the National

Board, cities such as Grenada, Mississippi, would no doubt have again instituted local quarantines. "Quarantines are catching, and if Grenada had started one, the probability is that other places would have followed suit," he speculated. "The railroads know, to their cost, what such quarantines mean, and I believe that it was the settled determination of some of the most important roads, in the event of their establishment as in 1878–79, to run their engines into the yard, and not turn a wheel until the people had come to their senses." Instead, 1880 had been a profitable year for his line, especially in contrast to 1879. Every railroad man he knew held similar opinions and likewise favored the continuation of the inspection service.[87]

The reply to Mitchell's query of Adriance Storm, superintendent of the St. Louis and Vicksburg Anchor line, echoed the railroad's satisfaction with the National Board. He stressed the uniformity and certainty that the inspection service ensured his shipping company, in contrast to the chaotic state of discovering "the regulations of a town only when the boat arrived at it and was met with a board of health order forbidding her to put off freight or passengers." He cited the case of the *Raven* as one about which "it would have been very easy to get up a panic," and noted the calm that instead ensued due to the National Board's rapid and sure intervention.[88] A letter from the superintendent of the New Orleans Anchor line voiced similar sentiments and at the same time captured the sense of one community of transportation men, engaged in trade throughout the Mississippi Valley, sharing a common outlook. "All steamboat interests south of St. Louis know that the confidence felt throughout the Mississippi Valley in the supervision and certificate system of the National Board of Health has been of signal benefit in preventing panic and local quarantines on several occasions during the past summer, which has been of immense benefit both to the steamboat interests as well as the shippers."[89] Similar words, written by railroad executive James C. Clarke in advocacy of the National Board, conveyed the same perception of regional, transportation route–defined, mercantile allegiance.[90]

The burst of mercantile involvement in public health matters near the end of the 1870s had manifold roots. Certainly the fact that the 1878 epidemic was more costly and widespread than any previous yellow fever visitation gave a powerful impulse to public health reform. The railroad network that made disease dissemination possible also exacerbated the financial impact of yellow fever by creating a regionally intermeshed economy for the epidemic's panic to destroy. Further, the 1878 epidemic occurred at a time of resurgence in the South's economic life, a time when businessmen in the region were publicizing the South as an ideal site for investment and immigration. Southern businessmen saw in yellow fever a formidable impediment to these regional aspirations, and its presence demanded action if commercial prosperity was to be restored. Yellow fever clouded the bright promise of commercial rebirth. In sanitation, businessmen found one direction into which to channel their investment dollars, with the hope that money thus spent would be returned tenfold in the resurrection of their cities from the degradation of disease and commercial isolation. Accustomed by the late 1870s to forming organizations with the purposes of furthering their commercial goals, businessmen in New Orleans and Memphis were optimistic that direct sanitary reform could make the detested quarantine obsolete, and finally effect the elimination of yellow fever from their cities.

4

THE SEARCH FOR CONFIDENCE: Southern Public Health, 1881–1900

During the last two decades of the nineteenth century southern boards of health strove to consolidate the spirit of emergency that had brought them about in the late 1870s. What they sought was a more permanent, solid mandate for continuing public health action grounded upon a broad base of public confidence and support. Although other diseases such as diphtheria, tuberculosis, smallpox and typhoid, attracted their professional attention during these years, yellow fever remained the most critical problem for southern public health authorities through the end of the century, especially in the Gulf coast states. In order to heighten the prestige and respect accorded their boards by lessening conflict among themselves, during the 1880s and 1890s southern public health officials actively promoted co-operation among southern boards. Still, such ambitions could not overcome the prevailing localistic orientation of public health officials in the South, who remained jealous of their local prerogatives and often indifferent to the regional impact of their actions. Throughout this period yellow fever persisted as the nexus of controversies both among southern public health officials and between the Marine Hospital Service and southern boards. The resulting discord accelerated the evolution of the Marine Hospital Service into a national quarantine agency.

During the 1880s and 1890s some sense of normalcy returned to the South. With the end of Reconstruction, white Democrats returned to power in southern state houses, and secessionist politicians like Isham G. Harris of Tennessee went to the U.S. Senate. In contrast to the tumultuous decades before, peace and prosperity fueled optimism that the "New South" would leave defeat behind and be able to catch up in the national economic competition. The depression of 1893 demonstrated the fragility of this new beginning. For black southerners these were decades of increasing repression, as Jim Crow laws and harsh sharecropping agreements ended the hopes of Reconstruction. "The negro question" continued to dominate discussions of the southern labor pool, attraction of capital, and provision of political rights. The period ended with a war just off the southern coast, drawing attention to the region's importance to the nation as a whole.

Although in the decade following 1885 most physicians, newspaper editors, and legislators tended to believe that southern state boards of health were for the most part capable of controlling yellow fever, by the late 1890s this confidence had all but vanished. The 1880s were years of maturation and optimism for southern public health: implementation of the Holt system of maritime sanitation promised to end both yellow fever and the burden of lengthy quarantines, and the scarcity of the disease bolstered faith in the new procedure. The technological prowess embodied in the process, which purported to destroy the yellow fever germ with powerful disinfectants, indicated to many that while administrative problems remained, the technical aspects of yellow fever control had been solved in theory, and, to a certain extent, in practice. When in 1888 a yellow fever epidemic swept out of Florida to threaten other southern states, instead of spurring great outcry for national quarantine, the epidemic pressured the Florida legislature to establish a state board of health. Contemporaries by and large did not consider the Florida epidemic as representative of southern public health as a whole, but rather as a weak link in an otherwise strong chain.

Attendant growth in federal quarantine also defused reform-
ist energies directed toward the establishment of a national
quarantine, for the system in place combined federal and state
quarantine jurisdiction into what many perceived as an adequate quarantine network. Then in 1897 yellow fever again
spread throughout the South, shattering the vision of regional
security and southern public health administration competency.
The century closed with a strong demand for an entirely national coastal quarantine, but the drive was diverted in part by
the exigencies of the Spanish-American War. The American
occupation of Cuba offered new hope that the question of quarantine authority would be rendered irrelevant by the conquest
of yellow fever on the island, with the eradication of the disease
there eliminating the major threat to the American mainland.

In 1884, Joseph Holt succeeded Joseph Jones as president of
the Louisiana State Board of Health, and inaugurated a course
of action that was to elevate public confidence in his and other
southern state boards to an unprecedented level. One of Holt's
first acts was to publish a circular letter distributed to the medical and general press announcing the new membership of the
board and promising cooperation with other state boards, especially in the publication of yellow fever information.[1] Holt left
no doubt, however, that like his predecessor he would resist any
federal interference in the public health affairs of Louisiana.
"We will maintain the prerogatives of the board as a department of State government, and will resent instantly an
encroachment from any quarter," stated Holt in a speech delivered two weeks into his tenure.[2] Evident as well in this address
was Holt's commitment to sanitation. Later, Holt would reiterate the theme "NEW ORLEANS, TO BE SAVED, MUST BE DRAINED
AND CLEANED!" but early in his administration he focused his
professional efforts on quarantine.[3]

During the summer of 1884 the state board enforced a
forty-day quarantine against ships from infected ports. Holt
combined the shock of this drastic quarantine with a superb
lobbying technique to coerce the legislature to fund a major
renovation of the Mississippi River quarantine station, the first
implementation of the Holt system of maritime sanitation. In
order to prevent the importation of the yellow fever germ,

Holt's new station employed elaborate machinery to pump sulfur gas into the holds of ships, spray disinfectant solution on exposed ship surfaces and sturdy items of cargo, and disinfect clothing and other delicate cargo with steam heat. The new system had critical features that guaranteed its success with legislators: (1) it was easy to understand (kill the germ!); (2) its scientific basis was not questioned (germs cause yellow fever); (3) it offered complete protection; (4) it only minimally interfered with commerce and personal liberty. From science had come a system that would solve the yellow fever problem.[4]

To publicize his new system, and strengthen rapport among southern boards of health (thus limiting the manifest need for federal intervention), Holt called representatives of southern boards together for a June 1884 conference in New Orleans. In his conference invitation Holt predicted that the meeting would establish "uniformity and precision of action among ourselves and confidence in the minds of the people in the interior," thereby demonstrating that "we are keenly alive to our duties."[5] The conferees elected Wirt Johnston of the Mississippi Board of Health as president and C. C. Fite of Tennessee as secretary, choices no doubt influenced by Holt's desire to make the earlier opponents of the Louisiana Board feel an integral part of his initiative toward regional cooperation. One reporter termed the meeting harmonious and full of amity, an accord due in part, he believed, to the exclusion of all questions about the federal government's involvement in public health. The meeting refused to extend conference membership to the attending Marine Hospital Service representative, for example, which meant he was not allowed to speak. In addition, when Stanford Chaillé mentioned the National Board of Health in a speech to the conference, Holt rudely ordered him to sit down and shut up. Holt held that the meeting's purpose was to promote regional solidarity, and he wanted neither federal agency to interfere. The conference approved a series of resolutions promising prompt mutual notification of yellow fever and cholera, the promotion of unity among southern boards of health, and permission for state board of health inspectors to visit other states for the purpose of reporting on health conditions to their home boards.[6]

The meeting also endorsed Holt's disinfecting quarantine system. G. B. Thornton of the Memphis Board of Health, an ardent foe of the Joseph Jones administration, said of the new Louisiana Board, the conference, and the Holt procedure: "As a result of the salutary change which was made within the past two years in the *personnel* of the Louisiana State Board of Health, the great reformations made in the public health administration of that state, with the disposition to cooperate with other state boards of health of the Mississippi valley, have created a confidence throughout the valley which has never heretofore existed."[7] Holt was not likely to repeat Jones's error of alienating his neighboring state health officers, thereby creating a constituency favoring federal intervention. On the contrary, Holt made peace with the former enemies of the Louisiana Board. His efforts were all self-consciously directed at bettering the economic and sanitary condition of New Orleans. "We have given to the people of New Orleans a new hope, —to the people of the Mississippi valley the highest known guaranty against the introduction of pestilence," Holt announced to the American Public Health Association in 1885, "while at the same time we have removed from commerce a bar heretofore insuperable."[8] Yellow fever had retarded the growth of New Orleans, and in Holt's view his combined agenda of quarantine reform and promotion of regional public health cooperation would liberate his city from the twin threats of epidemic disease and federal domination.

John Godfrey, the silenced Marine Hospital Service representative at the conference, sent Surgeon General John Hamilton a report that belied the harmonious image of the gathering painted in the press. Godfrey believed that the public health officials of Tennessee and Mississippi had greater trust in the Marine Hospital Service than in the Louisiana Board.[9] Hamilton, who had been instrumental in destroying the National Board of Health, must have received the news with satisfaction. Ever since he had successfully wrested the epidemic fund from the National Board in 1882, he had been assiduously working to consolidate his Service's power, to avoid the mistakes that had helped to topple the National Board, and to curry favor with southern boards of health.

Hamilton sought to increase the popularity of the Marine Hospital Service with the state boards by studiously cultivating a reputation for largess and generosity. In Brownsville, Texas, the Service used the entire federal epidemic fund of $100,000 in battling a yellow fever epidemic during the fall of 1882; Alabama's Jerome Cochran noted later that $5,000 would have sufficed for the work, but commented wryly that "doubtless the money was appreciated by those who got it."[10] When yellow fever broke out in Pensacola that same year, a struggle ensued between the National Board and the Marine Hospital Service for the allegiance of local health authorities. The National Board maintained its jurisdiction in 1882, but Hamilton successfully wooed the local authorities into his camp the following year, in part by promising ample funds for city sanitation that neither he nor the National Board had any authority to deliver.[11] Hamilton had acquired the epidemic fund for 1883 as well, however, and was able to claim that in Pensacola, as in Brownsville, his Service had successfully protected the country from yellow fever. His major tool for epidemic control, much criticized by those who favored disinfection and inspection, was the cordon sanitaire, a ring of armed guards who prohibited both entrance to and egress from the infected town. Until 1887 the Service had only to deal with these two limited outbreaks, so that Hamilton could take liberal credit in his reports for having tamed the yellow beast.[12]

An important factor in the relationship of southern boards of health to the Marine Hospital Service was the location and operation of the Ship Island quarantine station that Joseph Jones had so opposed. Having inherited the Ship Island site from the National Board, Hamilton hoped to please the Louisiana State Board by moving the station to Chandeleur Island, further out in the Gulf and closer to Louisiana. The Alabama and Mississippi Boards of Health fought this transfer, however, and the station was not moved until 1889.[13] Officials of these latter two boards, after viewing the remodeled Louisiana quarantine station in 1885, urged Hamilton to have Ship Island upgraded to the standard of the Louisiana system instead. The inspector Hamilton sent to view the Holt procedure in operation reported that the advantage of the new method was only apparent if a station handled a large volume of traffic; as matters stood with the Ship Island station he did not believe that the expense of renovation was justified.[14]

The Ship Island station was at the center of the controversy that first tested the covenant formed among southern boards at the 1884 conference. In August 1886 a suspicious fever appeared in Biloxi, Mississippi. Local physicians treated the disease as malaria, and only a few persons, already weakened by ill health, died. On 1 September Holt visited eight sick and convalescent patients, and telegraphed back to Louisiana that the disease was in fact yellow fever. Drs. Godfrey and R. D. Murray of the Marine Hospital Service disagreed, as did Felix Formento, a member of the Louisiana Board on vacation in Biloxi at the time. But Holt persisted in his diagnosis and declared that Louisiana would quarantine any person coming from the town, causing many summer visitors to flee from the vicinity. Some other regional boards, such as that in Mobile, temporarily followed suit. Holt presented the affair in a letter to Cochran as an example of the 1884 compact's strength, and the inadequacy of the Marine Hospital Service. He accused the Service of allowing "clandestine communication" between the quarantine station at Ship Island and the Mississippi shore, thus allowing yellow fever to slip into Biloxi.[15] Formento condemned Holt's behavior in the Biloxi affair, charging that in announcing yellow fever he had acted in haste and on the basis of too little evidence. There is perhaps some truth in Formento's implication that Holt rather too greedily seized the opportunity to make himself appear the guardian of the South's health, fighting the ineptitude, bureaucracy, and deceit of the federal government.[16]

The first epidemic to severely challenge the Marine Hospital Service's ability to control yellow fever occurred in Florida during 1887 and 1888. It began in Key West sometime in the spring or summer of 1887, and by the fall of that year had spread to Tampa and other towns in southern Florida. Because the disease showed no disposition to spread further than the southern peninsula, these epidemics were of only minor concern throughout the rest of the South. However, in March of the following year the disease surfaced again, this time at a railroad junction between Tampa and Orlando, and by mid-summer yellow fever was advancing steadily northward through Florida. It reached Jacksonville in early August, and the city became a focal point for distribution of the disease during the course of the autumn months. "The city of Jacksonville is the commercial metropolis of Florida, and her relation during the epidemic of 1888 to the towns and hamlets of the State was identical with that of New Orleans during the year of 1878," asserted a physician chronicling the yellow fever epidemic of MacClenny, Florida, a small town thirty miles west of the city.[17] In September yellow fever cases were discovered in Decatur, Alabama, and Jackson, Mississippi. Both outbreaks were traced to immigrants from Jacksonville. Although much more limited in mortality and scope than the 1878 epidemic, the epidemic of 1888 was the first region-wide epidemic in ten years. As such, it generated national attention, anxiety, and calls for strengthening the country's defenses against yellow fever.[18]

While numerous towns experienced yellow fever in 1888, it was in Jacksonville that the toll was heaviest and the epidemic most severe. The Duval County Board of Health, unprepared for the epidemic and hesitant about what measures should be taken, was overshadowed by a voluntary organization of local businessmen and physicians, the Auxiliary Sanitary Association. The Association spent half a million dollars providing food and medical care, disinfectants, guards to ensure the isolation of houses with yellow fever patients, and crews whose task was cleansing the town. Joseph Porter, a physician from Key West who had managed earlier yellow fever outbreaks during his Army duty and who was also a surgeon of the Marine Hospital Service, volunteered his services in organizing the relief effort; he would later serve for nearly thirty years as the state's health officer. Funding for the Jacksonville work came from the Marine Hospital Service and from nationally collected contributions.[19]

The governor of Florida appealed to the Marine Hospital Service for help when the magnitude of the Jacksonville situation became apparent, and the Service quickly responded. Their chief strategy was to depopulate the city as quickly and completely as possible. In order to protect the surrounding countryside, refugee camps were set up at which emigrants were to spend days under observation and have their luggage disinfected. If no sign of yellow fever appeared, refugees then received a certificate attesting to their good health. Charles Faget of the New Orleans medical clan, whom the Surgeon General placed in charge of the hospital at the largest of these camps, called the plan "a new departure in the history of epidemics," for the refugee camp system constituted a veritable inland quarantine on the Holt model. During the epidemic the camp processed about eight hundred refugees, among whom thirty cases of yellow fever developed, with one death.[20]

While the detention camp plan seemed ideal on paper, allowing as it did the containment of yellow fever and the safe depopulation of a stricken area, practical difficulties soon squelched hopes that a panacea for epidemic visitations had been found. The first problem was to find a location for the camp: no community welcomed such a potential source of infection in its neighborhood. Another was to convince people to go to the camps, instead of fleeing independently. The Marine Hospital Service based its plan on the assumption that the freedom guaranteed by the health certificates would lure emigrants into the camps, but few towns were willing to accept refugees once the epidemic was underway, regardless of their credentials. A refugee would face the same desolate situation with or without the certificate, so ten days detention in the company of possibly infected people held little appeal. The alternative was to set up camps for continuous residency, as had been done in Memphis in 1878 and 1879, where emigrants would remain for the duration of the epidemic. But to provide food and shelter for two months or more for some 15,000 people—the population remaining in Jacksonville—was beyond the means and vision of the Marine Hospital Service in 1888.[21]

The Service's other major activity in Jacksonville was its funding of a massive disinfection of the town during the winter months following the epidemic. At the request of the Jacksonville Board of Health, the Service appropriated $50,000 for fumigating all the houses in the city with burning sulphur, boiling or disinfecting infected bedding or clothing, and buying and burning any materials not subject to such treatment that might be carriers of the yellow fever germ.[22] Porter later claimed that the thoroughness of this procedure prevented the return of yellow fever to Jacksonville in 1889; other testimony indicated that the work was sloppily done and the money extravagantly wasted.[23]

In the ten years that separated the Jacksonville epidemic from that of Memphis in 1878, the approach to yellow fever control had shifted subtly but perceptibly. While sanitarians called in 1879 for a thorough cleansing of Memphis as the way to prevent a recurrence of the disease, in 1889 public health officials recommended a disinfecting campaign specifically aimed at the yellow fever germ. In 1879 the federal government's yellow fever aid resulted in the construction of a sewer system for Memphis; in 1889 federal authorities bought up possibly infected objects and otherwise funded the disinfection of Jacksonville. During both epidemics physicians argued that a filthy environment was necessary for the propagation of the yellow fever germ, but in 1889 public health authorities were more concerned with stopping that germ at its source—the dejecta of the yellow fever patient—than with sanitizing the city. This approach weakened arguments for urban sanitary reform, as was the case for other diseases that public health officials sought to control by breaking up their specific etiological chains rather than by cleaning the overall environment. Although in 1889 sanitarians still castigated communities such as Jacksonville for tolerating filth and thereby encouraging the visitation of yellow fever, public health officials tackled the disease with the specific intention of eradicating not generic filth but the yellow fever germ.

The 1888 epidemic "caused an alarm without precedent and an interruption of commerce without example," according to the secretary of the Tennessee State Board of Health.[24] Practically every state and city in the South quarantined against Jacksonville, and in many cases, against each other. Early in the epidemic, Chattanooga, Memphis, Meridian, Vicksburg, and scores of other southern cities did not allow suspicious trains to even pass through their environs, much less discharge passengers. The Texas health officer detained and disinfected every person and train traveling from east of the Mississippi River, and even temporarily quarantined New Orleans. As the Crescent City had no cases of yellow fever, the Texas official yielded to pressure from the indignant Louisiana State Board of Health and lifted the quarantine.[25]

This widespread reaction attests to the unusually intense panic that accompanied the 1888 epidemic. Especially after cases turned up in Mississippi and Alabama—no matter that their number was few and mortality low—southern public health officials feared that a repetition of the epidemiological pattern of 1878 was imminent. State boards were not alone in their response to this fear; most cities and towns throughout the South instituted their own quarantine restrictions, which were often at variance with the state requirements and were in many cases illegal. Anyone unfortunate enough to be traveling in the South during the fall of 1888 had little idea what documents or evidence of surety the next town on his or her itinerary might require, or indeed whether entrance might be refused altogether. C. P. Wilkinson, who became president of the Louisiana State Board of Health in 1888, judged the actions of such local boards harshly. "In the vast majority of instances local boards of health did nothing to quell the agitation, but on the contrary led the panic and excitedly quarantined against the world," he charged. Wilkinson regretted that the southern people felt so little confidence in either their state boards of health or the principles of modern quarantine. "Throughout the breadth of the land there were outrages perpetrated, and cruelties shown, and brief authority arbitrarily and shamefully exercised, and all this continued until the chilling frosts of late October."[26] The epidemics in Florida, and the small outbreaks in Decatur and Jackson, caused an estimated 50,000 southerners to flee (according to reports, hysterically) to the safety of the North.[27]

The chaotic eruption of quarantines in 1888 had a severe impact on commerce. It was indeed a hallmark of the epidemic that, although many fewer lives were lost than were ten years earlier, the effect on business was equally, if not more disastrous. "An epidemic of yellow-fever, almost entirely confined to the boundaries of one sparsely settled and feasibly isolated state, has caused widespread panic, the loss of millions upon millions of dollars in paralyzed business and embarrassed industries," noted John Rauch of the Illinois Board of Health in 1889.[28] In the same year another commentator pointed to the

extensive expansion of railroad lines in the South that had occurred over the previous decade, and to the rapid industrial
growth that had swelled the population of the region's cities
and towns. He estimated that if an epidemic on the order of
1878 had stricken the South in 1888, it would have had double
to triple the financial impact of the earlier decade.[29] The more
money that was invested in southern business enterprises, the
more vulnerable was the region's economy, not so much to yellow fever itself but to the panics and quarantines that followed
in its wake. The events of 1888 reinforced the lessons of the
earlier epidemic about the value of making the public believe
that the state was in control of the disease, whatever the actual
state of affairs.

Another prominent feature of the 1888 epidemic was heightened anxiety about the peril inherent in the South's commercial
intercourse with Cuba and Florida. "Do Sanitary Interests of
the United States Demand the Annexation of Cuba?" asked the
secretary of the Pennsylvania State Board of Health in 1889.[30]
He calculated that the purchase price of the island would be
much below the cost of just one yellow fever season, and argued
that only the United States could or would ever clean up the
filthy home of yellow fever and hence oust the disease from its
endemic habitat.[31] As Key West had nearly the same climate as
Havana (and, some charged the same foul sanitary habits),
there appeared to be no reason why it should not offer a soil as
fertile for the yellow fever germ as that of Cuba. With the
growth of regular commercial exchange between Key West and
mainland Florida, public health officials warned that the 1888
disaster might easily recur unless the present system of protection were reformed.[32]

Florida, and more particularly the southern section of the
state, had assumed the position in the eyes of the South and the
nation that Louisiana and New Orleans had occupied only ten
years earlier. Now it was Florida that threatened the security of
the region by ignoring sanitary precautions and quarantine
regulations, and by being overly generous in its attitudes toward unrestricted trade with Cuba. The harshest charge against
Florida's public health officials in 1888, however, and one that
echoed earlier criticisms of the Louisiana Board, was that for

weeks in the spring and summer of 1888 they did not report the existence of yellow fever. "The barbarous plan of concealment has been so generally practiced by every county board of health which has been called upon to deal with the disease," pronounced one medical editor late in 1888, that steps to eradicate the Florida epidemic were perforce taken too late. If such practices continued, Florida would become a "continual menace to the whole country."[33] An Ocala, Florida, farmer's letter to a relative in July 1888, provides further testimony to the policy of secrecy. "I think that it is nothing but right that you should know a good many facts that everybody here are trying to conceal from the public outside of the state," he confessed. After instructing the recipient of his letter not to tell his mother, he went on to reveal that a man was dying of yellow fever in Tampa.[34] Hamilton claimed that the Florida authorities were more interested in suppressing information than in suppressing the disease, which earned him no friends among the editors of Florida's newspapers.

The universally prescribed remedy for Florida's health woes was the creation of a state board of health. Spokesmen for the boards of health of Tennessee, Louisiana, and South Carolina all sang the virtues of state boards as bulwarks in the fight against yellow fever, noting smugly that no yellow fever had entered their states that year. If Florida had had a state board in 1888 instead of the medley of competing, inefficient county boards, they reasoned, then the disease could have been easily contained.[35] Organization, not technical knowledge, was the essential factor missing from Florida's efforts to control yellow fever in 1888. Especially in the early months of 1889, southern public health officials urged the formation of a Florida Board of Health, for they feared the reappearance of yellow fever the following summer. "As to yellow fever we must not conceal the fact that the outlook is ominous," reported the secretary of the Tennessee State Board of Health in January 1889. "All sanitarians in the Southern States familiar with the past are very uneasy about the coming summer."[36]

Governor Fleming of Florida became convinced of the need for a state board while attempting to campaign in the fall of that year, for his travel arrangements were continually stymied by local quarantines. He called the state legislature into special session and signed the law founding the State Board of Health on 20 February 1889. The new board succeeded by their own account in gaining the confidence of the people. Porter was appointed state health officer, a post he retained until 1917. The public calm that prevailed throughout the state in 1889, despite yet another yellow fever epidemic in Key West, demonstrated that the new Florida board could at least control limited episodes of yellow fever and prevent commerce-crippling panic.[37]

Although there was some discussion of the need for a national quarantine following the 1888 epidemic, there was by no means as powerful a movement for federal involvement as the one that had resulted in the creation of the National Board of Health in 1879. This was due in part to a preoccupation with the need for a Florida state board. Southern public health officials did not view Florida's weakness as symptomatic of a larger southern problem, but as an isolated local break in the otherwise strong southern defenses against yellow fever. Southern boards of health pointed proudly to their 1888 accomplishments: only a few locations outside Florida experienced yellow fever, even if the epidemic did result in the virtual cessation of southern commerce. Many believed that the main difficulty in the 1888 epidemic had been the mutual lack of acceptance by southern state boards of each other's competency, the refusal of one state to honor the health certificates issued by another. With this situation in decline, the public's confidence in their state health authorities would grow, and shotgun quarantines would correspondingly diminish.[38]

Early in 1889 Cochran invited his southern public health colleagues to a quarantine conference in Montgomery, which officials from Texas, Florida, Louisiana, Mississippi, South Carolina, North Carolina, Georgia, Tennessee, Kentucky, and Illinois attended. The professed purpose of the conference was to establish a set of regional quarantine rules and regulations to be adhered to by all the southern states. The conference approved the Holt system of quarantine, ten-day detention of travelers leaving an infected area, immediate interstate notification of yellow fever, and the value of isolating yellow fever patients. The conference delegates also promised to accept each others health certificates.[39] Although some critics attacked the conference for not stressing the value of sanitation in preventing yellow fever, most observers saw the agreements as a positive step toward regional security. The conference established a standard of optimal southern public health practice that remained in force for the next decade.[40]

The fact that squabbles among southern boards of health during the next few years were rare can in large measure be attributed to the scarcity of yellow fever, but the standard of behavior set down in Montgomery also deserves some of the credit. When in the fall of 1889 Texas imposed what Florida health officials believed were "unnecessarily onerous" quarantine requirements on ships from Key West, the president of the Florida board could point out to the Texas state health officer, "You are violating the conditions formulated and agreements therein established by action of the Quarantine Conference held at Montgomery, Alabama."[41]

Florida health officials again cited the Montgomery Conference a year later, after learning that Louisiana public health authorities were treating persons who had passed through Florida on their way from Cuba as if they had come directly from Cuba to Louisiana. The president of the Louisiana Board strongly defended his board's actions, claiming that the agreements of the Montgomery conference on mutual acceptance of health certificates did not apply to passengers from Cuba. Florida did not follow the procedures of disinfection and detention that Louisiana did, and it had become all too common for travelers to purchase through tickets to New Orleans in Havana, make one stop in Tampa, and then attempt to evade Louisiana's quarantine requirements by proclaiming their status as "from Tampa" rather than "from Havana." Louisiana placed an inspector in Florida to provide information on the yellow fever situation there, an action which Porter termed "offensively suspicious." Porter saw in the Louisiana attitude an attack upon the integrity of his board. "The power to make a sweeping denunciation of this State, and injure her commerce, has never been questioned by this Board on the part of the Louisiana State Board of Health," he said in his annual report, "but the *right* in the sense of equity and fairness is questioned."[42] When the

Florida Board opened a detention and disinfection plant at Tampa a year later and began enforcing rules similar to those of Louisiana, the controversy ceased. The Montgomery conference rules had at least provided some basis for just behavior, but the veneer of solidarity evident in Montgomery was easily stripped away by suspicion and local jealousy.

The most compelling explanation for the relative dearth of sentiment supporting national quarantine in 1889 was the position of the Marine Hospital Service as a quasi-national quarantine agency. Its existence stymied plans for the resurrection of the National Board. Since 1884, advocates of a national board of health had urged Congress to create some sort of national health body, but with little effect. In 1888 and 1889 especially, several bills appeared proposing the establishment of a national bureau of health under the auspices of the Department of the Interior. Unlike the old National Board of Health, each of the proposed agencies included state public health officials as integral contributors to the national policy-making process. The American Public Health Association, and especially John Shaw Billings, George Sternberg, and Henry Pickering Walcott of the Massachusetts State Board of Health, lobbied for Congressional approval of a new national public health agency.[43]

Two major ambitions fueled this drive for a national health agency: a desire to elevate the prestige of public hygiene, and to limit the power of the Marine Hospital Service while retaining control of federal public health initiatives for state health officials. Southerners took part in this movement, but were by no means alone; in fact the leadership of the movement during the 1880s was composed almost entirely of Northerners, reflecting the geographic location of the main figures in the American Public Health Association. The effort paralleled a similar push for the establishment of a national department of science, a department that was to both coordinate the government's many scientific endeavors and heighten the status of the scientific professions.[44] Public health officials badly wanted the recognition that such national public health legislation would give to the value of their work, which was often effective only to the extent that they were able to capture public respect and confidence. Fear of the ever-expanding powers of the Marine Hospital was an even more substantial motivation of the movement. State board of health officials realized that the Service had taken over from the National Board the execution of federal public health directives. By creating a national public health body with direct input from state boards they hoped to reduce the power of the Marine Hospital Service, an agency over which they had no control.

John Hamilton took advantage of the Service's position to convince Congress that it would be foolish to create a new agency when his organization was already in existence and staffed with well-trained officers experienced in dealing with epidemic diseases. Congress accepted his argument that if federal involvement in public health were to increase, then money could most efficiently be spent by improving the system that had already proven its value. Instead of creating a new national public health bureau, Hamilton urged, national quarantine stations should be built on the pattern of the Holt system at key points on the East and West coasts. The stations would free the affected states from the expense of maintaining quarantine stations, and benefit commerce by removing the burdensome fees that those stations currently operating were forced to charge for their services. On 1 August 1888 President Grover Cleveland signed a bill appropriating over half a million dollars for the construction of quarantine stations for Delaware Bay, Chesapeake Bay, the Georgia coast, Key West, San Diego, San Francisco, and Puget Sound, all to be administered by the Marine Hospital Service. Earlier in the year Congress had approved funds for the transfer of the Gulf Quarantine Station from Ship to Chandeleur Island.[45]

There was no widespread demand for a national public health or quarantine service in 1889 because in the minds of many public health officials the United States already had one. As Walter Wyman, who was to become Surgeon General of the Marine Hospital Service one year later, noted in 1890, the completion of the stations authorized in 1888 amounted to the establishment of a national quarantine service, even though the stations of Louisiana, New York, Boston, and Baltimore, for example, remained under state control. Now, however, they were parts of a national string of defensive outposts. Content with this amalgamation of overlapping state and federal authority, Wyman stated that the National Board's attempts to override the states had been "un-American," and that the Marine Hospital Service always sought to work together with the states for the general good.[46] Eminent Chicago physician Nathan Smith Davis told the American Medical Association in 1888 that the Marine Hospital Service was "in some degree at least, a National health department, without the name," while J. Berrien Lindsley of the Tennessee Board of Health suggested renaming the Marine Hospital Service the "United States Public Health Service" since it performed all the functions of such a bureau.[47] Opponents of the Service continued to hope that its evolution into *the* national health service could be reversed, but many accepted by 1889 that escalation of the federal government's commitment to public health should most logically come from the nurture of the Marine Hospital Service and not the conception of a new agency.

In October 1892, Jerome Cochran of the Alabama Board of Health perceptively depicted the position of the Marine Hospital Service and its development into a national health service at a time when agitation for the complete federal assumption of coastal quarantine was again active. In a lengthy letter to Walter Wyman, he advised that instead of seeking to acquire "the whole management of maritime quarantine," which would generate considerable opposition, why not "allow the evolution that is now going on to continue? There is no doubt as to the ultimate outcome." Cochran was sure that "the attempt to legislate the local quarantine authorities out of existence will fail." Wyman would be wiser to strengthen those quarantine stations already under Marine Hospital Service control, and make them as efficient or better than the model stations of New Orleans, Mobile, and Florida. "The result will be that which is abstractly the most to be desired—a system of earnest and friendly cooperation between the States and the national government," claimed Cochran. "The National Board of Health dashed itself to pieces in its effort to supercede the New Orleans board in the control of quarantine at the mouth of the Mississippi," and the Marine Hospital Service would be foolish to challenge state boards directly. Cochran said that he personally hoped for a commissioner of public health who would rally the state boards and bring their leaders together for annual conferences. But he otherwise had little idea of what a separate national department of public health would do, and thought it unlikely that Congress would create such a body. Wyman's actions in the following months, when under his influence a bill was passed establishing the supremacy of the Service in questions of coastal quarantine, indicate that he was sympathetic both to Cochran's perception of the dangers of direct confrontation with state quarantine authority, as well as to his belief in the inevitable centralization of quarantine power into the hands of the federal government.[48]

Cochran's letter was written at a time when the imminent invasion of a frightening epidemic disease had once again brought the question of national quarantine into public view. The great menace in 1892 was cholera, and the most-feared entrepôt New York City. Cholera killed thousands in Russia in the early 1890s, and floods of immigrants escaping from that country brought the disease to American ports, especially New York. The cases at New York's quarantine station in the fall of 1892, and the controversy that followed, pitting state, municipal, and Marine Hospital Service officials against each other with accusations of lying and ineptitude, had made American public health authorities nervous about the nation's security. "The recent experience at the port of New York sent a shudder throughout the whole country," commented the editor of the *New Orleans Medical and Surgical Journal* in 1893, "and did more than anything else to direct public attention to the shortcomings of the State quarantine defenses and to crystallize public sentiment into a demand for national control of matters pertaining to the exclusion of epidemic diseases."[49] This anxiety was expressed in a spate of national quarantine bills introduced into Congress in the fall of 1892, ranging from the creation of a department of public health that would provide funds to help state boards, to plans for the complete assumption of national quarantine by the Marine Hospital Service.[50] Although the feared epidemic never materialized, its threat had a marked impact.

President Benjamin Harrison signed into law the bill that grew out of the concern over cholera on 15 February 1893. It granted authority over national quarantine to the Marine Hospital

Service, but left to the states the administration of existing quarantine stations where that function was being efficiently performed. The law required the Surgeon General of the Marine Hospital Service to examine the quarantine codes of all state and municipal boards of health and to cooperate with them in the execution of their laws. If in his opinion their rules were not sufficient, then he could make additional regulations. Should the local board choose not to enforce the supplementary rules, then the President was empowered to see that they were enforced. This provision in effect gave the Marine Hospital Service the right, with the President's approval, to intervene in any situation in which a local board's quarantine measures were judged too weak. The act required that all ships bound for the United States be inspected at the port of departure and be issued a bill of health detailing the ship's sanitary history. The ship then had to pass through quarantine inspection before entering a United States port. The act also granted to the Marine Hospital Service the authority to buy and maintain any quarantine station a state or local government was willing to sell, provided the Secretary of the Treasury was convinced of its usefulness. The formulators of the bill perhaps anticipated one of its outcomes, that the cost of enforcing a quarantine meeting federal standards would be beyond the means of smaller stations. Those stations would therefore pass into the hands of the federal government individually, without the need for a piece of sweeping legislation creating a national quarantine service.[51]

The 1893 law, which was to have a significant impact on the control of yellow fever, resulted from an amalgamation of the interests of those wishing to exclude diseased immigrants with the ambitions of those who sought to enlarge the federal government's role in public health. Foremost among the latter was Isham Harris, the Senate sponsor of the original National Board of Health bill and chairman of the Senate Committee on Public Health and National Quarantine. The Senate report on the measure submitted by Harris's committee explained the need for the legislation in terms of protecting the country from both cholera and yellow fever. Although some ports had ample quarantine defenses, the report admitted, at others quarantines were non-existent or rudimentary, and some form of national quarantine was urgently needed to patch these gaps. Harris's committee was grudging but pragmatic in its choice of which organization was to run the national quarantine; while preferring the creation of a national department of health, the committee concluded that it was "compelled to adopt, not what it regards as the best policy, but the only policy which it thinks can be made successful." The committee believed that only if the Marine Hospital Service were named as the quarantine administrator would the bill be acceptable to Congress.[52]

Some opponents of the law feared that it was too weak. Congress would repent its "pusillanimous course of inaction," warned one senator who wanted a completely national quarantine.[53] But the more frequent objection was framed within the familiar anguish over the invasion of states' rights. "The lines of State rights have been almost obliterated, in my opinion, by legislation on this floor. It is time that State right lines were reestablished, and I intend to give my little quota of effort toward reestablishing them," proclaimed one New York representative, to the loud applause of the Democratic side of the House chamber.[54] Edwin LeRoy Antony of Texas joined in this offensive, stating that "the local authorities can control these things better. They are familiar with the situation. They are on the ground and can protect themselves better than any officer of the Federal Government."[55] The officer whose mismanagement and despotism were most feared was the Surgeon General of the Marine Hospital Service, whom some congressmen regarded as power hungry and prone to bias, with the likely result that some regions, especially the Northeast, would be favored over other sections. "It is a power which is going to sow the dragon's teeth of centralization," cried Senator Edward Douglass White of Louisiana, who led the opposition to the bill.[56]

According to its president, S. R. Olliphant, the Louisiana State Board of Health "took the initiative in antagonizing this proposed Federal legislation."[57] The Louisiana board took the firm stance that as the "duly constituted guardian of the public health" of New Orleans, the board's duty was to resist any "abridgement or abolition of any of the powers vested in it by the aforesaid State laws, or any usurpation thereof by the Federal government." The memorial argued against the dreaded "evils of centralization," which would allow certain localities to be favored at the expense of others. For example, according to the research of Joseph Holt, the National Board of Health had been influenced by eastern railroad interests to the South's detriment. A clause introduced into the 1893 bill, which required national quarantine rules and regulations to apply uniformly to every port, climate permitting, eased this worry. Olliphant was proud to note that "the bill finally passed was not so sweeping in its provisions as was proposed, leaving the control of health and quarantine matters in the hands of each of those individual States whose authorities were prepared to enforce efficient quarantine service."[58] Texas, Alabama, and South Carolina public health officials joined those of Louisiana in lobbying for the less nationalized version of the bill.

Open friction between the Louisiana State Board of Health and the Marine Hospital Service continued for the next several years. Wyman proposed what Olliphant believed were unnecessarily meddlesome changes in the Louisiana quarantine code, and sent inspectors to the famous Mississippi River quarantine station too frequently to suit Olliphant's sense of propriety. "How are you and the M. H. authorities agreeing this year?" Olliphant asked Cochran in an 1894 letter. "I have had occasion to come in conflict with them several times this past summer— they are reaching out more and more every year & in my opinion it is only a question of time before they absorb all state health & quarantine powers unless something is done to check their career."[59] Olliphant felt particularly self-righteous because of the accolades recently granted the Louisiana system at the Chicago Columbian Exposition of 1893. The exhibition's sponsors had requested that the Louisiana State Board of Health submit an entry displaying its revolutionary new quarantine design, and the board was happy to oblige. The working scale model they submitted received awards at the fair. For Wyman to challenge the integrity of the quarantine station that had become the model for all American quarantine plants built in the previous decade was insufferable.[60]

Another opponent of the ambitions of the Marine Hospital Service emerged in the years following 1893: the Florida State Board of Health. By 1896 Joseph Porter was openly supporting the latest version of a department of public health bill. He also expressed concern that the Marine Hospital Service was not cooperating well with state boards but was instead seeking total control of coastal quarantine. The Florida board's president claimed in his report for 1896, "It seems to be the determined purpose of the Marine Hospital Service to supercede the authority of the states in charge of the public health, and new rules and regulations are being gradually formulated, which encroach more and more upon the power of the states as sovereign keepers of the physical welfare of the citizen."[61]

Alabama's Jerome Cochran, on the other hand, had by this time abandoned hope for a national department of health. As he had said two years earlier, "in the long run the Marine Hospital Service will win the fight."[62] He had been chairman of the American Medical Association committee that had drafted and supported department of public health bills since 1891, but his committee decided in 1896 to give up the effort. The committee urged the American Medical Association to channel its energies into bettering the Marine Hospital Service rather than trying to replace it. So while a Florida congressman again introduced national public health legislation in 1896, Cochran had decided that the battle was bootless.[63]

The Mississippi Board of Health was the Marine Hospital Service's sharpest critic in the mid-1890s. In 1893 a hurricane destroyed the Gulf Quarantine Station on Chandeleur Island. Instead of rebuilding in such an exposed location, the Service again established a quarantine station for the Gulf coast on Ship Island. H. H. Haralson of the Mississippi Board of Health expressed his board's anger and misgivings about the move. The federal government had ceded control of Ship Island to Mississippi after the national quarantine station had been transferred in 1889, and since that time Mississippi had been using the island for its own quarantine station, which now had to be relocated.

Haralson argued that the proximity of Ship Island to Biloxi, coupled with the Service's reputation of inefficiency, made the new station a threat to the Mississippi coast. Haralson raised the ghost of the 1886 Biloxi epidemic, including the accusations that the disease had originated at Ship Island, and then added the charges recently leveled over the Brunswick affair. The Mississippi Board went so far as to build a rudimentary station on Cat Island, a few miles from Ship Island (and just as near the mainland), and issued a proclamation declaring Ship Island an infected port. All ships destined for Mississippi ports were thus required to undergo two inspections, and if necessary, two disinfections before reaching the Mississippi coast. Wyman, who saw this action as motivated by animosity toward the Marine Hospital Service, and by the desire for the aggrandizement and enrichment of the Mississippi Board, ordered United States customs agents in Biloxi to require only Ship Island certificates and to ignore the state regulations. His firm stand caused Haralson to back down, and the quarantine against Ship Island was abandoned on 11 July 1897.[64]

When yellow fever appeared in Ocean Springs, Mississippi, in the fall of 1897, Haralson and other opponents of the Marine Hospital Service triumphantly claimed that their suspicion of Ship Island was fulfilled, and that the station was surely the source of the infection. Although Wyman traced the epidemic to a traveler from Guatemala, more considerate opinion later established the probability that the disease was imported by Cuban rebels who operated out of the small Mississippi seaside resort town.[65] Both federal and state investigations conducted in 1898 absolved the Marine Hospital Service of negligence at Ship Island and of responsibility for the epidemic, although enemies of the Service continued to cite the Ocean Springs epidemic as evidence of the Service's shortcomings.[66] According to Wyman, the allegations against Ship Island were "bruited for the double purpose of directing criticism from other stations, places, and persons, and casting discredit on a service which had been previously attacked, with the result of the utter defeat of its assailants."[67]

The epidemic that first appeared in Ocean Springs spread rapidly throughout the Gulf coast region. In apologizing for yellow fever's wide dissemination, public health authorities in Louisiana, Mississippi, and Alabama all pointed to the difficulties that accompanied the epidemic's initial diagnosis. There were several hundred cases of the fever in Ocean Springs before the first death occurred; physicians in the town concurred that the disease was dengue, and two investigating parties of yellow fever experts from the Louisiana, Mississippi, and Alabama Boards of Health were required before the diagnosis of yellow fever was announced. New Orleans and the rest of the South immediately quarantined the town, but it was too late. Hundreds of vacationers had already returned to New Orleans from Ocean Springs, for example, and the mild form of the disease was firmly entrenched in the city before it was recognized. Many other towns and cities in Louisiana, Alabama, and Mississippi were likewise visited by yellow fever, and a few cases appeared in Memphis, Pensacola, several Texas towns, and even Louisville. Altogether nine states were affected, with over 4,000 cases and nearly 500 deaths.[68] In New Orleans, a city that had been accumulating a non-immune population since the last epidemic nearly twenty years earlier, 300 people died in the epidemic. Louisiana, Mississippi, and Tennessee asked the Marine Hospital Service for assistance in setting up detention camps, isolating patients, maintaining inland quarantines, and disinfecting premises infected by the yellow fever germ.[69]

The initial mildness of the epidemic startled public health officials, for the 10 percent case mortality rate was starkly different from the more common 30 or 40 percent rate familiar from past epidemics. One plausible suggestion, offered by G. M. Guiteras of the Marine Hospital Service, was that mingled with the epidemic of yellow fever was a concurrent epidemic of dengue, a rarely fatal disease resembling yellow fever. The inclusion of cases of dengue in the tally of yellow fever patients would consequently have lowered the case mortality rate. Another explanation was that in earlier years milder cases of yellow fever went unreported, amplifying the former mortality rate. Still, whether dengue or yellow fever, mild or not, the disease retained its terror, and had its traditional effect of inducing panic throughout the South.[70]

A collage of conflicting quarantines was thrown together in the southern states during the fall of 1897. Natchez was, in the words of one newspaper editor, "closed up like an oyster" until the frost, and other cities in the state, such as Jackson and Vicksburg, followed suit.[71] During the 1897 epidemic, "cities and towns were quarantined against rival communities, producing bitter controversy," the Senate Committee on Public Health and National Quarantine reported. "Railway trains passing from one State to another were prohibited from proceeding, the passengers in many cases being forcibly taken from the cars and carried to improvised fever camps, where they were exposed to hardship and contagion."[72] A crowd near Jackson, Mississippi, tore up the tracks of the Atlanta and Vicksburg Railroad because they believed the company was violating quarantine procedures; the governor had to order out the national guard to restore order. Senator Don Caffery of Louisiana described vividly his personal experience with the shotgun quarantines in Louisiana. "Local quarantines were everywhere," he told the Senate. "It looked like a country in a condition of war. You were met at every 5 or 10 miles by a guard, armed to the teeth, challenging, questioning, examining into your every movement."[73] That the panic was more exaggerated and deeply felt than in 1888 was due in large measure to the greater extension and consequent mortality of yellow fever in the deep South during 1897.

The 1897 epidemic was marked by disputes among local, state, and federal authorities over the proper means of public health action. The continuing antagonism between the Mississippi State Board and the Marine Hospital Service, for example, made cooperation in the control of the epidemic difficult to achieve. The persistent claims by local boards of health in Ocean Springs and other afflicted towns, that the disease was in fact dengue and the quarantine fuss misguided, also added to the confusion.[74] In another acrimonious interchange, the Louisiana State Board of Health quarantined Mobile on the mere suspicion that yellow fever was in the city, basing their decision largely on the fact that Mobile refused to admit a Louisiana-appointed investigator.[75] The president of the Florida Board of Health accused the Alabama Board of "a total lack of assistance" in limiting the spread of yellow fever, which had forced the Florida Board to spend large sums protecting its borders.[76] The inability of state and local officials to syncopate their efforts, a failure aggravated by open disputes among themselves and with the Marine Hospital Service, made it appear that the southern strategy for controlling yellow fever was hopelessly inadequate.

Few commentators writing on the 1897 epidemic challenged the effectiveness of the Holt-model quarantine stations operating near New Orleans, Mobile, Pensacola, and Tampa, but they feared the large stretches of undefended coastline in between. In addition, land quarantines apparently could not contain the disease. It seemed inevitable that the presence of yellow fever in the South would be followed by conflicting, ineffective quarantines that harassed trade but did little to hinder yellow fever. The chaos attendant on the 1897 epidemic bore witness to the inefficiency of southern state boards. They quarrelled pettily among themselves and were unable to restrain the formation of shotgun quarantines within their borders, while in the meantime yellow fever raged unchecked. Confidence in the power of state boards of health to control yellow fever was destroyed.

Emblematic of this crash in popularity was the resignation of the entire Louisiana Board of Health in the face of overwhelming public recrimination. In the opinion of the newspapers and leaders of the commercial exchanges, the board had both let in yellow fever and then responded inappropriately to its presence. With benefit of hindsight it seemed clear by late fall that when the board's members had inspected Ocean Springs in August they missed cases of yellow fever. That ten days later the board reversed this opinion on a return trip earned them scant credit with the local press. By then vacationers fleeing the Mississippi coast had brought ample disease into the city, unhindered by the state board. Having failed so dismally to protect the city from invasion, the board's critics charged, it then set about to cause the most misery possible for very little benefit. Particularly unpopular was the house quarantine imposed when a case of yellow fever was recognized; locking healthy people up with those infected with yellow fever was heartless and did not appear to slow the epidemic. In his report for 1897, board president Olliphant defended his record while acknowledging the public hostility that caused the board to resign. He reiterated the inexact signs of yellow fever, and pointed out that if they had incorrectly diagnosed it, commercial interactions would have been badly hurt with no benefit to the public health. His was a classic instance of damnation without options, but he tried to put the best possible face on the resignation.[77]

The commercial impact of the 1897 epidemic was staggering. "Although there has been comparatively little loss of life in yellow fever districts of the South," wrote one observer, "there has been a tremendous loss of money to the community because of the contagion." He estimated that New Orleans businessmen alone lost 25 million dollars, and that another 38 million was consumed elsewhere in the South by quarantine costs and the destruction of trade. "Most of this loss is the result of the wild and unreasonable excitement of the neighboring towns and villages that have shut off all supplies shipped from New Orleans and have absolutely paralyzed business in that city," he concluded.[78] The editor of the *Mobile Sunday Item* declared that the shotgun quarantines of 1897 "killed trade, progress, production, personal liberty, and interstate commerce in one fell swoop," while his colleague at the *New Orleans Picayune* contended that the two hundred deaths that had occurred up to that point had had the same damaging impact on trade as two thousand.[79] The business losses of this epidemic raised commercial public health consciousness to a level reminiscent of 1879; something had to be done to avert the disruption wrought by yellow fever epidemics.

The necessity of a uniform national quarantine enforced by the federal government was trumpeted from many quarters following the 1897 epidemic. The Georgia and Mississippi legislatures passed resolutions urging federal action, and newspapers throughout the South—in Atlanta, Pensacola, Mobile, Memphis, Montgomery, New Orleans and Houston—repeated the message in editorials.[80] Medical journals, northern and southern, discussed the national quarantine solution as if there could be no other answer to the annual threat of yellow fever. After viewing the animosity among state boards and the harm done by chaotic quarantine regulations, many medical editors believed that only the federal government could force the state and local authorities into line by overriding jealousies and commercial rivalries with a uniform set of regulations impartially applicable to all. "Whatever side-issues may exist, and whatever personal ambitions may be secretly at work, the general sentiment of physicians, of sanitarians, and of the great commercial interests, is that it is the duty of the national government to protect us against the invasion of infection from abroad as well as from armed invasion," wrote the editor of the *Philadelphia Medical Journal*, aptly summing up the public health consensus of 1898. "The events of the past few months have greatly deepened these convictions, especially in our southern states, which have suffered so seriously from the inefficiency of certain local health-authorities and the insane and murderous activity of others."[81]

Although dissent still abounded on the question of which agency should be chosen to administer national quarantine, near unanimity existed on the imperative for federal quarantine supremacy. Southern public health officials backed the renewed movement for a national department of health. The most prominent bill to this end before Congress in 1897 sought to create a commissioner of public health, whose department was to take over all the public health duties of the Marine Hospital Service, oversee research on health and disease, gather vital statistics, and establish a uniform national quarantine system. The commissioner was to meet twice a year with representatives of state and territorial boards of health, and together with them decide upon the rules and regulations that would govern federal public health action.[82] Another variation on the department of public health theme proposed that a separate commission on maritime and domestic sanitation—with representatives from the state boards—be established, which would set quarantine rules. These bills were similar in their inclusion of state public health officials in the decision-making process and in their hostility toward the Marine Hospital Service, which both bills would have reduced to its former status as an agency with one concern, the care of sick sailors.[83]

Although the department proposal had its supporters, especially among southern public health officials seeking input into national health administration, by 1897 most sanitarians had come to believe with Jerome Cochran that the creation of a new federal agency was an unlikely and unwanted event. Instead, they held that the powers of the Marine Hospital Service should be supplemented. Critics depicted the department of public health plan as "an untried scheme," "a retrograde measure" that would require consultation with forty-five probably contentious public health officials before action could be taken against an epidemic.[84] Furthermore, such a department was open to political pressures, since the commissioner was likely to change with every president. "How much more just and fair, and how much better for the country, therefore, it seems to us," decided the editor of one Georgia journal, "to draft a bill imposing additional duties and enlarging the field of usefulness of that very important Department of Public Health (*which it now is*), the Marine Hospital Service."[85]

The Senate committee charged with examining the public health bills that were before Congress in the winter following the 1897 epidemic agreed. After describing the two department of public health bills before them, the committee concluded that "taking away the jurisdiction over quarantine matters from the Marine Hospital Service and vesting it in a department of health" would be "both impolitic and dangerous." Given that the southern states would again shortly be exposed to the threat of yellow fever, it would be unwise to make a sudden transition to a new, untried, and "necessarily crude system." Yellow fever was "the only contagious disease from foreign countries to be really dreaded," and the committee felt constrained to view the bill in light of its principal applicability to this disease. "In our opinion," the committee reported, "it is wise and necessary to retain the present system of quarantine under the management of the Marine-Hospital Service, with its hospitals, quarantine stations, improved apparatus for the investigation of disease germs, and corps of officers, 25 per cent of whom have experience in the prevention and treatment of infectious diseases, and especially of yellow fever." The committee voted favorably on a bill introduced by Senator Caffery of Louisiana that expanded the powers of the Marine Hospital Service.[86] In the House, the Committee on Interstate and Foreign Commerce similarly rejected the department of public health bills and approved a bill very close in its provisions to Caffery's, which followed the logic and language of the Senate report.[87]

Caffery's bill established the Surgeon General of the Marine Hospital Service as the supreme quarantine authority for the United States. The Surgeon General was to write the quarantine code, and the states were to enforce it. The provision of the 1893 bill that required the Marine Hospital Service to assist the states in the enforcement of their quarantine regulations was deleted. The new quarantine rules were to "operate uniformly, so far as climatic conditions will justify," and if the states refused to cooperate in their execution, the President was empowered to see that the regulations were implemented. The most revolutionary of the bill's provisions was its transferral of authority over inland quarantine to the federal government. The law gave the Marine Hospital Service the right not only to stop trains, vessels, other vehicles, and their passengers for the purpose of controlling epidemic disease, but also to require communities to receive the same when the Service's approval of passage had been granted. This section of the bill, which essentially outlawed shotgun quarantines, was designed for the prevention of the commercial disruption so characteristic of yellow fever epidemics. Senator Stephen R. Mallory of Florida, who alone on the Senate committee in opposing the measure, did so because he disagreed with this provision. He did not believe that the federal government had the constitutional right to force a community to hand over to others its prerogative of self-protection. The inclusion of this provision demonstrates that one of the primary purposes of the bill was to protect commerce; this section was its most powerful tool to that end.[88]

The House minority report on the bill concurred with Mallory that quarantine was a negative power, and the federal government could stop but not impel the movement of goods or people. Other senators also spoke in opposition to the bill, citing its invasion of states' rights and the dangers of investing power over coastal quarantine, and hence national commerce, into the hands of one man. Southern public health officials testified against the bill in committee, with Porter, Olliphant, R. M. Swearingen of Texas, John R. Hunter of Mississippi, and W. H. Sanders of Alabama all speaking in favor of the department of public health alternative. "[The Caffery bill] is really the most autocratic measure every introduced into an American Congress," said Porter in his annual report. It created "a quasi-military power, fastening its invidious grasp upon the private concerns of a people, under the plea of serving the public health."[89] Porter went on to accuse Wyman of aspiring to medical dictatorship, when what was needed was greater cooperation among state boards and the elevation of public confidence in their local and state public health officials. That confidence, not the rude imposition of federal power, would prevent panics and stop shotgun quarantines. State boards of health outside of the South opposed the bill as well, and continued to seek an alternative measure that would ensure them a greater voice in national public health policy. But southern health authorities led the fight; the bill was prompted by the fear of yellow fever, and they would be most directly affected by its implementation.[90]

The Caffery bill never came up for a vote. It was not killed so much as ignored. On 15 February 1898 the U.S.S. *Maine* exploded and sank in Havana Harbor, and Congress continually postponed consideration of the Caffery bill for the more urgent debate over the appropriate United States reaction to the purported Spanish aggression. The Marine Hospital Service, the Army, the Navy, and southern boards of health braced for the concentration of American troops in the southern states. Anxiety was rampant over the communication of yellow fever by troops returning from Cuba. With the nation's political and public health attention directed elsewhere, the Caffery bill expired with the second session of the Fifty-fifth Congress.[91]

Southern state boards of health did not remain passive in the face of charges that they were inefficient, disorganized, and lacking in unity. While Congress debated the Caffery bill in the early spring of 1898, southern public health officials again attempted to create among themselves the harmonious system for which so many were clamoring. A series of conferences whose membership included both state public health officials and representatives of commercial interests met in New Orleans, Mobile, and Atlanta during April and drafted a new set of regulations concerning the shipment of freight while an epidemic was in force. Affirmations of friendship and trust were likewise renewed among southern boards.

Edmond Souchon, newly appointed president of the Louisiana State Board, proudly pointed out that the subsequently termed Atlanta freight regulations were practically identical to those recommended by his board, although Wyman claimed the same influence over their formulation. The rules were designed to alleviate that feature of the 1897 epidemic which businessmen found most disturbing—the refusal of communities or states to allow freight trains to discharge cargo or even continue through the area. The southern officials agreed upon certain categories of safe freight, such as agricultural produce that had been loaded far from epidemic sites, or non-absorbent materials like iron, wood, and ore. Other regulations required the fumigation of railroad cars and set up a certification system for manufactured goods loaded away from infectious areas. The state delegates reasoned that the danger of transmission came from germs carried in heavily infected air, in articles that had come in contact with a yellow fever patient, possibly in fruit shipments and perhaps in passengers. Trains carrying none of these items were adjudged safe. Although strong states' rights advocates attended the conferences, they did not succeed in convincing their colleagues to endorse the department of public health bill or oppose that of Caffery, and instead the conventions merely voted for greater federal involvement in public health.[92]

The capabilities of southern boards were again tested when yellow fever returned to the South in 1898. Early in the summer the disease appeared in McHenry, Mississippi, a town similar to Ocean Springs in character and location. As a result, much of the South again quarantined the Mississippi coast. That episode proved short-lived, but in August the disease broke out in Franklin, Louisiana, and from there spread extensively throughout Louisiana and into Mississippi. Although around 4,000 cases were reported, fewer than 200 deaths occurred among them. The usual panic accompanied the epidemic, with the corresponding detriment to trade, but the partial observation of the Atlanta regulations helped somewhat to ease the burden on commerce.[93] Still, according to a Boston medical editor, the panic, at least in Mississippi, was "out of all proportion to its [the epidemic's] severity," a response that obstructed the provisioning of infected areas and caused food shortages, especially among poor blacks.[94]

In addition to the epidemics in Mississippi and Louisiana, another outbreak, this one in Key West, Florida, generated great excitement during 1898. "There seemed to be a conviction that it would be impossible for Florida to escape a visitation of yellow fever," recounted the president of the Florida Board of Health in his report for that year.[95] It appeared inevitable to many public health officials that the proximity of non-immune American troops to Havana would lead to a major yellow fever epidemic in Florida. So, when dengue broke out among troops stationed in Key West, the nervous naval physician there diagnosed yellow fever, although Porter and two Marine Hospital Service physicians familiar with yellow fever disagreed. The subsequent tally of 6,000 cases with no deaths lends credence to Porter's diagnosis. But the Navy pulled its men out of Key West anyway, taking its troops to more northern ports and spreading the disease to their new residences.[96]

Although the terror and mortality of the 1898 epidemic was comparable to that of 1897, and expressions of support for a national quarantine again proliferated, the force compelling the 1897 movement for an enlarged federal role in public health was lacking. In part this may have been due to a dulling of sensibilities by the repetition of events and ideas, but it is likely the preoccupation of the country's sanitarians and politicians with events in Cuba was more significant in the enervation of the national public health drive. Certainly it reflected no credit on southern boards of health. As the president of the University of Tennessee wrote a Louisiana friend, "When we have cleaned up Cuba we will have no more yellow fever, and you poor people will be rid of this curse anyhow."[97] After American troops occupied Cuba in 1898, and the United States began to administer the island's civil affairs, public health officials throughout the U.S. expected the federal government to clean up Havana and thus eliminate the breeding ground of yellow fever, effectively ending the threat of the disease for the Gulf coast.[98] New Orleans had controlled the threat from Mexico and points south; with yellow fever now seen as principally a Florida problem, controlling Cuba was now the answer. The eradication of yellow fever in Cuba had become the new solution, overshadowing disputes about inland and coastal quarantine authority.

This activity in Cuba was also to provide the context for a discovery that would fundamentally redirect yellow fever control efforts. Reed's and Carroll's striking demonstration that mosquitoes spread yellow fever created a lull in calls for national quarantine, while public health officials on both the local and national level explored the application of the new techniques aimed at destroying mosquitoes instead of germs. Yet the discord among southern boards of health in 1897 and 1898 had made it evident to many contemporaries that these state authorities were not capable of controlling yellow fever. The inability of southern boards to work together suggested that only the federal government could muster the organization and power a successful fight against yellow fever would demand. Not until the first decade of the twentieth century, though, would the struggle between state and federal public health officials for authority over coastal quarantine finally be resolved.

THE LAST CAMPAIGN:
Yellow Fever, Southern Public Health, and Federal Authority in the New Century

Y ellow fever is recognized by the public at large as the most dreaded disease which visits our Gulf coast states," a rural Mississippi physician told the Gulf Coast Medical and Surgical Society meeting at Pass Christian, Mississippi, in November 1899. "It keeps capital away, drives commerce from our door and keeps immigration at a minimum—thereby leaving millions of acres of fertile land lying idle, which if cultivated would make of this one of the most prosperous portions of the Union."[1] On the eve of the new century, the South's health, commerce, and reputation appeared to be as vulnerable to and as victimized by yellow fever as ever. The history of yellow fever in the South during the next decade illustrates the persistence of the intimate relationship among commercial expectations, federal ambitions, the disease, and the southern public health endeavor.

During the first few years of the 1900s, southern public health officials struggled to regain the public's confidence by presenting an image as conservative, stalwart guardians of the southern coast. They were hesitant to accept the mosquito as the sole vector of yellow fever, and clung to the notion that the yellow fever germ might in addition be transmitted by infected air or material objects. Southern boards of health were unwilling to abandon, on the basis of yet another theory about yellow fever, the disinfecting quarantine methods which had brought so much prestige to the southern quarantine system. This attitude changed slowly, as the control of yellow fever in 1903 in Havana and Laredo, Texas, impressed American sanitarians with the power of anti-mosquito action. By the end of 1905, when the last American yellow fever epidemic was successfully limited by a control effort founded on the mosquito doctrine, few doubters remained. Unlike the changing ideas about the germ of yellow fever, the new information about yellow fever's transmission fundamentally altered yellow fever control.

Their performances in the 1903 and 1905 epidemics brought southern public health officials little credit, while those same years provided a context within which the Marine Hospital Service showed itself to be efficient and capable in controlling yellow fever. The first decade of the twentieth century saw the denouement of the long struggle between state and federal public health authorities for the right to administer coastal quarantine. With the usurpation of maritime quarantine control, the federal victory that followed the yellow fever epidemic of 1905 deprived southern coastal boards of health of a fundamental component of their professional duties, an ingredient long central to the professional identity of the southern public health official. Boards that had come into existence with the charge to protect commerce and the people's health from yellow fever by the appropriate administration of quarantine now had to find new reasons for deserving public support and legislative funding.

The century began with the publication by Reed and Carroll of their work on the transmission of yellow fever, work that had immediate implications for public health practices. Preventive measures that had heretofore targeted the elusive yellow fever germ were now turned on the mosquito. In 1901, William Crawford Gorgas set in motion the first mosquito destruction campaign in Havana, which established the procedures that would become standard features of future anti-mosquito programs. A central aspect of his plan was the elimination of all mosquito breeding places. The yellow fever mosquito, *Aedes aegypti* (then labeled *Stegomyia fasciata*), was known to favor relatively clean water for laying eggs, so its larvae were abundant in cisterns, water barrels, house gutters, and any upturned vessel such as a broken bottle or flower pot in which rainwater had accumulated. Since the larvae rose to the water's surface for respiration, a layer of oil on top of the water suffocated them quickly.

Acting under the authority of the United States Army and the Mayor of Havana (who made it a crime to allow mosquitoes to breed on one's property), Gorgas oversaw crews of men who poured oil on the tops of cisterns, inspected premises to detect mosquito breeding grounds, ordered land drained, stocked ponds with larvae-eating fish, and otherwise attempted to remove all possible breeding habitats while educating the public about the mosquito peril. When cases of yellow fever were discovered, Gorgas implemented more strictly focused actions. The patient was covered with mosquito netting and the sick room screened for the duration of the severe stage of the illness. When the case had terminated, either by death or convalescence, Gorgas's crews would seal the patient's room by pasting paper strips over any cracks that offered possible escape routes for mosquitoes, and burn pyrethrum powder inside the room to kill or stun the insects. They shined a light in one small area of the floor, toward which the mosquitoes gravitated; any mosquitoes surviving the pyrethrum were then killed directly by the fumigation team. The crew also fumigated the rest of the house and nearby buildings, and kept a sharp watch on the people surrounding the patient for any sign of fever. Using this technique, Gorgas was able to banish yellow fever from Havana, where it had been endemic for decades. Contemporaries hailed his accomplishment as one of the great achievements of modern medical science.[2]

Gorgas's success in Havana inspired scattered but intense interest in the destruction of mosquitoes in the United States. The mayor of Winchester, Virginia, was one of the first to apply the Havana methods to the mosquito problem in his town, where there was little fear of yellow fever but where malaria was a recurrent problem and mosquitoes generally an aggravation.[3] It was in New Orleans that the anti-mosquito measures were first employed as a means of reducing the threat from yellow fever.

There in August 1901 the health officer of the municipal board of health (established in 1898) proclaimed a crusade against the mosquito menace. Health officer Quitman Kohnke demarcated a section of New Orleans as an experimental zone, and announced his intentions in the newspapers. He then proceeded to send board of health crews to each household in the section to pour oil into cisterns and teach the populace not to allow water to stand undisturbed in either the house or yard. Even though his plan initially met with considerable enthusiasm from householders pleased by the prospect of eliminating mosquitoes, a few people refused the oil, largely in the belief that it altered the taste of the water. Kohnke claimed that, on the contrary, the oil had no affect on the water's potability. By 18 September the newspapers were reporting that eight percent of the householders included in the experimental district had disallowed the mosquito control measures.[4] In November, Kohnke finally admitted that the oiling project had been inconclusive and ineffective, since full public compliance was not forthcoming. He recommended instead that the City Council pass an ordinance requiring that screens or mosquito-proof covers be fitted on all cisterns.[5]

It was spring before the City Council debated Kohnke's ordinance. The measure drew broad support from the medical community of New Orleans, particularly from the Orleans Parish Medical Society, which had passed resolutions in its favor in March and April 1902.[6] Kohnke vigorously attempted to educate the council and the public about the mosquito theory. He became famous for his talks on the mosquito and disease, illustrated by lantern slides. However, in spite of his efforts, the City Council voted down the screening ordinance after much debate. The chief objection to the measure was the burdensome expense it would entail for property owners, especially for landlords with extensive holdings.[7]

The New Orleans City Council again considered the enactment of a screening ordinance against mosquitoes in the spring of 1903. Since its defeat a year earlier, open ridicule of the mosquito theory had become increasingly common in the public press. Cartoons depicted Kohnke battling a giant mosquito for the defense of New Orleans; one newspaper claimed that in

1903 the movement against the mosquito had "beached high among other medical fads and theories."[8] Opponents of the ordinance could cite the opinion of respectable scientists that the mosquito larvae in cisterns never developed, because their food supply in such a habitat was severely limited, and in addition that they improved the water by cleansing it of impurities. Or they could quote one New Orleans physician who wrote in a letter to the *Picayune*, "The mosquito theory is a fad, just as the unproven discovery of the yellow fever germ," which was promulgated as another scheme to spend the people's money.[9]

In response, the ordinance's proponents argued that the experiences in Havana had proven the efficacy of the actions that the law sought to require, and pointed to endorsements of the mosquito theory by the Louisiana State Board of Health and the American Medical Association as evidence for its scientific acceptability. A survey of New Orleans physicians conducted in July 1903 found that only twenty-one of one hundred and nine respondents did not believe in the mosquito vector. There is some evidence that the reason for the defeat of the ordinance again in 1903 was financial and not due to differences in medical theory. The law's main spokesman on the City Council called its opponents the "anti-improvement league," noting that the same men had opposed water and sewage reforms. He claimed that their status as property holders caused them to act from personal greed rather than for the good of the community. Kohnke despaired that "after more than two years of earnest and persistent effort, in spite of ridicule and interested opposition, in the advocacy of the mosquito as an important factor in disease and the desirability of its destruction for the prevention of certain diseases," so little had been accomplished. The citizens of New Orleans were slow to act in the absence of an actual epidemic, and were complacent that the great quarantine station operated by the Louisiana State Board of Health ensured their protection from yellow fever.[10]

Public health officials were not long in exploring the implications of the Reed commission's work for maritime and land quarantine as well. Reed and Carroll themselves presented recommendations for the reformation of quarantine procedures to the American Public Health Association in the fall of 1901. Their advice was based on the assumption that only mosquitoes, and not any form of soiled clothing, bedding, or baggage, could convey yellow fever. They began with the proposition that quarantine officers could trust the Marine Hospital Service to inform them when a port was infected, which implied that ships and passengers from non-infected ports should suffer no restrictions at quarantine whatsoever. If there had been yellow fever on board a ship during passage, the patients were to be moved to a screened hospital, their quarters fumigated and the ship then allowed to proceed to the wharf. If on the other hand the vessel had been twenty days at sea with no yellow fever, Reed and Carroll thought that it was unlikely that infected mosquitoes were aboard, so there was no cause for detention or fumigation, even if the ship had come from an infected port. In their view, there was clearly no point in disinfecting baggage, and only non-immune passengers should be detained if their total time from port to port was less than five days. If no yellow fever had appeared by the fifth day, the passenger was free to go. These criteria, although sketchy and lacking the detail that one familiar with the administration of quarantine (as Reed and Carroll were not) would expect, were hailed by the press of New Orleans as portending the end of obstructive quarantine measures.[11]

Although the elegance of the experiments establishing the mosquito's role in transmitting yellow fever impressed most physicians, many were reluctant to accept their demonstration of the innocence of fomites—articles such as bedding, clothing, or mattresses infected by contact with the yellow fever patient. "While I believe that Drs. Reed, Carroll and Agramonte have proved that yellow fever is transmitted by the mosquito," a Shreveport physician typically commented, "yet there are other methods of conveyance which these experimenters have ignored, because the peculiar atmospheric condition and temperature necessary for the propagation of the germ, were lacking at the time their experiments were conducted." The Army investigators had tested bedding from yellow fever patients in December, when yellow fever spread only with difficulty. The experiment would have been much more conclusive had it taken place in the acute yellow fever months of August or September, critics argued.[12]

A. N. Bell, the doyen of American sanitationists, similarly

doubted that fomites were harmless or that their safety had been demonstrated by the Cuban experiments. He was particularly puzzled about how the mosquito theory could explain the existence of infected houses, which retained their infectious qualities from one year to the next if not disinfected, or the case of the U.S.S. Plymouth, which had preserved its disease-generating power through an icy Boston winter. Surely the ship's mosquitoes must have been killed by the subfreezing temperatures of the season.[13] Even the Marine Hospital Service was slow to adopt the mosquito as the sole agent in the communication of yellow fever, and its representatives opposed a resolution favoring such a position at a conference in Havana in 1901.[14]

The southern public health officials most actively concerned about the admission of yellow fever into their states responded with skepticism to the Reed commission assertion that fomites were non-infectious. There was too much evidence indicating that such fomite transmission was possible and had taken place, claimed both George R. Tabor, health officer of Texas, and John R. Hunter, secretary of the Mississippi State Board of Health. "I cannot accept these conclusions [regarding fomites], nor do I believe that they are accepted by many of the health authorities of the Gulf States, who, from long experience, know that yellow fever has been and believe it may be now conveyed by fomites," wrote Tabor in his 1902 annual report. He was, furthermore, unwilling to change his state's quarantine procedures against fomites until more was known about yellow fever's transmission. Like his fellow southern health officers he believed that "the mosquito can convey the disease, but I do not concede that it is the sole distributor thereof."[15] Florida's Joseph Porter expressed like sentiments, and stressed that experiments conducted somewhere other than Cuba were necessary to decide the fomite question for the southern states.[16]

President Edmond Souchon of the Louisiana State Board of Health emerged as the leading spokesman for southern health officials in maintaining that a cautious retention of disinfection methods targeting fomites was the most responsible course. With so much at stake, he was "unwilling to accept the dictum of the experimenters" that yellow fever was only conveyed by the

mosquito. When in May 1903 the Louisiana State Board of
Health passed a resolution supporting a campaign of mosquito
destruction in New Orleans, Souchon coupled it with a statement asserting the persistent value of traditional quarantine
measures. "The methods of disinfection practiced at the Mississippi River Quarantine Station in 1902 and 1903 have included,
whenever deemed advisable by the physician in charge, the
application of steam heat and bichloride solution [a disinfec-
tant], under the conviction that officers charged by law with the
grave responsibility of excluding infection are not warranted by
theoretical beliefs in neglecting known and proved methods of
safety."[17]

The Louisiana State Board of Health had invested heavily in
the form of maritime sanitation which Souchon was defending.
Before 1900, their Mississippi River Quarantine Station was the
model of modern scientific quarantine, not just for the United
States but for the world. Louisiana's public health officials had
invented "rational quarantine" and taught the world how to
implement it. "Of all quarantines, the masterpiece stands at the
mouth of the Mississippi river," one admittedly partisan New
Orleans physician exclaimed at a meeting of the Louisiana State
Medical Society in 1903. "As it stands it is one of the greatest
monuments in the world to sanitary science."[18] This prestige was
clearly threatened by a theory that denied the validity of one
major part of the station's function. The Louisiana board was
not only proud of its preeminence in quarantine, but also very
self-conscious of the importance of its work. "We believe we are
protecting the whole Mississippi Valley from this very terrible
disease," stated one board member in response to criticism that
the board's continued actions against fomites were too stringent
and unfounded.[19] Such a position of responsibility meant that in
their eyes experimenting with an established method of protection that had the imprimatur of almost twenty years of successful operation was very risky indeed. Walter Reed acknowledged
the influence of the Louisiana board's resistance to his ideas
when he wrote Gorgas in 1902, "If you could only bite the La.
State Board of Health with a few 'loaded' stegomyia, you will be
doing a public service."[20]

The discovery of the mosquito vector raised other issues relating to quarantine as well. Whereas Reed had contended that mosquitoes in boxes or trunks could rarely survive beyond the fifth day of captivity, a Marine Hospital Service investigator found that if even a small amount of moisture were present in the container, as in sweaty clothing, the mosquito could prosper several days longer. He concluded that infected mosquitoes could be transported in baggage, but that it seldom happened and was not a cause for concern.[21]

More serious was the question of whether mosquitoes transported from infected ports on ships were a source of danger in transmitting yellow fever. Alvah H. Doty, health officer of the Port of New York, argued that during the days of slow and filthy sailing vessels, which carried large supplies of water in which mosquitoes could breed, yellow fever mosquitoes were imported in dangerous numbers, igniting the epidemics in the Northeast of the early nineteenth century. But he believed that the contemporary steamship that carried an infected stegomyia was rare, since travel was brisk, water reserves correspondingly minimized, and the yards surrounding the docks grown so large as to reduce the available number of mosquitoes for immigration. This last conclusion he based on the fact that the stegomyia was known to be a house mosquito, and so it followed that where there were no houses, only loading areas and warehouses, there would be few yellow fever mosquitoes. Henry R. Carter questioned the incautious attitude Doty displayed in his determination not to molest debarking mosquitoes. The numerous instances of secondary infections that had occurred during the course of voyages convinced Carter that mosquitoes must be available on board to transmit infection. Souchon similarly pointed out that while Doty's practice of not fumigating vessels to kill mosquitoes might be safe in a northern climate inhospitable to the development of yellow fever, it was requisite that southern quarantine officials thoroughly exterminate all mosquitoes on board.[22]

During the early years of the twentieth century, southern boards of health again found themselves in frequent disagreement, if not open confrontation, with the Marine Hospital Service. The struggle for control over national public health administration persisted in these years as well. Early in 1902

Walter Wyman engineered an attempt to expand the power and change the name of the Marine Hospital Service. Introduced into the Senate by George C. Perkins of California and into the House by William P. Hepburn of Iowa, the Perkins-Hepburn bill changed the name of the service to the Public Health and Marine-Hospital Service, provided for additional staff to assist in the hygienic laboratory, renamed Wyman's position "surgeon general" (instead of the official, but seldom-used, designation of "supervising surgeon general"), and directed the service to collect and publish vital statistics.[23] The Louisiana State Board of Health quickly responded with a resolution condemning this new manifesteation of federal lust for power.

Souchon called a conference of state public health officials in 1902 to consider action against the Perkins-Hepburn bill.[24] The offspring of the conference was an addition to the Perkins-Hepburn bill, included as Section 7, which required the Surgeon General of the Marine Hospital Service to call yearly conferences of state health officials in order to elicit their advice on public health matters. The Senate committee report on the bill stated bluntly, "This section we regard as by all means the most important section in the bill."[25] The inclusion of the section gave the bill the almost unanimous backing of state health officials and eased its way through Congress. This compromise at least ensured that state health officials would have an official role in the establishment of federal public health policy, although the preference of state health officers, both northern and southern, was still for the creation of a national department of health with heavy state representation.[26]

The congressional advocates of the Perkins-Hepburn bill dwelled heavily on the value of Section 7 for readying the nation to fight epidemic disease. "This bill will unite, harmonize, and rationalize the work of the State and Federal health officers in the interests of public health and commerce of our country," proclaimed one Alabama congressman.[27] Since it was the "joint product of the earnest labor of both Federal health officers and State health officers," argued another representative of the same state, it would help rid the South of "shotgun policy" and "destroy the opportunity for the fearful and frightful panics and the prostration of public business that take place in many sections of this country on the first announcement that yellow fever has appeared in a given place."[28] Opponents of the measure thought it unlikely that such significant results would follow from the mere calling of conferences, which the Surgeon General was certainly free to assemble at present. One Missouri representative considered the bill to be primarily "for the aggrandizement of the present head of the Marine Hospital,"[29] while a like-minded colleague from Illinois was puzzled about what the bill would actually accomplish other than increasing the prestige, pay, and staff of the Marine Hospital Service. Nevertheless, the bill became law on 1 July 1902.[30]

The newly named Public Health and Marine-Hospital Service (henceforth, for brevity's sake, the Public Health Service), was soon furnished with the opportunity to display its competence in controlling yet another yellow fever epidemic, this time in Laredo, Texas. In July, news of severe yellow fever in Mexico reached Souchon and Tabor, who consequently became especially watchful of travelers and vessels from Mexico.[31] By mid-September epidemic dengue had appeared in Nuevo Laredo, a Mexican town across the Rio Grande from its American namesake, and late in the month Wyman detailed G. M. Guiteras and R. D. Murray to Laredo to assist the Texas health authorities. Wyman wired Guiteras the following message: "Believed here good opportunity for demonstrating possibility of restricting spread of fever by new methods, as at Habana [sic], screening patients and destroying mosquitoes."[32] After seeing two cases of yellow fever upon his arrival, Guiteras met with Tabor to allot responsibility. They agreed that Guiteras and his assistants were to take charge of local efforts to stamp out the disease and to maintain the border quarantine against Mexico already established. Tabor would set up a detention camp for those leaving out of Laredo, using equipment furnished by the Public Health Service, and take action to protect the rest of the state.[33]

Within Laredo, Guiteras attempted to apply the anti-mosquito methods proven so effective by the Havana experience. He discovered that a crucial factor in the proliferation of mosquitoes in the Texas town was the near-universal habit of keeping drinking water, which came from the muddy Rio Grande, in barrels so that sedimentation would clarify the murky liquid. Guiteras sent "mosquito brigades" out to oil these barrels and then fit them with wooden faucets which would allow water to be drawn from underneath the oil layer. By the end of the epidemic the crews had oiled 3,500 barrels, but the results were discouraging. Yellow fever continued to spread, not only within Laredo but also to other nearby Texas towns. In the final count, there were a over a thousand cases and 107 deaths reported in Laredo (out of a population of 18,000).[34]

The reason for this failure, according to Guiteras, was the limited cooperation and ignorance of the Mexican population living in Laredo, and the Public Health Service's lack of authority in dealing with them. "A large part of the people, particularly the ignorant class, were filled with the idea that the doctors and the authorities were in a conspiracy against them," Guiteras explained in his report. "It was quite generally believed that the physicians poisoned their patients to get rid of them as soon as possible and in this summary manner end the epidemic." They also feared the toxicity of the oil used on water barrels, and removed it when the oiling crew departed. Nor could a hospital be established for the isolation and treatment of impoverished patients, for the Mexican population concealed cases when they could. Guiteras concluded that the wisest action a government could take at the onset of an epidemic was the declaration of martial law; thereby the conditions of military control that had made the anti-mosquito campaign in Havana so triumphant could prevail in American cities stricken with yellow fever.[35]

Military power did not ensure success against yellow fever, though, as the experience of an Army surgeon sent to Fort McIntosh, Texas (near Laredo), to cope with the epidemic demonstrated. When Roger Post Ames, a physician who had worked with Reed and Carroll in Cuba, arrived at the fort, he had Laredo declared off-limits and began anti-mosquito measures. But he apparently failed to convince the post commandant of the seriousness of the situation, for the commandant continued to visit Laredo himself, and issued passes to soldiers granting free passage through the quarantine lines. This attitude changed, and the military authorities began to heed Ames's admonitions, when several soldiers became ill. Even with strict compliance, however,

Ames believed that the threat of yellow fever could never be entirely eradicated until the water supply was furnished in some other way than in open barrels. "The open top water vessels of our near neighbors lately in great distress, will continue very probably to the end of time," he predicted dismally in a letter to his superior. "[A]nd Mrs. Stegomyia when infected will disseminate Yellow-fever, to soldiers and civilians alike, Sister Anopheles, favor all with distressing malaria fever, Cousin Culex, will ever be about to assist in the general innocent biting, and annoyance."[36]

The work of the Public Health Service in Laredo earned it mixed evaluations, although the Service was generally credited with having controlled an unwieldy situation to the best of its abilities. During the course of the epidemic, public health officials in other southern states were alarmed when the disease spread from Laredo to other Texas towns, and feared that the epidemic would escape from the state. The two contemporary methods of constraining yellow fever were tested simultaneously in 1903—mosquito control in Laredo and traditional disinfection along the state's quarantine lines—so no clear image of the superiority of one method over the other resulted from the experience. Most observers blamed the persistence of yellow fever in 1903 on the laxity of the Mexican authorities in Nuevo Laredo; since no anti-mosquito work was undertaken there, a constant source of new infection remained within a short distance of Laredo's residents. For the most part, the medical press credited the Public Health Service with slowing the epidemic through mosquito control. Later medical authors cited the Laredo case as the first demonstration of the effectiveness of anti-mosquito measures for limiting yellow fever.[37]

In 1905, epidemic yellow fever struck the United States for the last time. On 22 July the presence of yellow fever in New Orleans was announced publicly, and the local authorities launched a vigorous anti-mosquito campaign. A principal component of the control effort was the issuing of proclamations to physicians, householders, and even clergymen, urging them to practice and preach the creed of reporting suspicious cases, screening any fever patient for at least the first three days of the disease, and oiling/screening cisterns and other possible mosquito breeding areas.[38] Kohnke gained some grim satisfaction from the fact that on 2 August the City Council unanimously passed an ordinance that ordered all cisterns screened within forty-eight hours, and encouraged that other water receptacles be drained, oiled, or stocked with fish. The ordinance was enforced with vigor, and by the middle of the month violators were being jailed. After debating the move for four days, the Louisiana State Board of Health sealed New Orleans off from the rest of the state on 28 July, and instituted a system of detention and fumigation of outgoing passengers and trains with the assistance of the Public Health Service.[39]

On 4 August a combined appeal from the governor, mayor of New Orleans, Souchon, Kohnke, the Orleans Parish Medical Society, and local business organizations requested that President Theodore Roosevelt instruct the Public Health Service to assume charge of the yellow fever epidemic in New Orleans. The reasons later given for the transfer of authority were varied. According to Kohnke, because internal bickering endangered the final outcome, the Public Health Service was invited to bring unity to the fight against yellow fever.[40] Certainly one source of the animosity Kohnke felt was the Orleans Parish Medical Society, whose president attributed the call for federal intervention to the local physicians' perception that the City Board of Health's fumigation work was ineffective and poorly managed. "We regard this as the first crucial test in America [of the mosquito theory], and it must be absolutely perfect in its working to be efficient," the medical society stated in its letter justifying its call for federal control.[41] Souchon offered yet another explanation for the appeal. "By the beginning of August it became apparent that the fever had obtained such a foothold in New Orleans as to threaten an epidemic unless the sanitation could be undertaken on a scale of much greater magnitude than had been practicable up to that time," he recalled in his report for 1905. "The plan of invoking the aid of the Federal Government had been freely discussed by leading citizens, with the idea that if invited to take full charge in the City of New Orleans the United States Public Health and Marine Hospital Service would not only send an adequate force of its trained men to carry on the work, but would also defray all expenses."[42]

There is irony in the fact that one of the first things that J. H. White, the physician Wyman installed as commander of the New Orleans campaign, did was to reveal that the Public Health Service did not have enough money to battle the fever, and that a quarter of a million dollars was needed for the work to be carried out. In a few days the citizens of New Orleans raised $150,000, and the state contributed the remaining $100,000. Also, while Wyman sent over twenty of his men to New Orleans, forty more were recruited as temporary Public Health Service officers from the local physician population.[43] But even if the federal agency did not contribute the funds and manpower so confidently expected by those who originated the plea for Public Health Service assistance, White's sovereignty apparently brought calmness, regularity, and almost military authority to the city and the mosquito control effort. He openly admitted that his service merely took over the activities in progress— screening patients, destroying mosquito breeding grounds, and fumigating houses—that had been begun by the local authorities. Only six cases occurred after the first of November (although the first frost did not appear until mid-December), with a total of 452 deaths resulting from 3,402 cases of the fever.[44]

The achievement of the public health authorities in New Orleans in ending the epidemic before the first frost was widely heralded as a great vindication of modern sanitary ideas. Professor Rubert Boyce of the University of Liverpool, who participated in the New Orleans campaign, judged that the reliance on the mosquito theory "resulted in complete victory; and constitutes, in my opinion, *one of the most brilliant examples of the practical applicability of the teachings of medical science to the prevention of disease.*"[45] Wyman, never one to hide his light under a bushel, predicted that the 1905 campaign would "be recorded on the brightest page of sanitary history."[46] Celebrants pointed to the similarity of the epidemic in its early weeks with those of 1853 and 1878, and confidently calculated that, were it not for the measures taken, a similar disaster would have followed.

One outcome of the epidemic's defeat was the near universal acceptance among medical thinkers that the mosquito, and only the mosquito, communicated yellow fever. "It is safe to assert that the experience gained during the prevalence of yellow fever in Louisiana and Mississippi in 1905 had the effect of banishing the last lingering belief in the conveyance of the disease by fomites so far as the vast majority of medical men in the South were concerned," wrote G. Farrar Patton, professor of clinical medicine at Tulane and secretary of the state board of health from 1896 to 1906. "During that outbreak no attention whatever was paid to the disinfection of the clothing and bedding of patients by the State and Federal authorities who conducted the campaign," yet the disease was conquered before the coming of frost. Such a "vast and costly object lesson" could not be slighted, as the Havana investigations had been, on the grounds that it was too limited or inapplicable to the Louisiana situation.[47]

With the radical change in etiological theory that resulted from the discovery of the mosquito vector of yellow fever came a marked shift in the perception of the disease's victims. It had been far easier in 1878 to see yellow fever as the logical, and perhaps just, consequent of a life lived amidst filth. Cleanliness was, in the eyes of many contemporaries, next to godliness, and if a person ignored the laws of God and nature, tolerated filth in his/her surroundings, and probably exacerbated the situation by intemperate habits, then the occurrence of disease followed naturally. But a person's responsibility for the presence of mosquitoes in his/her habitat was much more problematic. Public health workers derided the ignorance of the immigrant population with whom they had to deal in 1905, yet they never associated this ignorance with immoral behavior. This is not to say that public health officials refrained from disparaging the squalor in which the poor population lived or from holding them in part responsible for it, but their exposure to yellow fever was viewed as in large measure beyond their control and moral judgment.

In 1905, probably for the first time, blacks were suspected as carriers of yellow fever. C. M. Brady, a physician who wrote on the characteristics of yellow fever in the Negro race, pointed out that while blacks contracted mild forms of the disease, they nevertheless suffered from genuine yellow fever, and in large numbers. In New Orleans, there were only six blacks among the 452 recorded yellow fever deaths in 1905, and elsewhere in Louisiana where figures for black cases of yellow fever are available, the evidence is even more striking: according to one report, there were 1,684 cases of yellow fever among blacks in Louisiana (outside New Orleans) during 1905, but only twenty-six deaths.[48] But the many black yellow fever patients played a significant role in spreading the epidemic, Brady maintained. Their part in exacerbating the 1905 epidemic was heightened by the fact, in Brady's words, that they "associate with the Italians on certain terms of social equality," thus having plentiful opportunities for the transfer of infection. Blacks were like Italians, he continued, in shunning authority, moving stealthily by night, and on the whole existing in a subculture distant from the purview of public health authority.[49]

C. B. Young, the Public Health Service coordinator for Mississippi who was located at Jackson, received reports from his subordinates stationed in towns around Mississippi and Louisiana that induced him to believe that the concept of the black carrier provided a crucial clue in unraveling the course of yellow fever's dissemination in both the present and previous years. "The history of these mild outbreaks of fever among negroes is strongly suggestive of the idea that many of the outbreaks of fever in times gone by, where the fever appeared suddenly and most mysteriously among the white population in places hitherto apparently un-infected, and where an explanation was sought by the suggested transmission by means of letters, etc., really owed their origin to fever imported by negroes," Young postulated in a September 1905 note to Wyman. "It is a notorious fact that in the country towns of the South, negroes habitually move about from place to place in spite of quarantine restrictions, and it being a popular belief that they did not have the fever, any slight sickness passed un-noticed."[50]

The possibility of well (or in this case, only lightly ill) carriers had been recognized only in the previous decade for diphtheria and typhoid, and was slow to be accepted for blacks and yellow fever, perhaps because their immunity to yellow fever had been so widely held since the early years of the century. It may be, too, that the acceptance of the mosquito theory of transmission contributed to the development of the idea of the black carrier. The infection theory had postulated the communication of the disease through clothing or air drenched in the germs of yellow fever, which then came in contact with the victim. If the critical germ dosage was so massive, surely the mildly infected black emitted innocuous amounts of the poison, compared to his virulently ill white neighbor. But the mosquito clearly transmitted only a tiny amount of matter, making this dosage argument appear unfounded. This theoretical alteration may have opened the way for seeing the black patient as a dangerous reservoir of the yellow fever germ, whose movement during an epidemic should be as strictly controlled as that of a white person.[51]

Many physicians had predicted that the confidence resulting from the application of the mosquito theory would eliminate the blind panics that had so often arisen during previous epidemics of yellow fever. One Mobile practitioner noted, after reviewing the fundamentals of yellow fever prevention based on mosquito control, "Yellow fever is not a dangerous disease provided there is no delay in its recognition." On the contrary, it was now simple to stamp out; once the public could be educated to that fact, the only response to a case of yellow fever would be cool, deliberate action.[52] G. M. Guiteras agreed, commenting in 1905, "An intelligent conception by the people of what is yellow fever and how it is transmitted would eliminate such absurdities as 'shot-gun' quarantine and other irrational measures;—commerce and traffic would go on with but little interference, and above all, much suffering and many lives saved."[53] But he and his fellow Public Health Service workers found that the inhabitants of the rural communities with which they were dealing were largely ignorant of the mosquito theory, and knew little of either the Havana or Laredo successes. Educational lectures convinced infected towns to take up the anti-mosquito crusade, but were ineffective in limiting the declaration of local quarantines by towns not yet affected. Local and state quarantines against New Orleans proliferated as enthusiastically as in earlier epidemics.

Confidence in the power of the public health officials of Louisiana or the Public Health Service could not develop merely from conviction about the mosquito theory. As earlier, if the people were to trust the public health authorities, it was necessary first that the assorted public health agencies involved demonstrate their mutual trust. But southern public health officials had little confidence in each other's reliability or truthfulness.

The Mississippi Board of Health excoriated Souchon for concealing the New Orleans epidemic for so long. The New Orleans press retaliated by accusing officials in Gulfport, as well as the Public Health Service, of suppressing knowledge of yellow fever cases there. When the Alabama State Board of Health declared absolute quarantine against the coast of Mississippi, Eugene Wasdin invited state health officer W. H. Sanders to inspect the coastal cities and discover for himself that they were not infected. Instead of being reassured enough to lift the quarantine, Sanders found a suspicious case, and returned home to crow about discovering a nest of yellow fever within the Public Health Service's jurisdiction.[54] When Wasdin then criticized the Alabama State Board for the unnecessary stringency of its quarantine, the editor of the *Mobile Medical and Surgical Journal* jumped to its defense, citing Wasdin's "indiscretion, if not crass ignorance," and asserting that "beneath all his aspersions is an offended ego."[55]

As a result of the myriad charges and countercharges, and the pandemonium of quarantines during the 1905 epidemic, the prevailing image of the South's public health administration was one of disarray, ineptitude, and ineffectiveness. The medical members of the Arkansas State Board of Health, for example, resigned in protest when their governor refused to accept their recommendation that passengers and freight from New Orleans certified by the Public Health Service be allowed to enter the state.[56] In addition, both the Louisiana State and New Orleans City Boards of Health resigned at the end of the epidemic, because they had so singularly failed in their duty by allowing yellow fever to enter the state and spread in the city. Even though the members of the New Orleans board tried to prove that it was their preliminary efforts in July and early August that "broke the back" of the epidemic, that the trend of the cases was already heading downward by the time the Public Health Service took over, the service emerged from the epidemic with a reputation of calm efficiency, in sharp contrast to the inept bungling and strong passions of the state health authorities.[57] The aura of capability surrounding the Public Health Service was much brightened by its victory over yellow fever in 1905.[58]

During the fall of 1905 the apparent incompetence of southern state and local public health officials in the control of yellow
fever brought new demands that the federal government assume complete control of maritime quarantine. In Memphis,
state and local public health authorities joined with the local
medical society in resolving that a truly national quarantine was
needed to prevent the importation of yellow fever. The governor and at least one senator of Louisiana expressed a like opinion, and by mid-October the New Orleans *Times-Democrat* could
report that all but five Louisiana newspapers favored a uniform, national quarantine.[59]

In 1905 the governor of Tennessee invited the governors,
other politicians, and representatives of leading railroad and
commerical interests to a quarantine conference in Chattanooga.[60] In a series of resolutions signed by representatives from
every southern state except Texas, the conference delegates declared that the mosquito theory of yellow fever transmission,
solidly established by the experiences of the past few years, provided the only acceptable foundation for quarantines against
yellow fever. The need for one uniform system, based on its
precepts to prevent both the introduction of yellow fever and the
dissemination of the disease from state to state after entry, was
clear. "Be it resolved," the delegates concluded, that "[we] hereby
respectfully request the Senate and House of Representatives, in
Congress assembled, to enact a law whereby coast maritime and
national frontier quarantine shall be placed exclusively under
the control and jurisdiction of the United States Government,
and that matters of interstate quarantine shall be placed under
the control and jurisdiction of the United States Government,
acting in co-operation with the several State Boards of Health."
The conference also urged Congress to fund programs for eradicating the yellow fever mosquito in the United States, and to
encourage the governments of Central and South America to do
the same. In addition, they called for state health authorities to
voluntarily bring their quarantine regulations in line with those
of the federal government, to guarantee uniformity of action.[61]

Senator Stephen R. Mallory of Florida and Representative
John Sharp Williams of Mississippi spoke, they claimed, for
the majority of southerners when in February 1906 they intro-

duced into their respective congressional chambers bills providing for the federal control of southern quarantine. The
Mallory-Williams bill, which President Roosevelt signed on 19
June 1906, instructed the Public Health Service to establish up
to four quarantine stations for the express purpose of preventing the importation of yellow fever. The legislation further
provided for the purchase of land, equipment, and buildings;
the prosecution and punishment of quarantine regulation offenders; and the investigation of the possibility that state-
owned quarantine stations might be procured for carrying out
this federal activity. Congress appropriated $500,000 to exe-
cute the bill's provisions, as well as for the general purpose of
excluding yellow fever or combatting it once imported.

The bill did not require state or local officials to accept the
certificates of good health granted to ships by such federal
stations, but in actuality the measure was designed to put the
remaining non-federal quarantine stations in Louisiana, Alabama, Texas, and South Carolina out of business. Once federal
quarantine stations were constructed for these states, then if
their officials proposed to maintain their own separate quarantine establishments, it would mean that shipping would have to
undergo inspection (and possibly disinfection and detention)
twice. This would clearly result in an unacceptable burden on
commerce. As the Public Health Service already administered
quarantine for Mississippi, Florida, Georgia, and Virginia, the
bill's intended and ultimate effect was to grant to the Public
Health Service complete sovereignty over quarantine on the
southern coast.[62]

Like the legislation creating the National Board of Health in
1879, the Mallory-Williams Bill was in its essence a yellow fever
bill, and was in addition undeniably a piece of sectional legislation, narrowly aimed at preventing the introduction of yellow
fever into the South. It called for federal hegemony over southern quarantine, but left intact the local quarantine systems of
Boston and New York.[63] The fear of yellow fever provided sufficient emotional force to effect the bill's passage; by excluding
the issue of northeast coastal quarantine, its sponsors avoided
stirring opposition from powerful northern commercial and
public health interests. "If gentlemen who have taken part in

this debate had gone through a yellow-fever epidemic, as I have, they would not stand here upon technicalities," declared Representative Robert C. Davey of Louisiana, waving the yellow shirt as dramatically as Isham Harris had in 1879. "I have taken part in every yellow-fever epidemic since my birth, during the great epidemic of 1853. . . . I have seen them dying, and I have seen them dead. Mr. Speaker, there is no law strong enough for me to vote for that would keep the yellow-fever plague from the boundaries of the United States." Davey, speaking in mid-April, further warned the lawmakers to act expeditiously, for the summer was approaching.[64] As Williams told the House, "It is mosquito time down in Dixie, and it is yellow-fever time in South and Central America."[65]

Proponents of the bill quite openly admitted that it was in part a pro-business measure, designed to ease yellow fever's impact on commerce. In a most explicit statement elucidating why Congress was considering a bill to control yellow fever, but not the many other deadly diseases affecting the American population, a Louisiana representative went to the heart of the relationship between yellow fever, commerce, and the federal control of southern maritime quarantine.

Though I was born and reared in the State of Louisiana, I was greatly surprised myself in examining the statistics of this subject to ascertain the very small percentage of deaths from yellow fever compared with other diseases. I wish to make some comparisons, and while they show that such diseases as typhoid fever, pneumonia, consumption, and scarlet fever carry off a great many more human beings than ever yellow fever does, that fact does not militate in the slightest degree against the necessity of this legislation, nor does it follow therefrom that similar legislation should be enacted to control these diseases, for *none of them interfere in the slightest degree with interstate commerce*, and it is under the commerce clause of the Constitution that we find our warrant and authority in enacting this bill.[66]

Yellow fever was a deadly disease, but the characteristic that set it apart from other major causes of mortality was its destruction of commercial intercourse, not lives.

The Louisiana delegation had been prominent in supporting the Mallory-Williams bill, and its governor remained an enthusiastic friend of national quarantine. As soon as the federal legislation was signed into law, a resolution was introduced into the Louisiana General Assembly that authorized the governor to sell the Mississippi River quarantine station to the federal government. Supporters of the move contended that this was the only way that the state could realize the value of its investment, for otherwise the station would be rendered obsolete by the certain construction of a federal quarantine station further down the Mississippi River. The Louisiana State Board of Health opposed the sale, but the resolution passed on 12 July 1906.

After much haggling with the Public Health Service, a deal was finally struck on 14 March 1907. For a payment of $100,000 the federal government bought from Louisiana the main station on the Mississippi River and four auxiliary inspection stations, thus entirely removing maritime quarantine from the purview of the state. The anguish of C. H. Irion, then president of the Louisiana State Board of Health, was evident in his closing remarks on the sale. "While there is not supposed to be any sentimental feeling in matters of business," he began, "and especially in such prosaic official work as the management of maritime quarantine, it was felt by many people in New Orleans and elsewhere in Louisiana that in selling the historic and splendidly equipped Quarantine plant, which has served as the model for other States and for the Federal Government, the State of Louisiana parted with something which was peculiarly her own, a monument to the genius of her sons, and the pride of her people."[67] The sale of the station was symbolic of the larger loss to southern public health officials of a source of prestige and professional identity.

Irion was not unaware of how intertwined were quarantine and the professional identity of southern public health officials and how closely tied was the protection of commerce with the preservation of the population from yellow fever. "While the State Board of Health realizes that its function is the preservation of the public health," he said in a speech given early in his tenure, which outlined the policy of the new board, "it also realizes that the vast commercial interests of the State must be protected by every means not inconsistent with that function.

Public health and commercial interests are so intimately related that the preservation of the one must be the greatest protection of the other."[68] Only a southern public health official would have that perspective on his role. In Irion, the ideas of Joseph Jones endured; Irion's ardent defense of the need for local control of quarantine in order to ensure the maximum protection from disease and the minimal obstruction of commerce recalled the fight against the National Board of Health over two decades earlier. Unlike Jones, however, Irion lost and the Public Health Service, whose cause Jones had furthered in its earlier incarnation as the Marine Hospital Service, won. In his report for 1906 and 1907, Irion made some attempt to recoup the state board's losses by emphasizing the vast amount of work waiting to be done in tuberculosis, diphtheria and typhoid control, and the protection of the public from food and drug adulteration. But the abrogation of what had long been the primary duty of the Louisiana State Board of Health, the protection of the state's commercial interests by the finely tuned administration of quarantine against yellow fever, left a large gap in the board's function and identity.

Yellow fever disappeared from the United States after 1905, except for isolated imported cases that did not generate epidemics. The eradication of yellow fever in Cuba by means of mosquito control measures and the establishment of rigorous quarantines targeting the right vector no doubt contributed heavily to this outcome. Yet the disease had been fading anyway, moving farther and farther south over the course of the nineteenth century. Most likely the biology of the virus or its vector changed in some way as yet to be elucidated. In any event, after 1905 it did not return. While public health officials fighting the epidemic of that year could not have known it would be their last, they did acquire a sense of mastery over the disease that caused them to look to the future with confidence. Yellow fever could be prevented and controlled.

Louisiana was not alone in feeling the impact of these events. The transfer of southern maritime quarantine to federal control, and the disappearance of yellow fever from the South, left other southern boards of health inactive as well. In Mississippi, where the state board had been all but dormant between the

1898 and 1905 epidemics, the state legislature refused to grant the board's requested appropriation for 1906, because the lawmakers assumed that now the federal government would take care of yellow fever.[69] The Texas legislature had never believed that the state needed more than a single health officer to coordinate yellow fever's exclusion, and certainly saw little immediate reason, especially after the passage of the Mallory-Williams act, to concede to the requests of state public health officials and create a state board of health. Florida's Joseph Porter was quick to realize that a new use would have to be found for the ample treasury that the state's public health tax placed at the discretion of the state board of health. After the Florida quarantine stations were sold to the federal government in 1901, with yellow fever reappearing only once since then (and that a light epidemic in 1905 affecting only Pensacola), Porter turned to hookworm as a disease upon which to refocus the energies of the state board. Understanding that the most pervasive and fundamental health problems of his agricultural state were associated with rural poverty, he was among the first southern public health officials to shift his professional attention from urban epidemics to the unhealthy conditions prevalent in the rural South.[70]

In a perceptive article written late in 1905, John Fulton of the Johns Hopkins Medical School revealed the fundamental weaknesses plaguing the structure of southern public health. Fulton grounded his analysis on the course of events that seemed to inevitably follow in succession during a yellow fever epidemic. He began by sarcastically asserting,

Prompt notification of the occurrence of yellow fever is not expected of Southern health officials. It is nothing new for the presence of yellow fever in New Orleans to be first published after a visit by the health officials of Mississippi. Alabama officials, on occasion, do the same courtesy for Mississippi, and Louisiana officials for Texas. Downright lying about yellow fever (if it be not) might be among the resources of some Southern health officials without grievous offense to normal consciences.

While Fulton found this attitude unconscionable, Souchon differed; he defended it on the grounds that his role was to protect commerce as well as health, by controlling unreasonable panic through the judicious release of information. Fulton went on to characterize the response of the people to the announcement of yellow fever as a form of madness, "an incoherent, raging, fierce delirium," which was "actuated only by the instinct of self-preservation." Fulton viewed the repeated occurrence of these shotgun quarantines "as a serious phase of social disorder," and he found it difficult to "distinguish such a state of affairs from revolution." It may be that the willingness of southern communities to take up arms in their own defense was one expression of the well-documented southern propensity for lawlessness and violence; certainly shotgun quarantines constituted a profession of independence from state and national authority.[71]

In the persistence of this violent discord Fulton saw evidence that southern boards of health were too feeble to be relied upon to control yellow fever. "The chaotic spectacle of public sanitation in the South at this moment," was due, in his opinion, to the fact that southern boards of health were "organized for no constant utility, but for emergency use only," a characteristic which he noted was unfortunately shared by many other boards of health across the country. Fulton believed that for a board of health to be effective in an emergency, it must gain the confidence of the people by its regular, year-round exercise of hygienic tasks to improve the healthiness of their lives. Yet in Alabama, Mississippi, Louisiana, and Texas the presence of yellow fever alone brought the public health authorities into active contact with the populace. "What else can they [the public health officials of these states] possibly hope to bring to rare emergencies, except stout hearts and willing bodies? Skill is no fairy gift, nor attainable otherwise than by use," Fulton advised. "When these four states [Alabama, Louisiana, Mississippi, and Texas] recognize the supreme importance of ever-present and familiar causes of death, when health officers can sharpen their wits in seeking out and relieving common needs of the people, there will be an end of delirious quarantine," and the beginning of modern public health in the South. Fulton recognized that a complete revolution in the orientation of southern public health officials, away from yellow fever and toward the multiplicity of endemic health problems afflicting their populations, was required before they could gain the prestige, authority, and trust so badly needed during the throes of an epidemic. He did not explain, though, how southern public health officials were to convince their legislatures to fund the new public health direction.[72]

The South's public health professionals did not lack the orientation toward modern disease control technology or the intelligence to combat their endemic health problems. By 1905, their fight against yellow fever was every bit as sophisticated and current as any northern campaign against diphtheria, tuberculosis, or typhoid. Like efforts against other diseases, their work was specifically targeted on one disease and designed to break the chain of communication of that disease from person to person. No longer did they blindly go about cleaning up the city or disinfecting streets and privies in a broadside attack against the disease, but instead relied on the latest entomological and etiological information to limit yellow fever's spread. If southern public health officials largely ignored the endemic diseases that so preoccupied northern health authorities, it was not because they lacked professional skills. Rather, diseases such as diphtheria and typhoid were seen as much less significant than yellow fever; in New Orleans these two diseases were not severe, and few cities in the South were large enough to be seriously threatened by the diseases common to northern cities. A larger shift in public health attention was required for the southern health official to comprehend his region's public health needs. It was not a matter of southern public health officials turning from one urban disease to another, but rather of their becoming aware of the toll of disease on the poorly fed, poorly clothed and poorly housed rural population.

"The incubus of easily preventable disease lies so heavy on the South that no southern state can afford to allow party or personal politics to exist in the department of health," judged Providence sanitarian Charles V. Chapin in his 1915 survey of state boards of health for the American Medical Association.[73] Chapin relentlessly catalogued the deficiencies of the southern public health effort in his state-by-state summary of their situations by using such indices of progressive public health as the

regulation of vital statistics; efficiency in controlling tuberculosis, typhoid, and diphtheria; purity of water; extensiveness of
sewage systems; and the freedom of public health appointments from political influence. His assessment of most southern boards as sorely lacking in these areas has been frequently
cited by historians discussing southern public health.[74]

Chapin's criticisms, which stressed the enlightenment brought
to the South by the Rockefeller Hookworm Commission, were
no doubt apt, but were not modified by an understanding that
this state of affairs came in the aftermath of the loss of quarantine responsibilities. Southern boards of health had each been
born in the turmoil or wake of a yellow fever epidemic, charged
by their organizers to prevent the introduction of epidemic disease. Although many of their northern counterparts had been
founded in response to cholera epidemics, southern boards of
health had the distinctive task of remaining on the alert against
the epidemic disease that had spurred their creation. Northern
public health officials had in contrast been quickly faced with the
problem of finding other occupations to prove their worth, as
cholera threatened only rarely. To assail southern boards of
health for not following the agenda established by northern sanitarians was perhaps too harsh a recrimination. Certainly, public
health officials of southern states were familiar with and often
shared the hygienic goals of their northern and European colleagues; if their vision was in practicality restricted largely to the
prevention of yellow fever and the protection of commerce, it
should be remembered that this was the only public health activity that their respective governments consistently acknowledged
with funding. By the twentieth century, at any rate, northern
critics of southern public health were becoming more sympathetic with the southern plight. Less was heard about the lazy,
uncaring attitude of southern public health officials, and more
often northern writers realized the depth and complexity of the
South's health problems.

"God Help Us, and Give Us One Clean Street in the South."
With these fervent words the Episcopal Bishop of Tennessee
opened a tuberculosis conference sponsored by the Tennessee
State Medical Association in 1906. His prayer headlined an editorial that lamented the poor sanitary condition of southern

cities, and asked how much longer this situation would be tolerated. Southern cities must awaken, the editorial declared, and join in the new public health crusade against preventable endemic causes of death, thus finding new reasons, other than fear of yellow fever, for keeping their streets clean.[75] Yet a vicious circle entrapped southern boards of health. Their assigned purpose had been, in actuality, to protect commerce from the people, from the terror before which the rule of law was impotent. Funding had been procured for the prevailing form of yellow fever prophylaxis, whether sanitation or mosquito eradication, as long as the fear of yellow fever predominated; but as this dread subsided with the advent of federal quarantine and the disappearance of yellow fever, the incentive for legislative support of boards of health withered as well.

The first priority of southern boards of health had never been the saving of lives but the saving of business, and it would take years before the South's lawmakers could be convinced that money spent on endemic health problems was a sound investment. Abundant urban and especially rural sources of disease robbed the South of industrious, productive workers, but it would take the educational efforts of outside influences, such as the Rockefeller campaign and the Public Health Service's crusades against malaria, pellagra, and syphilis, to impress upon indifferent southern legislators the region's unhealthiness and the costliness of a diseased population. They further needed to be convinced that public health measures could improve the welfare of their impoverished, mostly rural inhabitants. A mercantilist model of the cost-effectiveness of public health had to replace one measured by business losses to major epidemics. Support for even yellow fever work had been tenuous, even with all the arguments that could be mustered about the millions lost to commerce. Without yellow fever and the power to administer quarantine to prevent its introduction, southern public health authorities were bereft of that which had sustained their professional identity and legitimacy within southern society. With the new century, they had to start again to regain their status as important guardians of the South.

Almost thirty years separated the yellow fever epidemics of 1878 and 1905; over that time period the institutions and methods for controlling yellow fever in the South had changed markedly. Southern boards of health, largely non-existent in the antebellum period, had emerged in the late 1870s to battle yellow fever. The introduction of new disinfecting techniques in the 1880s had heightened respect for the public health official to a new level, but after the poor performance of southern boards of health in the epidemics of the late 1890s and 1905, little public confidence in the competence of southern public health officials remained. Although knowledge about the transmission of yellow fever had greatly increased the effectiveness of measures taken against the disease, federal authorities, and not southern boards, benefited from the subsequent elevation in status accorded the public health worker who controlled a yellow fever epidemic. Certainly one of the most striking differences between 1878 and 1905 was the changing role of the federal government in fighting epidemic disease. The decades had witnessed an incremental growth in federal public health involvement, and the evolution of a minor government agency into a national public health service. Both the decline of the southern boards and the expansion of the Marine Hospital Service can be traced to the vagaries of yellow fever. As a deadly disease with a devastating impact on interstate and foreign commerce, yellow fever had fundamentally shaped the course of southern and national public health administration during the nineteenth and early twentieth centuries.

. . . .

EPILOGUE

The story of yellow fever in the American south illustrates the extent to which public health reform in the nineteenth century was tied to the nature of the disease being fought. Yellow fever focused attention on the quarantine question, both internal and external, because it was so incredibly mobile. Simple sanitation did not help much, and its advocates repeatedly had to admit failure. Yellow fever was also a disease that riled commercial sensibilities, as it so blatantly interfered with the ordinary conduct of business. Southern politicians have never felt a strong responsibility for the health of the poor (Alabama still has the lowest medicaid benefits in the nation), and the connection has not yet been made between worker health and prosperity. It is unlikely that any other disease that merely killed without stopping trains could have led impoverished southern governments to support public health in the nineteenth century.

There are key features about yellow fever that made it a particularly strong fulcrum for moving the federal government into public health as well. It did cross state lines, making the "right to regulate interstate commerce" applicable. The location of the disease predominantly in the South was also crucial. The northern image of the South as weak, backward, wayward, and all together untrustworthy allowed the sort of massive federal intervention that would be hard to imagine in, say, Wisconsin. Well into the twentieth century the South was an area of federal public health experimentation. Having yellow fever as its first target, one which so threatened the rest of the nation as to make involvement mandatory, no doubt eased the path toward ever more expansive federal public health activity.

An interesting pattern emerges from the yellow fever experience that is more broadly applicable to the history of public health. When physicians were divided over quarantine versus sanitation, and the efficacy of neither appeared clear-cut, politicians were reluctant to fund large public health projects. Reform in any direction was stunted, and failed efforts at street cleaning or isolation were hailed loudly by those protecting the taxpayer's pocketbook from wasteful expenditures. Only when the disease was on the doorstep did politicians vote meager funds to bar the door. This changed in the 1880s. The concept of disinfection offered the possibility of a truly protective quarantine that was at the same time limited and relatively cheap. Businessmen compared the alternatives between commerce-disrupting epidemics and disinfecting quarantine stations, and chose the latter. Here was a technique that anyone could understand: acid gas would kill disease causing germs and purify the ship or train, allowing it to continue on its journey in a few days. The city was safe; the cargo was safe. Funds for such quarantine stations repeatedly appeared in state and federal budgets in the 1880s and 1890s. They probably did a fair job of killing mosquitoes, which accounts for their good record of success.

The yellow fever experience would suggest that in order to gain political support in the United States a public health measure had best meet the following criteria: (1) be grounded in undisputed medical theory; (2) be reasonably affordable; (3) afford minimal disruption of individual rights; (4) target a public health menace which threatens a significant portion of the population; and (5) have a mode of action that is fairly straightforward and comprehensible to the lay mind. By the latter I mean that cause and effect are direct and easy to visualize. By the 1880s the etiology of yellow fever, at least at the level of thinking "a germ causes this disease," was disputed only by the cranky few. The identity of the germ was eagerly sought, but no leading physician doubted its existence or that it would succumb to the disinfecting powers of chloride and sulphur as other germs did. The disinfecting station was expensive to establish, but less so than the cost of one epidemic, and certainly less than the old-fashioned "forty days in isolation" quarantine. While the scientific quarantine did interfere with the free movement of people and cargo, the loss of liberty was not felt to be too burdensome. Furthermore, yellow fever was a dreadful disease that clearly required prevention. Finally, the technique had clear analogies for the lay mind to latch on to. The disinfecting stations killed germs just as the army would kill invading soldiers. The combination was right for generating government action in public health.

This highlights my belief that the history of public health needs to be studied with sensitivity to the disease that instigates the reform. The history of public health in this country can be seen in part as the history of physicians and laymen committed to preventive medicine, attempting to convince politicians of the value of their activities. Preventive medicine is an extraordinarily difficult concept to convey, given that if one is successful, nothing happens. The disease does not come; the babies do not die. The case is established through statistics, not the easiest mode of thinking for the less-sophisticated to accept. In order to promote basic reform, public health advocates often have to call attention to dramatic cases—yellow fever, cholera, smallpox—in order to justify their own salaries and more mundane activities. It is clear that the most important features of public health reform evolve around the provision of clean water, the disposition of wastes, the inspection of food, and provision of basic health care. But it was by way of the dramatic epidemics that the organizations which ultimately effected these changes came to power. One can see each epidemic as the chance for public health reformers to gain a more secure place in society so that the everyday reforms could be carried out.

It was yellow fever that generated the base of power for boards of health in the American South, and in its beginning, for the United States Public Health Service. It was a fickle friend, which hindered as well as encouraged growth. In the South yellow fever gave a strong boost to the formation of boards of health in the late 1870s, but by its infrequent appearances in the 1880s and 1890s, it left those boards in doldrums, struggling to find a reason for existence. The most creative presidents of boards of health turned to other diseases, such as hookworm, after yellow fever disappeared in the first decade of the twentieth century. The first federal board of health sank into oblivion when yellow fever lay dormant for three years. It required the imaginative directors of the Marine Hospital Service to find ways to grow and secure power by expanding into immigrant issues, malaria, and hookworm as well, once yellow fever had faded.

Yellow fever was central to the origins of federal public health involvement, and it had a vast impact on southern state boards of health as well. Its very elusiveness made it the center of debates about public health theory and practice, spurring innovation in epidemiological techniques. The history of yellow fever provides a useful model for understanding the ways in which one disease can provoke research and reforms that have far-reaching implications for science and society.

NOTES

ABBREVIATIONS USED IN REFERENCES

Manuscript Sources

Matas Library: Historical Collection, Rudolph Matas Medical Library, Tulane University School of Medicine, New Orleans, Louisiana.

MHS Records: Incoming Correspondence, Records of the Marine Hospital Service, Record Group 90, National Archives and Records Service, Washington, D.C. The correspondence is arranged by place or by institution (e.g., state boards of health of Alabama [ASBH], Florida [FSBH], Louisiana [LSBH], and Mississippi [MSBH]; Ship Island Quarantine Station [Ship Is. Stat.]; or in one instance, by event (Yellow Fever Epidemic in Florida and Louisiana, 1905). Within these categories, the correspondence is largely chronological.

NHB Reel #: Letters Received by the National Board of Health, 1879–1884, National Archives Microfilm #753.

Periodicals and Government Documents

Appeal: Memphis Daily Appeal
APHA Reports: Reports and Papers of the American Public Health Association
Avalanche: Memphis Daily Avalanche
ASBH Report: Report of the Alabama State Board of Health
BMSJ: Boston Medical and Surgical Journal
CMJR: Charleston Medical and Surgical Journal
FSBH Report: Report of the Florida State Board of Health

JAMA: Journal of the American Medical Association
LSBH Report: Report of the Louisiana State Board of Health
MBH Report: Report of the Board of Health of the Taxing District of Shelby
    County (City of Memphis)
MHS Report: Report of the Surgeon General of the Marine Hospital Service
MSBH Report: Mississippi State Board of Health Report
NOMSJ: New Orleans Medical and Surgical Journal
Picayune: New Orleans Picayune
Times Democrat: New Orleans Times-Democrat
TSBH Report: Report of the Tennessee State Board of Health

INTRODUCTION

1. George K. Strobe, ed., *Yellow Fever* (New York: McGraw-Hill, 1951);
Wilbur G. Downs, "History of Epidemiological Aspects of Yellow Fever," *Yale
Journal of Biology and Medicine* 55 (1982): 179–185.

2. Thomas P. Monath, "Yellow Fever Virus," in Gerald L. Mandel, et al.,
eds., *Principles and Practice of Infectious Diseases*, 2nd. ed. (New York: John
Wiley & Sons, 1985), 923–926.

3. W. E. George to My Dear Friend, 4 November 1897, Van Dyke Collection, Mississippi Valley Collection, Memphis State University, Memphis, Tenn.
At the top of the letter are the words, "All mail fumigated with formalde-
hyde."

4. Kenneth F. Kiple, "Black Yellow Fever Immunities, Innate and Ac-
quired, as Revealed in the American South," *Social Science History* 1 (1977):
419–436; idem, "A Survey of Recent Literature on the Biological Past of the
Black," in idem, ed., *The African Exchange: Toward a Biological History* (Durham:
Duke University Press, 1987), 7–34; Todd L. Savitt, *Medicine and Slavery: The
Diseases and Health Care of Blacks in Antebellum Virginia* (Urbana: University of
Illinois Press, 1978), 240–246; D. C. Rousey, "Yellow Fever and Black Police-
men in Memphis: A Post Reconstruction Anomaly," *The Journal of Southern
History* 51 (1985): 357–374.

5. H. D. Geddings, "Yellow Fever from a Clinical and Epidemiological
Point of View and Its Relation to the Quarantine System of the United States,"
in *MHS Report*, 1897: 241.

6. Charles V. Chapin, *A Report on State Public Health Work Based on a Survey
of State Boards of Health* (Chicago: American Public Health Association, 1915).

7. Gordon E. Gillson, *Louisiana State Board of Health: The Formative Years*
(n.p., 1967). Jo Ann Carrigan, "The Saffron Scourge: A History of Yellow
Fever in Louisiana, 1796–1905" (Ph.D. dissertation, Louisiana State Univer-
sity, 1961); John Duffy, *The Sword of Pestilence: The New Orleans Yellow Fever
Epidemic of 1853* (Baton Rouge: Louisiana State University Press, 1966); idem,
ed., *The Rudolph Matas History of Medicine in Louisiana*, 2 vols. (Baton Rouge:
Louisiana State University Press, 1958–1962); John Ellis, "Yellow Fever and
the Origins of Modern Public Health in Memphis, Tennessee, 1870–1900"
(Ph.D. dissertation, Tulane University, 1962); Thomas Baker, "Yellowjack: the
Yellow Fever Epidemic of 1878 in Memphis, Tennessee," *Bulletin of the History*

of Medicine 42 (1968): 241–264; Barbara Miller, "Tallahassee and the 1841 Yellow Fever Epidemic" (M.A. thesis, Florida State University, 1976).

8. For example, the most recent account of the history of the United States Public Health Service only briefly mentions yellow fever, with little discussion of its importance. See Fitzhugh Mullan, *Plagues and Politics: The Story of the United States Public Health Service* (New York: Basic Books, 1989).

9. Morton Keller, *Affairs of State: Public Life in Late Nineteenth Century America* (Cambridge, Mass.: Harvard University Press, 1977), viii.

1. PURSUING AN ELUSIVE DISEASE

1. J. H. Powell, *Bring out Your Dead: The Great Plague of Yellow Fever in Philadelphia in 1793* (Philadelphia: University of Pennsylvania Press, 1949); Martin Pernick, "Politics, Party, and Pestilence: Epidemic Yellow Fever in Philadelphia and the Rise of the First Party System," in Judith Walzer Leavitt and Ronald L. Numbers, eds., *Sickness and Health in America: Readings in the History of Medicine and Public Health* (Madison: University of Wisconsin Press, 1978), 241–256; George David Sussman, "From Yellow Fever to Cholera: A Study of French Government Policy, Medical Professionalism and Popular Movements in the Epidemic Crises of the Restoration and the July Monarchy" (Ph.D. dissertation, Yale University, 1971).

2. Philadelphia physician René La Roche presented the most thorough version of the anti-contagionist perspective on yellow fever in *Yellow Fever, Considered in its Historical, Pathological, Etiological, and Therapeutic Relations* (Philadelphia: Lea and Blanchard, 1855). La Roche reveals that this viewpoint was still strong in the northern U.S. and Europe in the mid-1850s, when it was fading among southern physicians. Charles Rosenberg discusses etiological theory as it pertained to cholera in "The Cause of Cholera: Aspects of Etiological Thought in 19th-Century America," in Leavitt and Numbers, *Sickness and Health*, 257–272.

3. John Harley Warner describes the Philadelphia influence on southern medical thought in "The Idea of Southern Medical Distinctiveness: Medical Knowledge and Practice in the Old South," in Ronald L. Numbers and Todd L. Savitt, eds., *Science and Medicine in the Old South*, (Baton Rouge: Louisiana State University Press, 1989): 179–205. Chervin's influence is evident in the comments of Dr. Beugnot in C. H. Stone, "Report on the Origin of Yellow Fever in the Town of Woodville, Miss., in the Summer of 1844 . . . ," *New-Orleans Medical Journal* 1 (1844–45): 525.

4. See, for example, John Duffy, ed., *The Rudolph Matas History of Medicine in Louisiana*, 2 vols. (Baton Rouge: Louisiana State University Press, 1958–1962), 1:382–409; 2:160–197.

5. Medical student lecture notebooks are particularly good sources for the accepted knowledge about yellow fever. See, for example, Samuel Favel King, Notes on Lectures at the Medical College of South Carolina, Dr. [Thomas Y.] Simons on Practice, 1837, Waring Historical Library, Medical University of South Carolina, Charleston; and Titus Munson Coan, Lectures of Dr. Alonzo

Clark, 1859–60, Lectures Delivered at the College of Physicians and Surgeons, New York, New-York Historical Society, New York, N.Y.

6. P. M. Kollock, "Notes on the Epidemic Fever of 1854," *Southern Medical and Surgical Journal* 11 (1855): 469–470.

7. Luther Preston, "Aetiology of Bilious Fevers in Hot Climates" (M.D. thesis, Transylvania University, 1826), Special Collections and Archives, Transylvania University Library, Transylvania University, Lexington, Ky.

8. A. D. Crossman, et al., "Report of the Sanitary Commission of New Orleans on the Origin and Spread of the Epidemic," in idem, *Report of the Sanitary Commission on the Epidemic Yellow Fever of 1853* (New Orleans: The City Council, 1854), 493–503.

9. J. K. Mitchell, *On the Cryptogamous Origin of Malarious and Epidemic Fevers* (Philadelphia: Lea and Blanchard, 1849); Josiah C. Nott, "Yellow Fever Contrasted with Bilious Fever—Reasons for Believing It a Disease Sui Generis—Its Mode of Propagation—Remote Cause—Probably Insect or Animalcular Origin, &c.," *NOMSJ* 4 (1847–48): 563–601.

10. In addition to Nott, "Yellow Fever Contrasted," see, for example, W. J. Tuck, "An Essay on Yellow Fever," *NOMSJ* 11 (1854–55): 175–191.

11. Richard D. Arnold, "An Essay upon the Relation of Bilious and Yellow Fever—Prepared at the Request of, and Read before, the Medical Society of the State of Georgia, at Its Session Held at Macon on the 9th April, 1856," *Southern Medical and Surgical Journal* 12 (1856): 517.

12. William Selden, et al., "Report on the Origin of the Yellow Fever in Norfolk during the Summer of 1855," *Virginia Medical Journal* 9 (1857): 91.

13. "Health of Our City," *New Orleans Medical News and Hospital Gazette* 4 (1857–58): 358.

14. W. M. Carpenter, *Sketches from the History of Yellow Fever; Showing Its Origin; Together with Facts and Circumstances Disproving Its Domestic Origin, and Demonstrating Its Transmissibility* (New Orleans: J. B. Steel, 1844), 6. See also John W. Monette, *Observations on the Epidemic Yellow Fever of Natchez, and of the South-West* (Louisville: Prentice and Weissinger, 1842), and B. B. Strobel, *An Essay on the Subject of Yellow Fever, Intended to Prove Its Transmissibility* (Charleston: A. J. Muir, 1840).

15. Bennet Dowler outlined the various meanings of contagion and infection in *Tableau of the Yellow Fever of 1853* (New Orleans: Office of the *Picayune*, 1854), 45–46. Curiously, the term "contingent contagion," popular for describing the communication of cholera in a suitably foul atmosphere, is rare in discussions of yellow fever.

16. "Quarantine," *New-Orleans Medical Journal* 1 (1844): 83.

17. William G. Williams and James Andrews, "An Account of the Yellow Fever which Prevailed at Rodney, Mississippi, during the Autumn of 1843," *New-Orleans Medical Journal* 1 (1844): 40.

18. Stone, "Report on the Origin"; and Andrew Kirkpatrick, "An Account of the Yellow Fever which Prevailed in Woodville, Mississippi, in the Year 1844," *New-Orleans Medical Journal* 2 (1845–46): 40–57.

19. A. P. Jones, "Yellow Fever in a Rural District," *New Orleans Medical News and Hospital Gazette* 1 (1854–55): 207.

20. *Weekly Delta*, August 14, 1853. Cited in Gordon E. Gillson, *Louisiana State Board of Health: The Formative Years* (n.p., 1967), 40.

21. Crossman, "Report of the Sanitary Commission," 479.

. . . .

22. S. H. Dickson, "Epidemics," *CMJR* 10 (1855): 609–620; P. C. Gaillard, "On Some Points of Hygiene, and Their Connection with the Propagation of Yellow Fever and Cholera," *CMJR* 4 (1849): 280–295; "Yellow Fever in Charleston," *CMJR* 11 (1856): 845–850; "Yellow Fever at the South-West," *Southern Medical and Surgical Journal* 9 (1853): 705.

23. H. L. Byrd, "Observations on Yellow Fever," *CMJR* 10 (1853): 329–333, 329.

24. Selden, "Yellow Fever in Norfolk"; Edward C. Bolton, "The Yellow Fever at Norfolk" (M.D. thesis, University of Pennsylvania, 1858), Special Collections, Van Pelt Library, University of Pennsylvania, Philadelphia, Pa.; Richard G. Parker, "Yellow Fever in Portsmouth Virg: During the Summer & Fall of 1855 (M.D. thesis, University of Pennsylvania, 1858), ibid.

25. John W. Francis, remarks of 29 April 1859, *Proceedings and Debates of the Third National Quarantine and Sanitary Convention* (New York: Edmund Jones & Co., 1859), 141–142.

26. This observation is based on my reading of the yellow fever articles cited elsewhere in these notes. The anti-transportation writers were mostly either in New Orleans, Charleston, or north of the Mason-Dixon line. The pleasure that some of the pro-transportation writers took in attacking "northern ideas" suggests that sectional politics was stronger in shaping opinion than labels of liberalism or conservatism. However, I was not able to explore the particular politics of each writer in a way that would conclusively refute Acker-knecht's claim, as it applies to the southern case. See Erwin Ackerknecht, "Anticontagionism between 1821 and 1867," *BHM* 22 (1948): 562–593.

27. George A. Ketchum, "Report on the Diseases of Mobile for 1854," *Transactions of the Medical Association of the State of Alabama*, 8th session (1855), 114; E. D. Fenner, *History of the Epidemic of Yellow Fever at New Orleans, La. in 1853* (New York: Hall, Clayton & Co., 1854), 74.

28. C. B. Guthrie, remarks of 28 April 1859, in *Third National Sanitary Convention*, 25–29.

29. The vote on the quarantine question was recorded and discussed on pp. 220–224, ibid. This volume also contains discussions of the value of disinfectants, and a prescription for the new system of quarantine.

30. Stanford E. Chaillé, in "The Yellow Fever, Sanitary Condition, and Vital Statistics of New Orleans during Its Military Occupation; the Four Years 1862–65," *New Orleans Journal of Medicine* 23 (1870): 563–598, discussed the federal occupation controversy and denied any credit to the Yankee forces. For a presentation of the opposite point of view, see Barbara Gutmann Rosenkrantz, *Public Health and the State: Changing Views in Massachusetts, 1842–1936* (Cambridge, Mass.: Harvard University Press, 1972), 49. George Augustin provided a list of outbreaks of yellow fever in America from 1860 to 1880 in *History of Yellow Fever* (New Orleans: Searcy and Pfaff, 1909), 179–180.

31. William Coleman, *Yellow Fever in the North: The Methods of Epidemiology* (Madison: University of Wisconsin Press, 1987); C.E. Gordon Smith and Mary E. Gibson, "Yellow Fever in South Wales, 1865," *Medical History* 30 (1986): 322–340.

32. Marshall Wingfield, "The Life and Letters of Dr. William J. Armstrong," *The West Tennessee Historical Society Papers* IV (1950): 106–108.

33. The widespread acceptance of the germ theory of yellow fever is evident in the majority of articles on yellow fever from the 1870s onward. For comments on this acceptance, and the role of the 1878 epidemic in solidifying it, see, for example, H. D. Schmidt, "On the Pathology of Yellow Fever, with Some Remarks on Its Cause, and the Means for Its Prevention," *New York Medical Journal* 29 (1879): 151–152; and "Yellow Fever [reported by Simon McPherson from the Medical Section of the Academy of Sciences in the Polytechnic Institute of Kentucky, 24 July 1879]," *Medical Herald* 1 (1879–80): 147–156. By 1880 the faculty of the University of Louisiana Medical School, which would later become part of Tulane University, were solidly in favor of the germ theory of yellow fever, and taught it to their students (R. Matas, "Discussion of the Etiology and Pathology of Yellow Fever," *NOMSJ* 50 (1897–98): 211–213).

34. William Selden, "Views on the Subject of Prevention of Yellow Fever," *APHA Reports* 4 (1877–78): 286.

35. Jerome Cochran, "The Yellow Fever Epidemic of 1879," *Transactions of the Medical Association of the State of Alabama* 33 (1880): 128.

36. Yellow fever in Key West is discussed in Chapter 5, as is the massive disinfection campaign that followed the 1888 Jacksonville epidemic. For a description of the steps involved in carrying out the disinfection of a household, see Edmond Souchon, *Louisiana State Board of Health. Instructions to Laymen Who May Have to Manage Yellow Fever Cases in Default of a Physician* (New Orleans: L. Graham & Son, 1898), 13–14.

37. See, for example, Harvey E. Brown, *Report on Quarantine on the Southern and Gulf Coasts of the United States* (New York: William Wood & Co., 1873), 85–87, and George M. Sternberg, *Report on the Etiology and Prevention of Yellow Fever* (Washington: Government Printing Office, 1890), 13.

38. "Relative to Disinfection and Precautionary Measures," *NBH Bulletin* 1 (1879): 39. See also George M. Sternberg, "An Inquiry into the Modus Operandi of the Yellow Fever Poison," *NOMSJ* 3 (1875–76): 7.

39. C. B. White, "To the Editor of the New Orleans Medical and Surgical Journal," *NOMSJ* 3 (1875–76): 445.

40. These assumptions are common in the literature concerning yellow fever. See, for example, R. B. Maury, "Yellow Fever," *Memphis Medical Monthly* 18 (1898): 1–8; J. C. LeHardy, "The Yellow Fever Panic," *Atlanta Medical and Surgical Journal* 5 (1888–89): 605–616; and J. M. Clemens, "Etiology of Yellow Fever," *Louisville Medical News* 6 (1878): 134–138.

41. Reuben A. Vance, "Remarks on Yellow Fever," *St. Louis Medical and Surgical Journal* 37 (1879): 4.

42. George M. Sternberg, "The History and Geographical Distribution of Yellow Fever," *Janus* 1 (1896–97): 195–201.

43. "Natural history" is not used here in the sense that Sydenham employed the term; it does not mean just the study of the course of the disease in the patient, but rather encompasses the broader definition supplied in the text.

44. The most detailed histories of microbiology are William Bulloch, *The History of Bacteriology* (London: Oxford University Press, 1938), and Hubert A. Lechevalier and Morris Solotorovsky, *Three Centuries of Microbiology* (New York: Dover Publications, 1974; first pub. 1965). Also useful are W. D. Foster, *A History of Medical Bacteriology and Immunology* (London: William Heinemann Medical Books Ltd., 1970), and Patrick Collard, *The Development of Microbiology* (Cambridge: Cambridge University Press, 1976).

45. Abraham Jacobi, "Inaugural Address, Delivered Before the New York Academy of Medicine," *Medical Record* 27 (1885): 172–173.

46. "Yellow Fever Microbes," *The Alkaloidal Clinic* 4 (1897): 549.

47. George M. Sternberg, *Report on the Etiology and Prevention of Yellow Fever* (Washington: Government Printing Office, 1890). Biographies of Sternberg are by Martha Sternberg, *George Miller Sternberg: A Biography* (Chicago: American Medical Association, 1920); and John M. Gibson, *Soldier in White: The Life of General George Miller Sternberg* (Durham, N.C.: Duke University Press, 1958).

48. Margaret Warner [Humphreys], "Hunting the Yellow Fever Germ: The Principle and Practice of Etiological Proof in Late Nineteenth-Century America," *Bulletin of the History of Medicine* 59 (1985): 361–382. Biographies of Walter Reed, which include accounts of his yellow fever work, are by Howard A. Kelly, *Walter Reed and Yellow Fever* (New York: McClure, Phillips & Co., 1906), and William B. Bean, *Walter Reed: A Biography* (Charlottesville: University Press of Virginia, 1982).

49. James Carroll, "A Brief Review of the Aetiology of Yellow Fever," *New York Medical Journal and Philadelphia Medical Journal, Consolidated* 79 (1904): 244–245.

50. Walter Reed, et al., "The Etiology of Yellow Fever. A Preliminary Note," *Philadelphia Medical Journal* 6 (1900): 791–792. On Ross's discovery of the malarial mosquito vector, see Gordon Harrison, *Mosquitoes, Malaria and Man: A History of the Hostilities Since 1880* (New York: E.P. Dutton, 1978), 17–86.

51. Henry Rose Carter, "A Note on the Interval between Infecting and Secondary Cases of Yellow Fever from the Records of the Yellow Fever at Orwood and Taylor, Miss., in 1898," *NOMSJ* 52 (1899–1900): 617–636.

52. Carlos Finlay was born in Cuba in 1832 and received his medical degree from Jefferson Medical College in Philadelphia in 1855. He returned to Cuba where he had an active and prominent career as a physician and researcher. See François Delaporte, *The History of Yellow Fever: An Essay on the Birth of Tropical Medicine*, translated from the French edition of 1989 (Cambridge, Mass.: The MIT Press, 1991), both for an in-depth discussion of Finlay and for further references on his career. Charles-Edward Amory Winslow, *The Conquest of Epidemic Disease: A Chapter in the History of Ideas* (Princeton: Princeton University Press, 1943), 347–361, is a history of theories of insect transmission of disease.

53. Nancy Stepan, "The Interplay between Socio-Economic Factors and Medical Science: Yellow Fever Research, Cuba and the United States," *Social Studies of Science* 8 (1978), 397–423.

54. Charles Finlay, "Inoculations for Yellow Fever by Means of Contaminated Mosquitoes," *American Journal of Medical Sciences* 102 (1891): 264–268; George M. Sternberg, "Dr. Finlay's Mosquito Inoculations," ibid., 627–630.

55. Charles F. Ring [a physician of Urbana, Ohio], "Yellow Fever: Some Thoughts on Its Prophylaxis," *Medical Visitor* 16 (1900): 337–345.

56. James Carroll, "Yellow Fever: A Popular Lecture," *American Medicine* 9 (1905): 912.

57. George H. F. Nuttall, "On the Role of Insects, Arachnids and Myriapods, As Carriers in the Spread of Bacterial and Parasitic Diseases of Man and Animals. A Critical and Historical Study," *The Johns Hopkins Hospital Reports* 8 (1899–1900): 1–154.

58. Delaporte, *The History of Yellow Fever*.

59. The many publications resulting from the Reed Commission's investigations, which document the history of these experiments extensively, were collected in *Yellow Fever: A Compilation of Various Publications. Results of the Work of Maj. Walter Reed . . . and the Yellow Fever Commission* (Washington: Government Printing Office, 1911).

60. H. R. Carter discussed the use of analogical thinking in the establishment of the mosquito theory in "The Methods of the Conveyance of Yellow Fever Infection," *Yellow Fever Institute Bulletin* #10, July, 1902, 17–23. On the comparison of yellow fever with cholera and typhoid, see Stanford E. Chaillé, "Prevention of Yellow Fever and the Quarantining of Houses to Stamp It Out," *NOMSJ* 50 (1897–98): 625–648. O. L. Pothier described the continuing search for an animal yellow fever parasite in "The Etiology of Yellow Fever and Its Transmission by the Mosquito," *NOMSJ* 58 (1905–06): 326–329.

61. W. C. Gorgas, "Disappearance of Yellow Fever from Havana, Cuba," *Medical News* 82 (1903): 1–7, and James Carroll, "Yellow Fever," are both typical in their emphasis on the great commensurability of the mosquito theory with evidence from former epidemics.

62. C. Faget, "Confusion between the Terms 'Contagion' and 'Infection,' or the Mosquito Craze," *NOMSJ* 59 (1906–07): 254.

63. Ibid., 265.

64. Rubert Boyce, "The Yellow Fever Epidemic in New Orleans in 1905," *Transactions of the Epidemiological Society of London* 25 (1905–06): 275.

65. The reasons for the gradual disappearance of yellow fever from the United States would be fascinating to explore, but are beyond the scope of this study. The explanation most likely lies in viral mutation; changing modes of water transport aboard ship; and improved urban sanitation in the U.S. with consequent reduction in breeding areas. Climatic differences and the behavior of the *Aedes* mosquito might also be implicated.

66. "The Quarantine Conference," *NOMSJ* 58 (1905–06): 482–483; "The Transmission of Yellow Fever," *Memphis Medical Monthly* 23 (1903): 325–328; *Picayune*, 11 December 1902 [report on APHA meeting].

67. Herman B. Parker, et al., "Report of Working Party No. 1, Yellow Fever Institute. A Study of the Etiology of Yellow Fever," *Yellow Fever Institute Bulletin* #13, March, 1903.

68. Frederick G. Novy, "The Etiology of Yellow Fever," *Medical News* 73 (1898): 369.

69. Walter Reed and James Carroll, "The Etiology of Yellow Fever—A Supplemental Note," in *Yellow Fever: A Compilation*, 149–160. Hubert A. Lechevalier and Morris Solotorovsky quoted extensively from this paper and placed it within the broader field of bacteriological and virological research in the early twentieth century (*Three Centuries of Microbiology*, 280–332). On viral research on yellow fever, see Andrew J. Warren, "Landmarks in the Conquest of Yellow Fever," in George K. Strode, ed., *Yellow Fever* (New York: McGraw-Hill, 1951), 5–37.

70. One of the best and most detailed accounts of the employment of germicidal techniques against yellow fever is George M. Sternberg, et al., *Disinfection and Disinfectants: Their Application and Use in the Prevention and Treatment of Disease, and in Public and Private Sanitation* (Concord, N.H.: Republican Press Association for the American Public Health Association, 1888).

71. James Cassedy, "The Flamboyant Colonel Waring: An Anticontagionist Holds the American Stage in the Age of Pasteur and Koch," in Leavitt and Numbers, eds., *Sickness and Health*, 305–312.

2.   YELLOW FEVER, THE SOUTH, AND THE NATION, 1840–1880

1. On these movements, see John Duffy, *A History of Public Health in New York, 1625–1866* (New York: Russell Sage Foundation, 1968); Barbara Gutmann Rosenkrantz, *Public Health and the State: Changing Views in Massachusetts, 1842–1936* (Cambridge, Mass.: Harvard University Press, 1972); John M. Eyler, *Victorian Social Medicine: The Ideas and Methods of William Farr* (Baltimore: The Johns Hopkins University Press, 1979); William Coleman, *Death Is a Social Disease: Public Health and Political Economy in Early Industrial France* (Madison: The University of Wisconsin Press, 1982).

2. The early history of the Louisiana State Board of Health is discussed in John Duffy, ed., *The Rudolph Matas History of Medicine in Louisiana*, 2 vols. (Baton Rouge: Louisiana State University Press, 1958–1962), 2:160–197, and in Gordon E. Gillson, *Louisiana State Board of Health: The Formative Years* (n.p., 1967), 35–76. Information on other southern boards of health can be found in Wyndham B. Blanton, *Medicine in Virginia in the Eighteenth Century* (Richmond: Garrett and Massie, 1931), 396–399; idem, *Medicine in Virginia in the Nineteenth Century* (Richmond: Garrett and Massie, 1933), 224–271; Joseph Ioor Waring, *A History of Medicine in South Carolina*, 2 vols. (Columbia, S.C.: The South Carolina Medical Association, 1964–1967), 1:48–61, 147–159, 2:30–70; Carey V. Stabler, "The History of the Alabama Public Health System" (Ph.D. dissertation, Duke University, 1944), 1–42; Felix J. Underwood and R. N. Whitfield, *Public Health and Medical Licensure in the State of Mississippi, 1798–1937* (Jackson: Tucker Printing House, 1938), 13–21.

3. Blanton, *Nineteenth Century*, 238–243; "Board of Health of the City of Knoxville," *Southern Journal of Medicine and Physical Sciences* 3 (1855): 92–95. On cholera in the United States see Charles E. Rosenberg, *The Cholera Years: The United States in 1832, 1849, and 1866* (Chicago: The University of Chicago Press, 1962).

4. "Health of the City," *New-Orleans Medical Journal* 1 (1844): 94. George Augustin, ed., *History of Yellow Fever* (New Orleans: Searcy and Pfaff, 1909), 769–780, contains a table showing the years in which yellow fever invaded the seaboard cities of the United States. James Cassedy discussed the broader ecology of disease in the antebellum South in "Medical Men and Ecology in the Old South," in Ronald L. Numbers and Todd L. Savitt, eds., *Science and Medicine in the Old South* (Baton Rouge: Louisiana State University Press, 1989): 166–178.

5. Donald B. Dodd and Wynelle S. Dodd, *Historical Statistics of the South, 1790–1970* (Tuscaloosa: University of Alabama Press, 1973), 2, 18, 26. On the ubiquity of malarial fevers in Alabama, the Southeast, and the Southwest, respectively, see John P. Caffey, "A Thesis on Calomel in Southern Fevers" (M.D. thesis, Medical College of the State of South Carolina, Charleston, 1839), South Carolina Room, Main Library, Medical University of South Carolina, Charleston; Edmund Ravenel, "On the Medical Topography of St.

John's, Berkley, S.C., and Its Relations to Geology," *CMJR* 4 (1849): 697–704; and J. P. Evans, "An Essay on Intermittent and Remittent Fevers," *CMJR* 4 (1849): 675–697.

6. J. C. Nott, "An Examination into the Health and Longevity of the Southern Sea Ports of the United States, with Reference to the Subject of Life Insurance," *Southern Journal of Medicine and Pharmacy* 2 (1847): 15.

7. J. C. Simonds, "The Sanitary Condition of New-Orleans, As Illustrated by Its Mortuary Statistics," *CMJR* 6 (1851): 700–709. Henry E. Sigerist discussed Simonds's work in "The Cost of Illness to the City of New Orleans in 1850," *BHM* 15 (1944): 498–507.

8. Barbara Elizabeth Miller, "Tallahassee and the 1841 Yellow Fever Epidemic" (M.A. thesis, Florida State University, 1976), 5.

9. Diary kept by Dr. [R. F.] McGuire at Monroe, La., 1818–1852, typescript, Special Collections Division, Howard-Tilton Memorial Library, Tulane University, New Orleans, La. The original manuscript of this diary is in the collections of Northeast Louisiana University, Monroe.

10. "Sanitary Surveys and Hygiene," *CMJR* 4 (1849): 478; "Quarantine," *New-Orleans Medical Journal* 1 (1844): 83.

11. [E. D. Fenner,] "Introductory Address," in idem, ed., *Southern Medical Reports* (New Orleans: B. M. Norman; New York: Samuel S. and William Wood, 1850), vol. 1 for 1849, 7–13. John Harley Warner analyzed the reform animus of this effort in "A Southern Medical Reform: The Meaning of the Antebellum Argument for Southern Medical Education," *BHM* 57 (1983): 364–381.

12. J. C. Nott, "Sketch of the Epidemic of Yellow Fever of 1847, in Mobile," *CMJR* 3 (1848): 4. John Duffy described this appraisal in *Sword of Pestilence: The New Orleans Yellow Fever Epidemic of 1853* (Baton Rouge: Louisiana State University Press, 1966), 6–9.

13. Nott, "Health and Longevity," 145. On Nott's life insurance studies see James H. Cassedy, *Medicine and American Growth, 1800–1860* (Madison: University of Wisconsin Press, 1986), 199–203.

14. A. B. Williman, "An Account of the Yellow Fever Epidemic in Norfolk during the Summer of 1855," *CMJR* 11 (1856): 163.

15. The concern of Barton, Fenner, Gaillard, and Simons with endemic urban health problems is evident in their respective contributions to the *First Report of the Committee on Public Hygiene of the American Medical Association* (Philadelphia: T. K. and P. G. Collins, 1849).

16. E. H. Barton, Y. R. Lemonnier, and T. G. Browning, "Annual Report of the Board of Health," *NOMSJ* 6 (1849–50): 665–666; see also Cassedy, *Medicine and American Growth*, 108–113.

17. Waring, *South Carolina*, 2:67 and 104; Blanton, *Nineteenth Century*, 9; Gillson, *Louisiana State Board . . . Formative Years*, 97. J. C. Simonds, "A Memorial to the Legislature of the State of Louisiana, from the Louisiana State Medical Society, and the Physico-Medical Society of New Orleans—with Reference to the Registration of Births, Marriages and Deaths," *NOMSJ* 8 (1851–52): 606–620, is the product of one such futile Louisiana initiative.

18. George R. Grant, "The Vital Statistics and Sanitary Condition of Memphis, Tenn.," *NOMSJ* 8 (1851–52): 690.

19. Ibid., 692, 696.

20. Simonds, "Sanitary Condition," 677–678, 726.

21. Simonds compared average urban mortality rates, ibid., 687, and in "Contributions to the Vital Statistics of New-Orleans, " *CMJR* 5 (1850): 280. He found the following percentages of deaths per year in the time periods indicated for the populations of these cities: (1) New Orleans, 8.1%, 1846–50; (2) Savannah (whites only), 4.1%, 1840–47; (3) Charleston, 2.6%, 1822–48; (4) Baltimore, 2.5%, 1836–49; (5) Philadelphia, 2.5%, 1807–40; (6) Boston, 2.2%, 1830–45.

22. G. A. Smith attacked Grant in "On the Sanitary Condition of Memphis, Tenn.—Being a Reply to Dr. Grant's Paper, Preceding This," *NOMSJ* 8 (1851–52): 706.

23. See, for example, E. H. Barton, *Report to the Louisiana State Medical Society on the Meteorology, Vital Statistics, and Hygiene of the State of Louisiana* (New Orleans: Davies, Son, and Co., 1851), 38; and Joseph Johnston, "Some Accounts of the Origin and Prevention of Yellow Fever in Charleston, S. C.," *CMJR* 4 (1849): 154–169.

24. Quoted in Editor, "[Review of] 'An Act to Establish Quarantine for the Protection of the State:' Approved March 15, 1855," *NOMSJ* 12 (1855–56): 129.

25. Ibid., 132.

26. A. F. Axson, "Reply of the President of the Board of Health to the 'Memorial to the Legislature' Published in the Preceding Number of the N. O. Med. and Surg. Journal," *NOMSJ* 15 (1858): 360–362.

27. A. Mercier, "To the Honorable, the Members of the Senate and House of Representatives of the State of Louisiana, Now in Assembly Convened, at Baton Rouge," *NOMSJ* 15 (1858): 221–252. Mercier claimed that nineteen out of twenty New Orleans physicians supported his position.

28. Gaillard, "Some Points of Hygiene," 292.

29. On Charleston, see Simons, "Epidemic Yellow Fever," 364. Although admittedly praising his own efforts, Simons's evaluation of the improvement of Charleston was not singular. Duffy, *Sword of Pestilence*, 19–20, discussed the New Orleans street cleaning contract.

30. "[Review of] Annual Report of the Board of Health to the Legislature of Louisiana, January, 1860," *New Orleans Medical News and Hospital Gazette* 6 (1859–60): 927.

31. Francis Robbins Allen, "Public Health Work in the Southeast, 1872–1941: The Study of a Social Movement" (Ph.D. dissertation, University of North Carolina at Chapel Hill, 1946), lists the founding dates of southern state boards of health on pp. 25–26. Studies of individual southern state boards not already cited above are W. J. Breeding, "The History of the Tennessee State Health Organization," in Philip Hamer, ed., *The Centennial History of the Tennessee State Medical Association* (Nashville: Tennessee State Medical Association, 1930), 409–447; Marshall Scott Legan, "The Evolution of Public Health Services in Mississippi, 1865–1910" (Ph.D. dissertation, University of Mississippi, 1968); J. W. Roy Norton and Benjamin Drake, "History of Public Health in North Carolina," in Dorothy Long, ed., *Medicine in North Carolina: Essays in the History of Medical Science and Medical Service, 1524–1960* (Raleigh: The North Carolina Medical Society, 1972), 2:581–622; Howard L. Holley, *The History of Medicine in Alabama* (Tuscaloosa: University of Alabama Press, 1982), 267–311 [this chapter is, however, largely repetitive of the Stabler work cited earlier]; George W. Cox, *History of Public Health in Texas* (Austin: Texas

State Department of Health, 1950). On the national public health movement, see Wilson G. Smillie, *Public Health: Its Promise for the Future; A Chronicle of the Development of Public Health in the United States, 1607–1914* (New York: Macmillan, 1955), 284–320.

32. The North Carolina law is quoted in Allen, *Public Health in the Southeast*, p. 42, and Rice is quoted in the same work on p. 43.

33. Elisha Harris outlined the history, goals, and deficiencies of southern boards of health in his "Report on the Public Health Service in the Principal Cities, and the Progress of Sanitary Works in the United States," *APHA Reports* 2 (1874–75): 151–182.

34. John H. Ellis discussed the private philanthropic efforts that focused on sanitation and the care of the sick in "Businessmen and Public Health in the Urban South during the Nineteenth Century: New Orleans, Memphis, and Atlanta," *BHM* 44 (1970): 197–212, 346–371.

35. Robert A. Kinloch to Henry I. Bowditch, ca. March 1876, in "Appendix [consisting of responses to Bowditch's survey]," Henry I. Bowditch, *Public Hygiene in America* (Boston: Little, Brown and Co., 1877), 242. This appendix includes numerous other southern replies.

36. Two detailed histories of southern boards of health that illustrate these problems are John Hubert Ellis, "Yellow Fever and the Origins of Modern Public Health in Memphis, Tennessee, 1870–1900" (Ph.D. dissertation, Tulane University, 1962); Gillson, *Louisiana State Board of Health: The Formative Years*; and idem, *Louisiana State Board of Health: The Progressive Years* (Baton Rouge: Louisiana Health and Human Resources Administration, Division of Health, 1976).

37. One typical example of this sort of invective is found in the *Memphis Daily Avalanche*, 12 January 1879, in this case directed against New Orleans. Some coastal communities charged that while inland states were quick to criticize and urge vigilance, they were less ready to offer any financial support for quarantine. For one such argument, see the *Pensacola Semi-Weekly Gazette*, 4 July 1879.

38. See the state board of health reports and histories of southern boards of health cited elsewhere in these notes.

39. G. B. Thornton, "Memphis Sanitation and Quarantine, 1879 and 1880," *APHA Reports* 6 (1880): 198–199.

40. George Sternberg, "Letter," *Appeal*, 30 September 1880.

41. Rauch to Joseph Toner, 2 November 1879, NBH Reel 4.

42. Howard D. Kramer discussed the various attempts at regional organization in the South during the 1870s in "Agitation for Public Health Reform in the 1870s," *JHMAS* 3 (1948): 473–488; 4 (1949): 75–89.

43. J. D. Plunket, et al., "An Address to the Citizens of the Towns and Villages of the State of Tennessee," *TSBH Report*, 1877–1880, 346.

44. J. M. Woodworth, "A Brief Review of the Organization and Purpose of the Yellow Fever Commission," *APHA Reports* 4 (1877–78): 167–168.

45. J. M. Keating, *A History of the Yellow Fever. The Yellow Fever Epidemic of 1878, in Memphis, Tenn.* (Memphis: Howard Association, 1879), is the standard contemporary source on this epidemic in Memphis. The overwhelming fear that the rapid spread of the fever engendered is well-depicted in the daily journal kept by one minister in northeast Mississippi; see Samuel Agnew's Diary, Vol. 21, Samuel Agnew Papers, Southern Historical Collection.

46. J. P. Davidson, "Report of the Inspection of Morgan City and Surroundings," 8 August 1879, NBH Reel 15. One summary report of sanitary activity in the Mississippi Valley is M. S. Craft to Thomas J. Turner, "Report of Inspection of Y. F. Towns of 1878," ca. 1 September 1879, NBH Reel 15. Numerous inspectors' reports on NBH Reels 14–18 reiterate these findings. Most of the correspondence on these reels is addressed to Turner, who was secretary of the National Board from 1879 to 1882.

47. Many expressions of support for a national quarantine appeared during the winter following the epidemic. Most influential was the *Memorandum* circulated by the American Public Health Association to members of Congress and other public officials (*Memorandum of the American Public Health Association on Legislation Affecting Public Health*, Proceedings of the Select Committee on the Origin, Introduction, and Prevention of Epidemic Disease in the United States, 45th Cong., Legislative and Natural Resources Branch, National Archives and Records Service, Washington, D.C.). The Tennessee and Mississippi boards of health were among the proposal's staunchest supporters. See, for example, Wirt Johnston, et al., "Report of the Delegation from the Mississippi State Board of Health to the American Public Health Association," *APHA Reports* 4 (1877–78): 207–209.

48. Printed in Harvey E. Brown, *Report on Quarantine on the Southern and Gulf Coasts of the United States* (New York: William Wood & Co., 1873), 2.

49. In addition to Kramer, "Agitation for Public Health Reform," and Smillie, *Public Health*, see Bess Furman [in consultation with Ralph C. Williams], *A Profile of the United States Public Health Service 1798–1948* (Washington: Government Printing Office, 1973), 121–149, which contains a detailed account of the Marine Hospital Service–American Public Health Association rivalry over national health authority. Ralph Chester Williams discussed this period more cursorily in *The United States Public Health Service, 1798–1950* (Washington: Commissioned Officers Association of the United States Public Health Service, 1951), 71–74.

50. Comments of Representative Casey Young of Memphis, *Congressional Record*, 45th Cong., 3d Sess., 2264 (1 March 1879). Senator Isham G. Harris, also of Memphis, was the leading Senate spokesman for the bill.

51. *Avalanche*, 11 March 1879.

52. The *Congressional Record*, 45th Cong., 3d Sess., 1826–1856 (24 February 1879) and 2260–2273 (1 March 1879), reported the congressional debate on the "yellow fever bill."

53. *NBH Bulletin* 1 (1879): 1–3.

54. Ibid., 3–7; *NBH Report*, 1879, 5–26.

55. John S. Billings, the vice president of the National Board, vented his frustration over being caught between the expectations of the Treasury Department, which administered the National Board's budget, and the pressure of local boards, in Billings to Henry I. Bowditch, 12 July 1879, Scrapbook, Henry Ingersoll Bowditch Papers, Holmes Hall, Boston Medical Library, Francis A. Countway Library, Boston, Mass. Billings kept a scrapbook (Billings Papers, New York Public Library, New York, N.Y.), in which were glued clippings from northeastern newspapers that chronicle the history of the National Board, especially criticism of it.

56. An excellent account of the opposition to the National Board is found in Peter W. Bruton, "The National Board of Health" (Ph.D. dissertation, University of Maryland, 1974).

57. The medical literature of the 1870s is replete with articles on the etiology and prevention of yellow fever. Dr. Daniel C. Holliday of New Orleans claimed that the majority of New Orleans physicians believed yellow fever to be imported ("Remarks of Dr. D. C. Holliday, of New Orleans, on Yellow Fever, Made before the Baltimore Academy of Medicine at a Special Meeting Held November 26th, 1878," *Maryland Medical Journal* 4 (1879): 203–212), while the editor of the *BMSJ* characterized most physicians as localists ("Yellow Fever," *BMSJ* 99 (1878): 222–224). Another New Orleans physician, H. D. Schmidt, pointed out that the germ theory had not solved the contagionist-anticontagionist debate, because germs could either be local soil inhabitants or be imported ("On the Nature of the Poison of Yellow Fever, and Its Prevention," *New York Medical Journal* 29 (1879): 449–484).

58. J. L. Cabell, "Address in State Medicine and Public Hygiene," *Transactions of the American Medical Association* 29 (1878): 551–583; idem, "Brief Notice of the Rise and Progress of International Hygiene," *APHA Reports* 7 (1881): 16–31. In his 1878 paper Cabell devoted one paragraph to yellow fever and one sentence to quarantine. For a similar expression of the sanitary gospel, see Joseph M. Toner, "A View of Some of the Leading Public Health Questions in the United States," *APHA Reports* 2 (1874–75): 1–40.

59. John S. Billings, "The National Board of Health, and National Quarantine," *Transactions of the American Medical Association* 31 (1880): 435–455.

60. Bowditch to Billings, 2 June 1879, in Bowditch Scrapbook.

61. Turner to Bowditch, 29 May 1879, ibid.

62. Henry I. Bowditch, "Sanitary Organization of Nations," *BMSJ* 102 (1880): 25–30.

63. John S. Billings cautioned the Sanitary Council of the Mississippi Valley, "Don't let quarantine occupy the attention of your council to the exclusion of the securing of municipal cleanliness, which last is the great object to be secured." Billings to John Rauch, 13 July 1879, Records of the National Board of Health, Letters Sent, Vol. 1, Record Group 90, National Archives and Records Service.

64. "Inspection and Purification of Passengers, Baggage, and Freight," *NBH Bulletin* 1 (1879): 41. This article described the inspection and disinfection system of the National Board.

65. For doubts about the power of disinfectants, see *NBH Bulletin* 1 (1879): 39–40, 75–76. An extensive debate on the use of carbolic acid as a disinfectant was reported in "Meeting of Physicians to Discuss Carbolic Acid," *NOMSJ* 3 (1875): 414–440.

66. Printed in *NBH Bulletin* 1 (1879): 39.

67. *NBH Report*, 1879, and *NBH Report*, 1880.

68. J. D. Plunket, "Report of Committee on Yellow Fever in Tennessee during the Summer of 1879," *TSBH Report*, 1877–1880, 345–523. Memphis authorities annually renewed their request for National Board maintenance of the Memphis quarantine station (*MBH Report*, 1881, 10).

69. The product of the National Board's survey is the "Report of the Committee Charged with Making a Sanitary Survey of Memphis, Tennessee, March 1, 1880," Supplement no. 3, of *NBH Bulletin*. Two local accounts of the Memphis work are R. B. Maury, "The Sanitary Measures of Memphis and the Yellow Fever of 1878," *TSBH Report*, 1877–1880, 73–106, and *MBH Report*, 1879. Waring's summary of the Memphis sewer plan is in George E. Waring, Jr., "The Sewering and Draining of Cities," *APHA Reports* 5 (1879): 35–40.

70. Two local newspapers supported Jones in this perception. See the *New Orleans Democrat*, 31 August 1880, and the *Picayune*, 23 August 1881. While Jones spoke often of the "incompetent Yankees" that were interfering in Louisiana affairs, he had also to contend with two well-respected local physicians, Samuel M. Bemiss and Stanford E. Chaillé, who as active National Board associates weakened Jones's rhetoric about "Yankee spies" and "northern ignorance." For more detail on Jones, the National Board, and public health in late nineteenth-century Louisiana, see Duffy, *Matas History*, 2: 459–496.

71. Report of Finance and Conference Committee on National Board of Health Report for 1882, 15 December 1882, p. 15, in Official Records, 1881 [unbound but wrapped and labeled stack of papers], Matas Library.

72. Stanford E. Chaillé, Daily Records and Reports, entry for 20 July 1881, Stanford Emerson Chaillé Papers, Matas Library.

73. John Rauch, "Report Concerning Quarantine at New Orleans," 19 June 1879, NBH Reel 14, provides a good analysis of the shortcomings of the Louisiana quarantine system.

74. A. N. Bell, "Appendix P. Report on Quarantine at New Orleans," *NBH Report*, 1879, 463–467.

75. "Appendix: Dr. F. Formento's [Secretary of the Louisiana Board] Comments on Chaillé's Instructions, Appended by the Louisiana State Board of Health, 19 May 1881," in Supplement no. 15 of the *NBH Bulletin*, 17. This supplement contains a full account of the Ship Island controversy.

76. Jones related his side of the dispute in "Relations of the National and State Boards of Health to the Legal Authorities of the State of Louisiana. Ship Island Quarantine of the National Board of Health, Established by the Central National Authority in Washington," in *LSBH Report*, 1880, 45–63.

77. Jones wrote Billings on 30 April 1879 (NBH Reel 20) suggesting that an investigation of hemorrhagic malarial fever be sponsored by the National Board; it is clear that Jones had himself in mind as one of the project's necessary "quiet, honest, capable observers, activated by a love of truth." Apparently, no action was taken on this proposal. On 14 June 1879 Jones telegraphed Turner that he would "do what lies in my power to promote interests of NBH" (NBH Reel 12). In a letter of 11 July 1879 Jones told Billings that he would not inspect a neighboring town where yellow fever was suspected since his appointment had never been made official (NBH Reel 21). It is not surprising that Jones's later feelings toward the Board were less than amiable, given its members' lack of appreciation for his value as an expert on southern diseases.

78. Stanford Emerson Chaillé, Daily Records and Reports, entry for 20 July 1881.

79. James O. Breeden's biography of Jones's early career (*Joseph Jones, M.D.: Scientist of the Old South* (Lexington: University Press of Kentucky, 1975), characterized Jones as frequently obstinate, overly sensitive and unstable to the point of paranoia. His hypergraphia and frequent public displays of temper even suggest the diagnosis of temporal lobe epilepsy. On the retrospective diagnosis of this disorder see Shahram Khoshbin, "Van Gogh's Malady and Other Cases of Geschwind's Syndrome," *Neurology* 36, Supp. 1 (1986): 213–214.

80. Jerome Cochran et al., "The Memorial of the Board of Health of the State of Alabama," *Transactions of the Medical Association of the State of Alabama* 33 (1880): 124. Cochran had personal reasons to disagree with the National

Board. He went to Memphis as one of its representatives during the epidemic of 1879 to direct the isolation and disinfection of yellow fever patients and their environments. A complicated turn of events led to his activities being repudiated by the National Board. Due largely to poor communication and tact, the National Board made an enemy of an important southern public health figure. Cochran's published account of the Memphis affair is "The Yellow Fever Epidemic of 1879," ibid., 127–132, and many letters from him are found on NBH Reels 15–18.

81. In a 9 April 1880 circular letter to the Presidents and Secretaries of district societies of the Medical Society of New Jersey, Alexander Clendinen, a physician of Fort Lee, New Jersey, urged these societies to provide delegates and support for an upcoming convention that was to design a new representative National Board of Health (Joseph Jones Papers, Tulane University, New Orleans, La.). On 31 March 1880, a "Resolution" by Frank E. Rebarer was passed by the Savannah City Council condemning further congressional support for the National Board, as its centralized administration was unresponsive to local needs. The resolution accompanied a letter from the mayor of Savannah to the mayor of New Orleans, dated 17 April 1880, calling for concerted action ([mss.] Note Book of Joseph Jones, M.D., Board of Health, State of Louisiana—Sanitary and Quarantine Circulars, laws, etc., Correspondence Relating to Sanitary Matters [1880], Matas Library).

82. See, for example, B. F. Gibbs [Medical Inspector, U.S. Navy] to Joseph Toner, 27 October 1879, NBH Reel 4; and Henry Horton to Toner, 29 October 1879, NBH Reel 4. Both men were replying to Toner's survey questioning ways in which the National Board of Health could be improved.

83. NBH Reels 13–14 include numerous letters from midwestern public health authorities written during 1882 that discuss the National Board's smallpox inspection service, and New York's opposition to the plan.

3. DISEASE, DISORDER, AND DEFICIT

1. On the financial condition of Memphis and New Orleans in 1878 see, respectively, Gerald Capers, *The Biography of a River Town; Memphis: Its Heroic Age* (Chapel Hill: The University of North Carolina Press, 1939), and Joy J. Jackson, *New Orleans in the Gilded Age: Politics and Urban Progress, 1880–1896* (Baton Rouge: Louisiana State University Press, for the Louisiana Historical Association, 1969). For a more general view of the impact of Reconstruction on the southern economy, Emory Q. Hawk, *Economic History of the South* (New York: Prentice-Hall, 1934) remains useful. Gavin Wright's review of more recent post-war economic history ("The Strange Career of the New Southern Economic History," *Reviews in American History* 10 (1982): 164–180) demonstrates that the principle preoccupation of southern economic historians has been with issues of agricultural development, especially labor supply and capitalization. The recent literature is less rich on topics in business history, and offers little guidance for this study on how urban commercial and industrial figures wielded influence over municipal and state management.

2. C. Vann Woodward, *Origins of the New South, 1877–1913* (Baton Rouge: Louisiana State University Press, 1951) 20.

3. Jackson, *New Orleans*, p. 5, discussed the rise in cotton exports. In *Sugar*

Country: The Cane Sugar Industry in the South, 1753–1950 (Lexington: University of Kentucky Press, 1953), J. Carlyle Sitterson chronicled the rebirth of the sugar industry after the Civil War. For the history of southern railroads in the 1870s, see John F. Stover, *The Railroads of the South, 1865–1900: A Study in Finance and Control* (Chapel Hill: The University of North Carolina Press, 1955).

4. The best analysis of the "New South" movement is Paul M. Gaston, *The New South Creed: A Study in Southern Mythmaking* (New York: Alfred A. Knopf, 1970). Woodward's *Origins of the New South* remains the best single overall account of the first "New South" period.

5. Alfred L. Thimm, *Business Ideologies in the Reform-Progressive Era, 1880–1914* (Tuscaloosa: The University of Alabama Press, 1976), 90–94, documented the unprecedented appearance of businessmen in the political sphere in the 1880s. David J. Rothman has argued, however, that businessmen who became senators did not unreservedly favor business interests, and that the railroads were generally unsuccessful in their attempts to influence legislation in the 1870s and 1880s (*Politics and Power: The United States Senate, 1869–1901* (Cambridge, Mass.: Harvard University Press, 1966)).

6. Justin Fuller, "Alabama Business Leaders: 1865–1900," *Alabama Review* 16 (1963): 279–286; 17 (1964): 64–73.

7. On business involvement in the Memphis city government, see Robert Sigafoos, *Cotton Row to Beale Street, A Business History of Memphis* (Memphis: Memphis State University Press, 1979). A detailed account of the New Orleans "reform" party is Jackson, *New Orleans*, 55–110. John H. Ellis provides an insightful analysis of businessmen, municipal government in New Orleans and Memphis, and public health, in "Businessmen and Public Health in the Urban South during the Nineteenth Century: New Orleans, Memphis, and Atlanta," *BHM* 44 (1970): 197–212, 346–371.

8. Maxwell Ferguson, *State Regulation of Railroads in the South* (New York: n.p., 1916), detailed the history of the southern regulation movement.

9. *Report of the Howard Association of New Orleans, of Receipts, Expenditures, and Their Work in the Epidemic of 1878, with Names of Contributors* (New Orleans: A. W. Hyatt, 1878), 5–7. The Howard Association was named in honor of John Howard (1726–1790), the English prison and lazaretto reformer. F. Dolhonde (President of the New Orleans Peabody Subsistence Association), in a letter to Enoch Taylor (Secretary of the Citizens Relief Committee of Cincinnati) dated 30 August 1878, described the various relief agencies operating in New Orleans in 1878 and asked support for his organization (Cincinnati Historical Society, Cincinnati, Oh.). An excellent archive of one 1878 relief agency that was active in and near Grenada, Mississippi, is found in the Elizabeth Jones Library in Grenada. The items in this collection make appreciable the tremendous organizational problems incident upon epidemic relief efforts. For a broader view of American philanthropy in this period, see Robert H. Bremner, *American Philanthropy* (Chicago: The University of Chicago Press, 1960).

10. James E. Boyle, *Cotton and the New Orleans Exchange. A Century of Commercial Evolution* (Garden City, N.Y.: The Country Life Press, 1934), 69–72. Robert Wiebe discussed the extension of local business organizations to the national level, and their impact on progressive reforms, in *Businessmen and Reform: A Study of the Progressive Movement* (Cambridge, Mass.: Harvard University Press, 1962), 16–41.

11. Sitterson, *Sugar Country*, 250; H. S. Herring, *A Brief History of a Commercial Exchange: The New Orleans Board of Trade and Some of Its Most Important Activities* (New Orleans: Board of Trade, Ltd., 1930), chronicled the history of the Board of Trade (established 1889) and its predecessors, pp. 3–10.

12. *Picayune*, 22 November 1878. John F. Stover's *American Railroads* (Chicago: University of Chicago Press, 1961), a history of the development of railroads in the United States, revealed the fundamental shift in transportation patterns that the railroad instituted. On the railroad building ferment in Texas in the early 1880s see S. G. Reed, *A History of the Texas Railroads* (Houston: St. Clair Publishing Co., 1941), 518.

13. These sentiments were frequently expressed in the years 1878–1882. A particularly full account of the grievances of the New Orleans businessman is found in the *Picayune*, 22 November 1878.

14. For a discussion of competition in the shipping trade, especially among Mobile, Galveston, and New Orleans, see James P. Baughman, *Charles Morgan and the Development of Southern Transportation* (Nashville: Vanderbilt University Press, 1968), 174–235.

15. *Picayune*, 22 November 1878.

16. *LSBH Report*, 1879, 16–21; G. Farrar Patton, *The Louisiana State Board of Health, Its History and Work* (New Orleans: n.p., 1904), 6–16; *LSBH Reports*, 1870–76.

17. *Picayune*, 5 April 1878; 6 April 1878; 8 April 1878; 9 April 1878.

18. Stanford E. Chaillé, "The Foreign Commerce of New Orleans and the Epidemic of 1878," *NOMSJ* 9 (1881–82): 241–246; the estimate of the Board of Experts was cited in Jo Ann Carrigan, "The Saffron Scourge: A History of Yellow Fever in Louisiana, 1796–1905" (Ph.D. dissertation, Louisiana State University, 1961), 416.

19. Harris to Turner, 3 July 1882, NBH Reel 46.

20. *Picayune*, 22 November 1878.

21. Ibid.

22. Ibid.

23. Dennis East II, "Health and Wealth: Goals of the New Orleans Public Health Movement, 1879–84," *Louisiana History* 9 (1968): 245–275, is a history of the Auxiliary Sanitary Association.

24. Charles A. Whitney, et al., "To the Citizens of New Orleans," 31 March 1879, reprinted in *An Address from the Auxiliary Sanitary Association of New Orleans to the Other Cities and Towns in the Mississippi Valley* (New Orleans: Auxiliary Sanitary Association, 1879), 2–3.

25. *An Address from the Auxiliary Sanitary Association*, 2.

26. Ibid., 7, 9, 16; *Annual Address of Edward Fenner, Vice-President, with Remarks by Charles A. Whitney, President . . . at Regular Meeting of the New Orleans Auxiliary Sanitary Association, November 23, 1880* (New Orleans: New Orleans Democrat, 1880), 15.

27. On the sanitary condition of New Orleans in 1880, see George E. Waring, Jr., and George W. Cable, "New Orleans in 1880," in George E. Waring, Jr., ed., *Report of the Social Statistics of Cities* (Washington: Government Printing Office, 1887), 2:276. Ellis commented on the restriction of New Orleans businessmen to voluntary public health reform activity in "Businessmen and Public Health," 352–356.

28. Chaillé, "Foreign Commerce," 244.

29. *Annual Address of Edward Fenner*, 3.

30. Comments of Edward Fenner, *Proceedings of the New Orleans Auxiliary Sanitary Association, Meeting of November 8th, 1879*, printed pamphlet, Department of Archives and Manuscripts, Library, Louisiana State University, Baton Rouge, La. This pamphlet is unpaginated.

31. Ibid.; *An Address from the Auxiliary Sanitary Association*, 8; Joseph Holt, *The Evil and the Remedy for the Privy System of New Orleans* (New Orleans: L. Graham, 1879).

32. John Rauch, "Report Concerning Quarantine at New Orleans," 19 June 1879, NBH Reel 14.

33. *An Address from the Auxiliary Sanitary Association*, 20; Whitney, "To the Citizens of New Orleans."

34. Edward Fenner, "History of the New Orleans Auxiliary Sanitary Association," *APHA Reports* 7 (1881): 91.

35. *An Address from the Auxiliary Sanitary Association*, 20.

36. To arrive at the percentages of club membership, I compared the list of 210 individuals who signed the Association's first membership roll with the membership lists of the clubs. For the histories of these two clubs see Augusto P. Miceli, *The Pickwick Club of New Orleans* (New Orleans: The Pickwick Press, 1964), and Stuart O. Landry, *History of the Boston Club* (New Orleans: Pelican Publishing Company, 1938). The list's inclusion of prominent businessmen was discovered by matching its names with the leaders mentioned in Herring, *Board of Trade*, and Boyle, *Cotton and the New Orleans Exchange*, as well as Jackson, *New Orleans*, and other sources. East, "Health and Wealth," contains additional information on the commercial and social standing of Association members.

37. Rauch, "Report Concerning Quarantine at New Orleans." S. M. Bemiss described the confusing quarantine situation in a letter to T. J. Turner, 24 May 1879, NBH Reel 20.

38. M. S. Craft to T. J. Turner, 24 August 1879, NBH Reel 15.

39. Whitney, "To the Citizens of New Orleans," 2.

40. Devron to Dr. C. B. White, 15 November 1879, NBH Reel 40.

41. Joseph Jones, "The Relations of Quarantine to Commerce in the Valley of the Mississippi River during a Period of Eight Years, 1880–1887 Inclusive," in idem, *Medical and Surgical Memoirs* (New Orleans: n.p., 1890), 3: 2:285–327, is an extensive discussion of the Morgan case against the Louisiana Board. On Morgan's earlier successes against Mobile and Galveston, see Baughman, *Charles Morgan*, 160, 194.

42. Whitney to Bell, 1 November 1879, NBH Reel 40. Whitney was Charles Morgan's son-in-law. For his biography, see Baughman, *Charles Morgan*.

43. The National Board declared itself in favor of a quarantine based on cleanliness and disinfection, rather than time, in one of its earliest bulletins (*NBH Bulletin* 1 (1879): 40–41). In addition, the Board's inspectors were instructed to carry this message to the towns of the South. See, for example, A. A. Hornor to T. J. Turner, 10 September 1879, NBH Reel 15.

44. Comments of Edward Fenner, *Proceedings of the . . . Association, . . . November 8th, 1879*.

45. "Report of Stanford E. Chaillé, Supervising Inspector, National Board of Health. New Orleans, Louisiana, Oct. 12, 1881," in Supplement No. 15, *NBH Bulletin*, 19 November 1881, is a detailed account of this controversy from the National Board's perspective.

46. Henry G. Hester to President of the National Board of Health, 12 April 1881, contains a copy of the Association's resolutions, from which the quotation was taken.

47. "Report of Stanford E. Chaillé," 3. W. M. Clarke [Secretary of the Tennessee Board of Health] to Editor, *Memphis Daily Appeal*, 16 April 1881, reprinted the New Orleans Chamber of Commerce resolutions supporting the National Board. Hester's 12 April 1881 letter to the National Board's president included the Cotton Exchange's endorsement.

48. Edward Fenner to A. N. Bell, 13 November 1879, NBH Reel 40, was written on stationery with this letterhead. Jones pointed out that his enemy Whitney represented the Morgan company in "Relations of Quarantine," 288.

49. Mitchell to Cabell, 31 March 1881, NBH Reel 26.

50. See, for example, Chaillé, "Foreign Commerce"; S. M. Bemiss, "A Word of Explanation to My Professional Friends," *NOMSJ* 8 (1880–81): 476–482. *Proceedings of the . . . Association . . . November 8th, 1879* reported Chaillé's attendance. Stanford Emerson Chaillé, Daily Records and Reports, entry for 25 June 1881, recorded his $50 subscription "for self and Laura," Matas Library.

51. Joseph Holt, *Quarantine and Commerce, Their Antagonism Destructive to the Prosperity of City and State. A Reconciliation an Imperative Necessity, How This May Be Accomplished. Remarks . . . Before the Representatives of the Exchanges and Other Commercial Bodies* (New Orleans: L. Graham, 1884); and idem, "The Sanitary Protection of New Orleans, Municipal and Maritime," *APHA Reports* 11 (1885): 89–97.

52. Ibid. Also see chapters five and six.

53. These events are discussed in chapters five and six.

54. Gordon E. Gillson, *Louisiana State Board of Health: The Progressive Years* (Baton Rouge: Louisiana Health and Human Resources Administration, Division of Health, 1976), 110–112; Jackson, *New Orleans*, 145–161.

55. *Appeal*, 27 October 1878.

56. *Appeal*, 24 April 1880.

57. *Appeal*, 13 November 1878.

58. Ellis described mercantile involvement in Memphis public health in "Businessmen and Public Health." On public health in Memphis, see John Hubert Ellis [idem], "Yellow Fever and the Origins of Modern Public Health in Memphis, Tennessee, 1870–1900" (Ph.D. dissertation, Tulane University, 1962).

59. The *Appeal* of 25 June 1878 mentioned this earlier interest.

60. *Avalanche*, 1 August 1878.

61. Ellis, "Yellow Fever" thoroughly recounts the experience of Memphis with the 1878 epidemic. See also Thomas H. Baker, "Yellowjack: The Yellow Fever Epidemic of 1878 in Memphis, Tennessee," *BHM* 42 (1968): 241–264.

62. Charles H. McDougal [of Powell, McDougal & Co., Commission Merchants] to Frank H. Lawson, 2 September 1878, Cincinnati Historical Society, Cincinnati, Oh.

63. *Appeal*, 10 May 1879, suggested that Memphis merchants form an Auxiliary Sanitary Association like that of New Orleans to fend off future epidemics with sanitary reform.

64. Quoted in *Appeal*, 22 May 1879.

65. *Avalanche*, 31 May 1879; 4 June 1879; 12 June 1879; 1 July 1879; 3 July 1879; 4 July 1879.

66. Quoted in *Avalanche*, 25 June 1879.

67. *MBH Report*, 1879, 33.

68. For one such discussion of the connection of sewage reform with the prevention of yellow fever, see *Appeal*, 21 October 1879.

69. *Avalanche*, 23 September 1879.

70. *Avalanche*, 9 November 1879.

71. *TSBH Report*, 1877–1880, 388.

72. Ibid., 408; pp. 408–451 is a full history of this controversy.

73. E. M. Wight to T. J. Turner, 19 September 1879, NBH Reel 16.

74. *Avalanche*, 6 September 1879; 20 September 1879. See also *Appeal*, 6 September 1879; 28 September 1879; 4 October 1879.

75. *Avalanche*, 3 October 1879.

76. *Appeal*, 18 November 1879.

77. *Appeal*, 6 September 1879.

78. *TSBH Report*, 1877–80, 408–451.

79. Memphis Cotton Exchange, *Proceedings with Reference to the Public Health* (Memphis: Price Jones & Co., 1880), 4–5.

80. Remarks of Dr. Saunders, ibid., 6.

81. Maury Klein, "Southern Railroad Leaders, 1865–1893: Identities and Ideologies," *Business History Review* 42 (1968): 288–310.

82. Robert H. Wiebe, *The Search for Order: 1877–1920* (New York: Hill and Wang, 1967), xiii.

83. Stover, *Railroads of the South*, 122–154. Clarke is mentioned frequently in John F. Stover, *History of theIllinois Central Railroad* (New York: Macmillan, 1975), and a collection of his letters was printed in Thomas C. Cochran, *Railroad Leaders 1845–1890: The Business Mind in Action* (Cambridge, Mass.: Harvard University Press, 1953), 292–302. On Charles Whitney, see Baughman, *Charles Morgan*, 123–133.

84. Stover, *Railroads of the South*, 124.

85. Maury Klein, *History of the Louisville & Nashville Railroad* (New York: Macmillan, 1972), 151–152; idem, "The Strategy of the Southern Railroads," *American Historical Review* 73 (1968): 1052–1068.

86. Yellow fever also provided, however, an opportunity for public relations gestures whose purpose was to reform the public image of the railroads as evil monopolies. One railroad executive wrote another in the midst of the 1878 epidemic, "I have telegraphed you this morning suggesting a vote by the Board authorizing a contribution to the yellow fever sufferers. It will no doubt be of great benefit to us. What little has been done already by *your* Board has been extensively published." William K. Ackerman to William Osborn, 20 August 1878, printed in Cochran, *Railroad Leaders*, 239–240. Both men managed Illinois railroads.

87. Burke to Mitchell, 3 November 1880, in Memphis Cotton Exchange, *Proceedings*, 10–11.

88. Storm to Mitchell, 1 November 1880, printed in Memphis Cotton Exchange, *Proceedings*, 12.

89. James O'Neal to T. J. Turner, 9 November 1880, printed in *NBH Bulletin* 2 (1881): 689. That his letter is so strikingly close in wording to that of railroad manager Burke is curious; perhaps both were following a model submitted by Mitchell to those company officials from whom he sought letters of support.

90. Clarke to Turner, 27 April 1880, NBH Reel 40.

4. THE SEARCH FOR CONFIDENCE

1. Circular letter, S. S. Herrick [Secretary, Louisiana State Board of Health] to Dear Sir, 16 April 1884, MHS Records, LSBH. The resolutions were reprinted with favorable editorial comment in "The Policy of the New State Board of Health of Louisiana," *NOMSJ* 11 (1883–84): 876–877.

2. "Louisiana State Board of Health," *NOMSJ* 11 (1883–84): 890–896, is the published report on the proceedings of the meeting, and includes Holt's address. The quotation is from p. 891.

3. Joseph Holt, "The Sanitary Relief of New Orleans," *NOMSJ* 14 (1885–86): 444.

4. [G. Farrar Patton,] *The Louisiana State Board of Health, Its History and Work* (New Orleans: n.p., 1904), 23–27.

5. Circular letter, Holt to Dear Sir, 12 May 1884, MHS Records, LSBH.

6. The *NOMSJ* reported, for example, "We are pleased to chronicle the fact that perfect harmony and *entente cordiale* characterized all the proceedings" ("Conference of State Boards of Health," 12 (1884–85): 26–27). On the conference's treatment of national health agency representatives, see John Godfrey [to John Hamilton], 5 June 1884, MHS Records, Ship Is. Stat.

7. G. B. Thornton, quoted by G. P. Conn, chairman, in "Report of the Committee on State Boards of Health," *APHAReports* 11 (1885): 387–388.

8. Joseph Holt, "The Sanitary Protection of New Orleans, Municipal and Maritime," *APHA Reports* 11 (1885): 89.

9. Godfrey [to Hamilton], 5 June 1884, MHS Records, Ship. Is. Stat.

10. Jerome Cochran, "The Proper Relation of Federal, State and Municipal Quarantines," in *ASBH Report*, 1894, 28. R. D. Murray, "The Mexican-Texas Epidemic," *MHS Report*, 1883, 271–334, is a report on the Service's activities in Brownsville.

11. James L. Cabell presented the National Board of Health perspective in "A Plea for the Continuance of the Powers and Duties of the National Board of Health," *Sanitarian* 12 (1884): 396–411. The official Marine Hospital Service account was R. C. White, "The Florida Epidemic," *MHS Report*, 1883, 335–358. A letter from R. D. Murray to Hamilton (12 November 1883, MHS Records, Ship Is. Stat.), reveals in more depth the impact of complex local public health politics on the struggle between the two national agencies. For another viewpoint on the Pensacola epidemic, see Jerome Cochran, Report on Yellow Fever and Quarantine: Visit to Pensacola in 1882, William Henry Sanders Papers, Alabama State Archives, Montgomery, Ala.

12. A. N. Bell, for example, attacked the epidemic control methods of the Marine Hospital Service in "The U.S. Marine Hospital Service and Quarantine," *Sanitarian* 12 (1884): 324–331. Hamilton's *Reports* for 1883 through 1887 amply described the Service's experience with yellow fever during those years, and the measures used against it.

13. Jerome Cochran, et al. [Members of the Alabama State Board of

Health,] The Memorial of the Board of Health of the State of Alabama, 24 April 1883, MHS Records, ASBH; Cochran to the Secretary of the Treasury, 30 May 1883, ibid.; and Cochran to Hamilton, 3 July 1883, ibid., all importuned the Marine Hospital Service to leave the Gulf Quarantine Station on Ship Island and to improve it according to the Holt standard.

14. R. D. Murray to General [Hamilton], 8 July 1883, MHS Records, Ship Is. Stat. "The New Quarantine System of Our State Board of Health," *NOMSJ* 13 (1885–86): 137–140, described the quarantine tour conducted by Holt for invited public health officials and the media that Murray recorded in his letter.

15. Holt to Cochran, 24 September 1886, Sanders Papers. These events are chronicled in "The Biloxi Fever," *NOMSJ* 14 (1886–87): 298; "The Biloxi Fever," ibid., 391–393; Joseph Holt, *Outbreak of Yellow Fever at Biloxi, Harrison Co., Miss. and Its Relation to Inter-state Notification* (New Orleans: n.p., 1886). The Mississippi State Board of Health perspective on the Biloxi affair was presented in *MSBH Report*, 1886–87, 10–27.

16. Felix Formento, letter to the editors, 15 September 1886, in "Correspondence [on Biloxi Fever]," *NOMSJ* 14 (1886–87): 289. Shortly thereafter R. D. Murray diagnosed a case of yellow fever on a ship that had passed through the Louisiana quarantine station nearly a month earlier. Holt believed that Murray intended to discredit him personally, and wrote to both Murray and Hamilton decrying the petty act (Holt to Murray, 24 September 1886, MHS Records, Ship Is. Stat; Holt to Hamilton, 25 September 1886, MHS Records, LSBH). His bitter letter surprised Murray, who had heretofore considered Holt a friend. When Murray responded, he confessed himself "in the dark as to what impulses you are temporarily governed by," and then proceeded to defend the security of Ship Island's quarantine procedures (Murray to Holt [copy], 26 September 1886, MHS Records, Ship Is. Stat.).

17. J. L. Posey, "Yellow Fever at MacClenny, Fla.," *MHS Report*, 1889, 96.

18. On the 1887 and 1888 epidemics see *MHS Report*, 1887; ibid., 1888; Wirt Johnston, "The Outbreak of Yellow-Fever at Jackson, Mississippi, in September, 1888," *APHA Reports* 14 (1888): 51–54; W. E. Forest, "The Cost of Yellow Fever Epidemics—The Epidemic at Decatur, Ala., in 1888," *Medical Record* 35 (1889): 620–626; John P. Wall, "Observations on Yellow Fever, with Special Reference to Diagnosis, Prognosis and Treatment," *Proceedings of the Florida Medical Association*, 1888, 41–49.

19. Charles S. Adams, ed., *Report of the Jacksonville Auxiliary Sanitary Association of Jacksonville, Florida. Covering the Work of the Association during the Yellow Fever Epidemic, 1888* (Jacksonville: Executive Committee of the Association, 1889), is the best account of the epidemic. For a grasp of the immense bureaucratic tangle created by the epidemic, see the Correspondence of Dr. Joseph Porter as Surgeon in Charge of the Government Relief Measures for the Yellow Fever Epidemic in Jacksonville, 1888, Record Group 894, Florida Board of Health Papers, Florida State Archives, State Library, Tallahassee, Fla. See also Albert V. Hardy and May Pynchon, *Millstones and Milestones: Florida's Public Health from 1889* (Jacksonville: Florida State Board of Health Monograph Series, No. 7, 1964), 8–12.

20. Faget to Joseph Jones, 22 October 1888, Joseph Jones Papers, Manuscripts Department, Special Collections Division, Howard-Tilton Memorial Library, Tulane University, New Orleans, La.

21. Jerome Cochran, "Problems in Regard to Yellow-Fever and the Prevention of Yellow-Fever Epidemics," *APHA Reports* 14 (1888): 41–50.

22. MHS Records, Jacksonville, contains numerous letters in reference to the disinfection effort. D. Echemedia [Chief of the Disinfecting Corps] to Porter, 30 January 1889, ibid., is a concise summary of the disinfection routine and results.

23. Joseph Y. Porter, "Looking Backward over Fifty Years of Health Work in Florida," *Journal of the Florida Medical Association* 12 (1925–26): 40, is a positive appraisal of the disinfection work; "Yellow Fever Epidemic of 1887 and 1888 in Florida—Testimony of Dr. George Troup Maxwell.—Correspondence with Prof. Joseph Jones, M.D., of New Orleans, Louisiana," *Virginia Medical Monthly* 16 (1889–90): 266–286, presented the opposite point of view. Henry Ingersoll Bowditch was a vocal critic of the Service's handling of the 1888 epidemic, and in *MHS Report*, 1888, pp. 47–51, Hamilton both reported and rebutted his attacks. Hamilton's particular pride in the 1888–89 disinfection campaign was evident in *MHS Report*, 1890, 86–87.

24. J. Berrien Lindsley, "Proceedings of the Quarterly Meeting of the State Board of Health, October 16th, 1888," *[Tenn.] State Board of Health Bulletin* 4 (1888): 41.

25. "That Quarantine," *NOMSJ* 16 (1888–89): 311–313; *LSBH Report*, 1888–89, 30–31, 61.

26. *LSBH Report*, 1888–89, 30–31. A letter from Annie to Sa, 7 September 1888 (Robert O. Butler Papers, Department of Archives and Manuscripts, Library, Louisiana State University, Baton Rouge, La.), written from somewhere near New Orleans, described the frustrating experiences of family members attempting to travel through the South in the fall of 1888.

27. Forest, "Cost of Yellow Fever," 620.

28. John H. Rauch, "Yellow-Fever Panics and Useless Quarantines—Limitation by Temperature and Altitude," *APHA Reports* 14 (1888): 138.

29. Forest, "Cost of Yellow Fever," 620–621.

30. Benjamin Lee, "Do the Sanitary Interests of the United States Demand the Annexation of Cuba?" *APHA Reports* 15 (1889): 47–52.

31. Ibid. Jerome Cochran likewise called attention to Cuba as the greatest source of danger to the Gulf coast ("How to Prevent the Invasion of Our Gulf Ports by Yellow Fever," *Alabama Medical and Surgical Age* 3 (1890–91): 267–277).

32. Comments of John Guiteras, Minute Book of the Medical Society of South Carolina, 1881–97, Minutes for 1 December 1888, South Caroliniana Library, University of South Carolina, Columbia. John Guiteras, a Cuban who became prominent in the island's public health administration in the first decade of the twentieth century, should not be confused with G. M. Guiteras, a Marine Hospital Service surgeon and authority on yellow fever. Joseph Porter described conditions at Key West in *FSBH Report*, 1890, 25–26.

33. "Yellow Fever in Florida," *NOMSJ* 16 (1888–89): 223–224.

34. McIver to Mom McMaster, 18 July 1888, George McMaster Papers, South Caroliniana Library.

35. J. R. Bratton, "Report from the South Carolina State Board of Health," *APHA Reports* 16 (1890): 176–180; Lucien F. Salomon, "The Louisiana Quarantine System and Its Contemplated Improvement," *APHA Reports* 14 (1888): 110–115; "Lesson Not Lost," *[Tenn.] State Board of Health Bulletin* 4 (1889): 125.

36. J. Berrien Lindsley, report of the secretary in "Proceedings of the Quarterly Meeting of the State Board of Health, January 8 and 9, 1889," *[Tenn.] State Board of Health Bulletin* 4 (1889): 108.

37. *FSBH Report*, 1890, 3–5, 18; Joseph Porter to Hamilton, 17 February 1889, MHS Records, Jacksonville; J. E. Ingraham to Porter, 4 December 1888, Correspondence to Joseph Porter, 1888; R. P. Daniel to Porter, 16 October 1889, Florida Board of Health Records; ibid., 28 October 1889; Porter to Daniel, 9 November 1889, ibid.

38. See note 37.

39. *MHS Report*, 1889, 10–16.

40. J. C. LeHardy, "The Rational Method of Preventing Yellow Fever Epidemics on the South Atlantic Coast," *Transactions of the Medical Association of Georgia* (1889): 51.

41. R. P. Daniel [president, Florida State Board of Health] to Robert Rutherford [state health officer of Texas], undated copy, ca. November, 1889, Florida Board of Health Papers.

42. *FSBH Report*, 1891, 35. For the Louisiana perspective, see *LSBH Report*, 1890–91, 32–48.

43. The House of Representatives debate concerning the measure was recorded in *Congressional Record*, 50th Cong., 2d. Sess., 2129–2132 (20 February 1889). The bill's sponsor withdrew it at the end of the session. For a spectrum of opinions on the department of public health bills, see, for example, H. P. Walcott, "National Health Legislation and Quarantine," *BMSJ* 127 (1892): 307–308; "A New National Board of Health Proposed," *Maryland Medical Journal* 12 (1884–85): 142–143; "The Present Condition of National Health Legislation," *Medical Record* 28 (1885): 490–491; "A Bureau of Public Health," *Memphis Medical Monthly* 9 (1889): 33–37; "A National Quarantine Bureau," *NOMSJ* 16 (1888–89): 378–381; "The Marine-Hospital Service and the Proposed National Bureau of Health," *New York Medical Journal* 47 (1888): 324; and "The National Board of Health?" *Sanitarian* 20 (1888): 358–360.

44. A. Hunter Dupree described the drive for a national department of science in *Science in the Federal Government: A History of Policies and Activities to 1940* (Cambridge, Mass.: Harvard University Press, 1957), 215–231.

45. *MHS Report*, 1888, 12–14.

46. Walter Wyman, "Government Aids to Public Health," *JAMA* 15 (1890): 1–4.

47. N. S. Davis, "The American Medical Association and Its Relations to Public Health," *JAMA* 13 (1889): 125; J. Berrien Lindsley, "Popular Progress in State Medicine," *JAMA* 13 (1889): 45.

48. Cochran to Wyman, 10 October 1892, MHS Records, ASBH.

49. "National Quarantine," *NOMSJ* 20 (1892–93): 526–530; J. M. Byron, "Asiatic Cholera at Lower Quarantine in 1892," *Transactions of the New York Academy of Medicine* n.s. 9 (1893): 289–299.

50. On the efforts for a national department/bureau of health in the early 1890s, see H. P. Walcott, et al., "Report of Standing Committee on National Health Legislation," *APHA Reports* 18 (1892): 409–410; "National Health-Organization," *Medical News* 61 (1892): 739–740; "The Senate Quarantine Bill," *Medical News* 62 (1893): 79; "A National Board of Health," *Medical Record* 41 (1892): 661–662.

51. *MHS Report*, 1893, 1:265–271. The 1893 law superceded another bill, passed in 1890, which had given the Marine Hospital Service the power to make regulations concerning interstate quarantine when cholera, yellow fever, smallpox, or plague had already gained entrance into the United States. The Service found the law vague and difficult to enforce, and its provisions were made superfluous by the clarity and strength of the 1893 law. The 1893 act also officially repealed the legislation that created the National Board of Health, thus making its destruction final, although the board had been without funding and hence practically non-existent for years.

52. Report from the Harris Committee, read into the *Congressional Record*, 52d Cong., 2d Sess., 436–437 (9 January 1893). "Draft of a Proposed Bill to Establish a Bureau of Public Health," *Sanitarian* 31 (1893): 148–150, reprinted the most popular of the bureau of public health bills.

53. Comments of Marriott Brosius of Pennsylvania, *Congressional Record*, 52d Cong., 2d Sess., 798 (23 January 1893).

54. Comments of Amos Cummings of New York, ibid., 799.

55. Comments of Antony, ibid., 795.

56. Comments of White, ibid., 435.

57. *LSBH Report*, 1892–93, 18.

58. *LSBH Report*, 1892–93, 18–37, discussed this legislation; quotations are from pp. 19, 21, and 30.

59. S. R. Olliphant to Cochran, 9 September 1894, Sanders Papers. Other letters in this collection from Olliphant to Cochran elaborated on the former's attitude toward Marine Hospital Service meddling.

60. *LSBH Report*, 1892–93, 54–55. Perhaps in retaliation, that fall Olliphant questioned the effectiveness of the disinfection procedures in force at the Marine Hospital Service's Gulf Quarantine Station, and detained a vessel from there for observation as a sign of his distrust of the federal agency's thoroughness (Olliphant to G. M. Guiteras, 3 September 1894, MHS Records, Ship Is. Stat.; *MHS Report*, 1892, 69–70).

61. *FSBH Report*, 1895–96, 5. *MHS Report*, 1896, 938–939, described the strained relations between the Service and the Florida Board of Health. W. F. Brunner, health officer of Savannah, warned Wyman in a letter of 25 February 1896 (MHS Records, Savannah, Ga.) that Florida public health officials were plotting against the Marine Hospital Service, and would carry their fight into Congress.

62. Cochran, "The Proper Relation," 29.

63. *MHS Report*, 1896, 1042–1046; U. O. B. Wingate, "Some Thoughts Relative to Sanitary Legislation," *APHA Reports* 22 (1896): 138–142. Cochran's position was perhaps influenced by George Sternberg's opinion communicated in a letter of 12 July 1894 (Sanders Papers) that "there is no chance of any bill for a National Health Bureau passing this session. The idea of securing a cabinet minister is not likely to lead to any results and the Am. Med. Ass'n. is wasting its ammunition." Sternberg went on to recommend the less ambitious New York Academy Bill.

64. *MHS Report*, 1896, 948–954; *MHS Report*, 1897, 510–537; *MSBH Report*, 1896–97, 3–39. Marshall Scott Legan, "The Evolution of Public Health Services in Mississippi, 1865–1910" (Ph.D. dissertation, University of Mississippi, 1968), 84–107, is a more detailed account of the Ship Island controversy.

65. *MHS Report*, 1897, 528, 580; Edmond Souchon, "True Origin of the Epidemic of Yellow Fever," *JAMA* 35 (1900): 308–310.

66. "The Opinion of the Quarantine Officer of the Louisiana State Board of Health," *JAMA* 29 (1897): 974–975.

67. *MHS Report*, 1898, 532.

68. *MHS Report*, 1897, 580–621; *MHS Report*, 1898, 529–530; "Yellow Fever Situation," *NOMSJ* 50 (1897–98): 263–266. The New Orleans papers reported extensively on the disputed epidemic in Ocean Springs, and the subsequent region-wide epidemic. See, for example, the *Picayune*, 24 August 1897; *Times-Democrat*, 5 September 1897, 6 September 1897, 7 September 1897. Clippings from these and other papers on public health matters were pasted into the Louisiana Board of Health Official Scrapbook, 1894–1897, Matas Library.

69. *LSBH Report*, 1896–97, 24–43.

70. "The Yellow Scourge at Work," *Memphis Medical Monthly* 17 (1897): 471–472; "Dengue or Yellow Fever?" *NOMSJ* 50 (1897–98): 309–311. On Guiteras's ideas about the mixed nature of the epidemic, see the *Picayune*, 10 September 1897.

71. *Picayune*, 13 September 1897.

72. "Report of Senate Committee on the Foregoing Bill (S. 2680) and Also upon Senate Bills 1703 and 2343," *MHS Report*, 1898, 754.

73. Comments of Caffery, *Congressional Record*, 55th Cong., 2d Sess., 3091 (22 March 1898).

74. "The Gulf Quarantine Muddle," *Memphis Medical Monthly* 17 (1897): 279–281; *Ocean Springs Progress*, 15 June 1898.

75. *Times-Democrat*, 12 September 1897.

76. *FSBH Report*, 1897, 4.

77. *LSBH Report*, 1896–97, 18–22.

78. "The Cost of Yellow Fever," *JAMA* 29 (1897): 867.

79. Mobile *Sunday Item*, 2 January 1898; *Picayune*, 5 December 1897. Henry R. Carter of the Marine Hospital Service stated that many of the quarantines were commercially motivated, otherwise the "remarkable spectacle [that] was presented of places thoroughly infected quarantining against other places infected to a greater or lesser degree" was hard to comprehend. Carter reported that some merchants took advantage of quarantines to move large or old stocks of goods. Although some exorbitant profits were thereby made, the deficits of 1897 far outweighed the gains (H. R. Carter, "Report of Sanitary Work of Marine-Hospital Service in Southern Louisiana and in Montgomery, Ala.—Epidemic of 1897," *MHS Report*, 1897, 626).

80. Extracts from editorials published in newspapers throughout the country were read into the *Congressional Record* (55th Cong., 2d Sess., 3359–3376 (30 March 1898)).

81. "The Public Health Bills before Congress," *Philadelphia Medical Journal* 1 (1898): 39; "The Marine Hospital Service and National Quarantine," *New England Medical Monthly* 17 (1898): 128.

82. "A Bill to Establish a Department of Public Health and to Define Its Duties," *JAMA* 29 (1897): 751–754.

83. "Report of Senate Committee," 752.

84. "The National Government and the Public Health," *New York Medical Journal* 66 (1897): 876–877.

85. "The Department of Public Health Bill," *Georgia Journal of Medicine and Surgery* 1 (1897): 65.

86. "Report of Senate Committee," 753.

87. "Report of House Committee on House Bill 4363," *MHS Report*, 1898, 766–771.

88. Comments of Mallory, *Congressional Record*, 55th Cong., 2d Sess., 2922 (17 March 1898). The text of the Caffery Bill was printed in *MHS Report*, 1898, 749–752.

89. *FSBH Report*, 1897, 41.

90. R. M. Swearingen, "The Relation of Federal to State Quarantine," *Sanitarian* 39 (1897): 427–434.

91. See, for example, the postponement of debate on the bill on 17 March 1898 (*Congressional Record*, 55th Cong., 2d Sess., 2916).

92. *LSBH Report*, 1897–98, 27–29; "The Quarantine Convention in Mobile," *NOMSJ* 50 (1897–98): 539–541; "A Quarantine Convention," ibid., 542–545; "The Quarantine Controversy," *Memphis Medical Monthly* 18 (1898): 137–139.

93. *LSBH Report*, 1898–99, 35–37; *MHS Report*, 1898, 544–578; *MSBH Report*, 1897–1899, 8–111.

94. "Epidemics," *BMSJ* 139 (1898): 658.

95. *FSBH Report*, 1898, 4.

96. Ibid., 7–18.

97. Charles Dabney to George Ramsey, 23 November 1898, George Ramsey Papers, Duke University Library, Durham, N.C.

98. See, for example, the Resolutions of the Board of Health of City of New Orleans, 6 February 1899, in the Minutes of the Louisiana State Board of Health, 30 August 1898–29 December 1902, Matas Library, for one such plea to the federal government to clean up Havana.

5. THE LAST CAMPAIGN

1. J. A. Tabor, "Sanitation and Isolation As a Means of Prevention and Eradication of Yellow Fever," *Journal of the Mississippi State Medical Association* 3 (1899–1900): 797.

2. W. C. Gorgas, "The Practical Mosquito Work Done at Havana, Cuba, Which Resulted in the Disappearance of Yellow Fever from That Locality," *Washington Medical Annals* 2 (1903–04): 170–180; idem, *A Few General Directions with Regard to Destroying Mosquitoes, Particularly the Yellow Fever Mosquito* (Washington: Government Printing Office, 1904). L. O. Howard, a leading American entomologist who worked in the Department of Agriculture, provided Gorgas and Reed with essential information on the life cycle and behavior of mosquitoes. His ideas were codified in a book that became a manual for malaria and yellow fever control (*Mosquitoes: How They Live; How They Carry Disease; How They Are Classified; How They May be Destroyed* (New York: McClure, Phillips & Co., 1901)).

3. *Picayune*, 9 June 1903.

4. *Times-Democrat*, 18 September 1901. Quitman Kohnke, "Report of the Board of Health of the City of New Orleans," *LSBH Report*, 1900–01, 2:6–254, on pp. 46–56, outlined the anti-mosquito efforts of 1901. The *Picayune*

(19 August, 20 August, 23 August, and 30 August 1901) gave a good day-by-day account of Kohnke's first campaign.

5. *Times-Democrat*, 12 November 1901.

6. "Down with the Mosquitoes!" *NOMSJ* 55 (1902–03): 102–104, printed the medical society's resolutions on p. 103; for the report of the society's mosquito committee, which studied the mosquitoes of New Orleans, see *Transactions of the Orleans Parish Medical Society*, 1901, 151–228. The Progressive Union of New Orleans also supported the anti-mosquito plans (*Times-Democrat*, 8 June 1902).

7. *Times-Democrat*, 23 January 1902 and 24 April 1902; "Down with the Mosquitoes!" 104; Quitman Kohnke, "Mosquito Destruction in New Orleans," in *LSBH Report*, 1902–03, 2:139–164.

8. *New Orleans States*, 17 April 1903. Examples of cartoons are in *New Orleans Item*, 6 May 1902, and *Picayune*, 14 September 1902.

9. Letter from Dr. William Hencks, *Picayune*, 26 June 1903. For other claims, see *Times-Democrat*, 7 September 1902, and *New Orleans Item*, 12 September 1902.

10. The quotation is from "Biennial Report of Board of Health of the City of New Orleans," *LSBH Report*, 1902–03, 2:166. It prefaced a comment on the satisfaction Kohnke felt in seeing Laredo finally adopt a screening ordinance during their epidemic. The *Times-Democrat* reported on the anti–improvement league (15 June 1903), while the *Picayune* (25 and 26 June 1903) also provided details on the council fight.

11. Walter Reed and James Carroll, "The Prevention of Yellow Fever," in *Yellow Fever: A Compilation of Various Publications. Results of the Work of Maj. Walter Reed . . . and the Yellow Fever Commission* (Washington: Government Printing Office, 1911), 131–148. See also V. Havard's frequently cited, and more detailed, quarantine prescriptions based on the mosquito theory, in *The Transmission and Prevention of Yellow Fever* (Havana: Sanitary Department, 1902).

12. Joseph Waldauer, "The Efficacy of Quarantine and Fumigation in the Prevention of the Spread of Yellow Fever without Molesting the Mosquito," *American Medicine* 2 (1901): 534. It was not unusual for physicians to argue, when presented with a new explanation for the transmission of a particular disease, that instead of abandoning the old view it was more prudent to accept both until further evidence was gathered.

13. "Quarantine and Yellow Fever," *Sanitarian* 47 (1901): 143–144; A. N. Bell, "Fomites and Yellow Fever," *APHA Reports* 27 (1901): 144–151.

14. John Purnell, "The Mosquito As Insignificant Factor in the Propagation of Yellow Fever," *Philadelphia Medical Journal* 8 (1901): 189–193. J. B. Lindsley, "Quarantine Regulations Should Be Based against Yellow Fever upon the Doctrine that It Is Only Conveyed by the Mosquito," *APHA Reports* 29 (1903): 81–90, discussed the reluctance among many public health workers, including those of the Marine Hospital Service, to ignore fomites. Lindsley surveyed southern public health officials on their opinions about Reed's work, and published many of their replies in this article.

15. Quoted in Lindsley, "Quarantine Regulations," 86. Hunter's reply is on p. 87.

16. Ibid., 86.

17. *LSBH Report*, 1902–03, 91–92. The discussion of this resolution is

found in the manuscript Minutes of the Louisiana State Board of Health, 17 February 1903–10 June 1908, entry for 26 May 1902, Matas Library.

18. Comments of J. J. Archinard following paper by Arthur Nolte, "The Progress of Rational Quarantines," *Transactions of the Louisiana State Medical Society,* 1903, 224.

19. Comments of Arthur Nolte, ibid., 226.

20. Reed to Gorgas, 14 May 1902, William Crawford Gorgas Papers, Manuscripts Collection, University of Alabama, University.

21. S. B. Grubbs, "A Note on Mosquitoes in Baggage," *Yellow Fever Institute Bulletin* #6, March 1902, 1–6.

22. A. H. Doty, "To What Extent Are Infected Mosquitoes Present on Shipboard?" *APHA Reports* 32 (1906): 1:44–51; idem, "Are Vessels Infected with Yellow Fever? A Reply to Dr. Carter," *Medical Record* 62 (1902): 894–895; Henry R. Carter, "Are Vessels Infected with Yellow Fever? Some Personal Observations," *Medical Record* 61 (1902): 441–444.

23. The bill was printed in the *Congressional Record,* 57th Cong., 1st Sess., 7525 (27 June 1902).

24. Edward Souchon to the Louisiana State Board of Health, 18 March 1902 and 1 April 1902, Matas Library; *LSBH Report,* 1902–03, 82–83.

25. Senate Report 1531, printed in *Congressional Record,* 57th Cong., 1st Sess., 7758 (1 July 1902).

26. On northern support for section 7 and a national department of health bill, see, for example, *Nineteenth Report of the State Board of Health and Vital Statistics of Minnesota, 1901–1902* (St. Paul: Pioneer Press, 1902), 287–302; and *Nineteenth Report of the State Board of Health of Wisconsin, 1901–1902* (Madison: Democrat Printing Co., 1903), 91–95.

27. Comments of Henry D. Clayton, *Congressional Record,* 57th Cong., 1st Sess., 7758 (1 July 1902).

28. Comments of William Richardson, ibid., 7756.

29. Comments of David DeArmond, ibid., 7757.

30. Comments of James R. Mann, ibid., 7756–7757.

31. Telegrams from Souchon and Tabor about the danger of Mexican yellow fever were printed in *MHS Report,* 1904, 236.

32. Wyman to G. M. Guiteras, 25 September 1903, ibid., 255.

33. G. M. Guiteras, "The Yellow Fever Epidemic of 1903 at Laredo, Texas," *JAMA* 43 (1904): 115.

34. G. M. Guiteras, "Report of the Epidemic of Yellow Fever of 1903 at Laredo, Minera, and Cannel, Tex.," *MHS Report,* 1904, 303–325.

35. Ibid., 311–312.

36. Ames to the Adjutant Post, 6 December 1903, Roger Post Ames Letterbook, 1903, Matas Library. Other letters in this collection to the Chief Surgeon, Department of Texas, U.S. Army, and to the Surgeon General of the Army, described his experiences during the epidemic.

37. See, for example, James Carroll, "Lessons to Be Learned from the Present Outbreak of Yellow Fever in Louisiana," *JAMA* 45 (1905): 1079–1080.

38. A typical example of such anti-mosquito ordinances is Public Health and Marine Hospital Service, *How to Prevent Yellow Fever—No Mosquitoes, No Yellow Fever,* 31 July 1905, printed broadside, Matas Library.

39. The *Picayune,* 2 August 1905, reported the ordinance's passage. It is printed in Augustin, *Yellow Fever,* 1100–1101. The *Times-Democrat,* 18 August

1905, commented favorably on the incarceration of offenders. The decision to quarantine New Orleans was recorded in the Louisiana Board of Health Minutes, entries for 24 July and 28 July 1905. In addition to Souchon's account in the *LSBH Report*, 1905–06, other perspectives on the epidemic are S. L. Theard, "New Orleans Yellow Fever in 1905," in Augustin, *Yellow Fever*, 1093–1099; Louis G. LeBeuf, "The Work of the Medical Profession of New Orleans during the Epidemic of 1905," ibid., 1060–1077; and Charles Chassaignac, "Some Lessons Taught by the Epidemic of 1905," ibid., 1049–1059.

40. Quitman Kohnke, "The Sanitary Prevention of Yellow Fever," in Augustin, *Yellow Fever*, 1135.

41. Advisory Committee of the Orleans Parish Medical Society to the City Board of Health, 4 August 1905, printed in LeBeuf, "Work of the Medical Profession," 1074.

42. *LSBH Report*, 1904–05, 26.

43. Ibid., 27; T. D. Berry, "An Account of the Destruction of Mosquitoes in the 'Original Infected District' in the New Orleans Epidemic of 1905; Together with Yellow Fever Statistics of That District," *Medical Record* 72 (1907): 421.

44. *LSBH Report*, 1904–05, 34. Henry Dickson Bruns, "Experiences during the Yellow Fever Epidemic of 1905," *NOMSJ* 59 (1905–06): 196–216, is a very detailed account of one volunteer anti-mosquito crew's activities and experiences. Lazard, "Statistical Review," p. 1083, provided statistics on the New Orleans epidemic.

45. Rubert Boyce, "The Yellow Fever Epidemic in New Orleans in 1905," *Transactions of the Epidemiological Society of London* 25 (1905–06): 290. Stanford E. Chaillé spoke in similarly glowing terms: "This was one of the most triumphant demonstrations of the efficacy of the preventive measures adopted that has ever been secured." "Two Yellow Fever Topics," *NOMSJ* 58 (1905–06): 932.

46. [Walter] Wyman, "Yellow Fever—Its Origin and Prevention," *MHS Report*, 1905, 252.

47. G. Farrar Patton, "The Etiology of Yellow Fever. From the Standpoint of 1908 and in Retrospect," in Augustin, *Yellow Fever*, 1117–1118.

48. Lazard, "Statistical Review," 1085; data on black cases and deaths outside New Orleans are from comments of Representative Joseph E. Randsdell, of Louisiana, in the *Congressional Record*, 59th Cong., 1st Sess., 4701 (3 April 1906).

49. C. M. Brady, "The Prevalence and Diagnosis of Yellow Fever in the Colored Race," *NOMSJ* 58 (1905–06): 551. See also G. M. Guiteras, Report to the Surgeon General, 6 December 1905, MHS Records, Yellow Fever Epidemic, Louisiana and Florida, 1905. All following references to the MHS Records are to this collection of papers on the 1905 epidemic.

50. Ibid. G. B. Young, note dated 14 September 1905, on the back of C. H. Lavinder's letter to Young, 12 September 1905, which Young was referring to Wyman.

51. Public health authorities had argued since the 1870s that as many people as possible should be evacuated from a yellow fever–infected town, and this prescription included black residents. But before 1905 this recommendation had been applied to blacks largely for non-medical reasons. Municipal authorities feared the loss of civic order in the absence of such a large proportion of the

white population, and also argued that the relief required by blacks left destitute by a yellow fever epidemic could be best administered if all of the poor
were assembled in one place, preferably a camp outside of the city. With this
new awareness of the infectiousness of blacks, public health officials had even
stronger reasons for limiting the freedom of blacks during an epidemic.

52. Henry Goldthwaite, "Yellow Fever—Prophylaxis and Means to Prevent
Spread in a City or Unknown Focus," *Mobile Medical and Surgical Journal* 10
(1901): 322. For a similar expression of the view that the mosquito theory had
eliminated all reason to dread yellow fever, see "The Yellow Fever," *Atlanta
Journal Record of Medicine* 7 (1905–06): 302–306.

53. Guiteras, Report to the Surgeon General.

54. Wasdin, Report to the Surgeon General.

55. "The Board of Health of the State of Alabama," *Mobile Medical and
Surgical Journal* 7 (1905): 301–302.

56. "The Yellow Fever Situation," 285–286.

57. Theard, "New Orleans Yellow Fever," 1093–1099; Kohnke, "Biennial
Report for Board of Health of City of New Orleans, 1904–05," in *LSBH
Report,* 1904–05, 60–61.

58. Guiteras, report to the Surgeon General.

59. "Yellow Fever Resolutions," *Memphis Medical Monthly* 25 (1905): 541–
542; *Times-Democrat,* 3 October, 11 October and 7 November, 1905.

60. *LSBH Report,* 1906–07, 50–51.

61. "The Quarantine Conference," 483.

62. *MHS Report,* 1906, 201–203, reprinted this law; the quotation is from
pp. 201–202. The term "disinfection" included mosquito control measures,
for it had become customary by 1905 to use the term 'disinfect' in the context
of yellow fever control to mean the killing of mosquitoes by burning sulphur
or pyrethrum.

63. *LSBH Report,* 1906–07, 53.

64. Comments of Davey, *Congressional Record,* 59th Cong., 1st Sess., 5392
(17 April 1906).

65. Comments of Williams, ibid., 4698 (3 April 1906).

66. Comments of Joseph E. Randsdell, ibid., 4700 (3 April 1906); my emphasis.

67. *LSBH Report,* 1906–07, 67.

68. Ibid., 12.

69. Reported in the *Congressional Record,* 59th Cong., 1st Sess., 4669 (3
April 1906).

70. John Ettling, *The Germ of Laziness: Rockefeller Philanthropy and Public
Health in the New South* (Cambridge, Mass.: Harvard University Press, 1981),
123–124.

71. John Fulton, "Quarantine. The Delirium Ferox of American Sanitation," *APHA Reports* 31 (1905): 1:252–253. Violent reactions to public health
directives were not limited to the South. In Milwaukee, for example, an angry
immigrant community forcibly prevented the removal of smallpox patients to
the isolation hospital established by the board of health (Judith Walzer
Leavitt, *The Healthiest City: Milwaukee and the Politics of Public Health Reform*
(Princeton: Princeton University Press, 1982), 76–121). But instances of entire communities physically sealing themselves off from the world and defying
state and national authority were rare outside the South.

72. Fulton, "Quarantine," 253–254.

73. Charles V. Chapin, *A Report on State Public Health Work Based on a Survey of State Boards of Health* (Chicago: American Medical Association, 1915), 25.

74. See, for example, Ettling, *The Germ of Laziness*, 195–196.

75. "God Help Us, and Give Us One Clean Street in the South," *Memphis Medical Monthly* 26 (1906): 270.

ESSAY ON SOURCES

The sources explored in this project are abundant and varied, and have much to offer to future researchers. I relied most heavily on the collections of Countway Medical Library in Boston. There the researcher finds not only the essential indexes to start a project, but also a rich collection of nineteenth-century medical journals, books, and board of health reports. The holdings of southern antebellum medical sources there are unrivalled by any southern library.

Nineteenth-century medical journals published in the South were the main source for my description of yellow fever in that place and time. The *New Orleans Medical and Surgical Journal*, which spanned the years of this study, was the most long-lived and respected of the southern journals. Others, such as the *Charleston Medical Journal and Review*, the *Memphis Medical Monthly*, and the *Mobile Medical and Surgical Journal*, were briefer in appearance but useful for their spotlight on specific epidemics.

Once boards of health had been established in most of the southern states during the 1870s, their reports add considerably to the historical record. Often they contain not only the dry summaries expected in such documents, but also copies of fiery letters and controversial reports surrounding the always emotional events during epidemics. The reports of Louisiana, Mississippi, Alabama, Tennessee, and Florida shed considerable light on their states' public health activities and personalities.

The published record of federal public health activity during the 1878–1905 period is even more extensive. The National Board of Health printed both an annual report and a newsletter. It also commissioned special reports on given topics, such as that of the team sent to Havana in 1879, and published these as separate documents. As the Marine Hospital Service took over and expanded federal public health duties, it likewise created reports and newsletters. These frequently were fleshed out with letters from its agents in various southern ports, giving firsthand accounts of events there.

The thickest manuscript collections relate to these two federal agencies. The National Archives holds shelves of boxes on the Marine Hospital Service and has committed its large National Board of Health collection to microfilm. These records consist mainly of the letters and reports sent back and forth from federal inspectors in the South to their supervisors in Washington.

Manuscript archives throughout the South were visited in search of materials for this project. New Orleans has the densest grouping of collections, and also one of the best, that at Tulane Medical School's Matas Library. For years, someone at the Louisiana State Board of Health kept a scrapbook, containing newspaper clippings, letters, pamphlets, and other documents related to the board. The Matas library contains this as well as the papers of Joseph Jones, Stanford E. Chaillé, and other New Orleans public health figures. Countway Library has a similar scrapbook documenting the National Board of Health's career, which is housed in the Henry I. Bowditch collection.

While it is relatively easy to discuss primary sources for a work such as this, it is much harder to attribute the intellectual debt one owes other historians. References to the works of John Duffy, John Ettling, Gordon Gillson, Jo Ann Carrigan, and John Ellis, all of whom have written on some aspect of this subject, are noted throughout the text. More relevant to the way I approach both southern history and the history of public health are books which touch lightly on my specific topic, or not at all. Morton Keller's *Affairs of State* (Cambridge, Mass.: Harvard University Press, 1977) provided the framework for my understanding of federal politics in the Gilded Age. The broad conception of the social history of medicine in the nineteenth century as I have come to present it here can be found in the works of such scholars as Ronald Numbers, John Eyler, William Coleman, and John Warner. Barbara Rosenkrantz's *Public Health and the State* (Cambridge, Mass.: Harvard University Press, 1972) and Judith Walzer Leavitt's *The Healthiest City* (Princeton: Princeton University Press, 1982) served as specific models for the social history of public health. Yet at the same time these two books were what I contrasted my study against; that the issues facing "my" people were so persistently different from those facing "their" northern subjects continually stimulated my analysis.

INDEX

DEMCO